The Silent Day

Also by Max Arthur

The Busby Babes: Men of Magic

*Above All, Courage: First Hand Accounts from the Falklands
Front Line*

Northern Ireland: Soldiers Talking

Men of the Red Beret

Lost Voices of the Royal Air Force

Lost Voices of the Royal Navy

*When This Bloody War is Over: Soldier's Songs of the First
World War*

Symbol of Courage: A History of the Victoria Cross

Forgotten Voices of the Great War

Forgotten Voices of the Second World War

Last Post: The Final Word From Our First World War Soldiers

Lost Voices of the Edwardians

Faces of World War One

Dambusters: A Landmark Oral History

*The Road Home: The Aftermath of the Great
War Told by the Men and Women Who Survived It*

*Fighters Against Fascism: British Heroes of the
Spanish Civil War*

*The Last of the Few: The Battle of Britain in the Words
of the Pilots Who Won It*

Max Arthur

The Silent Day

*A Landmark Oral History of
D-Day on the Home Front*

HODDER &
STOUGHTON

First published in Great Britain in 2014 by Hodder & Stoughton

An Hachette UK company

1

Copyright © Max Arthur 2014

A CIP catalogue record for this title is available from the British Library

Hardback ISBN 978 1 444 78754 2
Trade paperback ISBN 978 1 444 78753 5
Ebook ISBN 978 1 444 78751 1

Typeset in Sabon MT by Palimpsest Book Production Limited,
Falkirk, Stirlingshire

Printed and bound in Great Britain by Clays Ltd, St Ives plc

Hodder & Stoughton policy is to use papers that are natural, renewable
and recyclable products and made from wood grown in sustainable forests.
The logging and manufacturing processes are expected to conform to the
environmental regulations of the country of origin.

Every reasonable effort has been made to acknowledge the ownership
of the copyrighted material included in this book. Any errors that may
have occurred are inadvertent, and will be corrected in subsequent
editions provided notification is sent to the author and publisher.

Hodder & Stoughton Ltd
338 Euston Road
London NW1 3BH

www.hodder.co.uk

For Martin Gilbert.
Friend and inspiration.

Contents

Introduction

In 2004 I was talking to Harry Patch who was to become the last British soldier to have fought on the Western Front in the Great War. He mentioned that in 1944 he was a maintenance engineer who worked on the camps in Devon occupied by several hundred American troops. He told me:

'In the weeks before D-Day, the camps became utterly chocked with American soldiers. I knew the time and date of all movements in and out of every camp in this area, except for one, and that was D-Day, 6 June 1944, which had been kept secret by everyone. I went away on the evening of the 5th; everything was normal, camps full of Americans, everything as it should be. I came back in the morning and not a soldier was to be seen, they were gone. It was quite eerie. Fires in the camp's ranges were still burning. There were urns of cocoa, coffee, tea, all hot. Cheese, butter, bacon, it was all there in the dining room, half-eaten meals on the table.'

His unusual story made me think of the consequences of having 180,000 men leave the UK without being able to tell anyone, even those close to them, that they were going and in many cases that they would not be returning. Armies are noisy and when they left, large areas of the UK, particularly the south became silent. Not only silent, but anxious, as everyone gathered around the wireless for news of the invasion. The United States and Canada also woke to the news that their servicemen, who in many cases had been in the UK for two years, were now fighting on the beaches of Normandy.

On D-Day 73,000 American, 61,715 British and 21,400 Canadians were transported by ships manned by close on 200,000 naval men. This, the largest amphibious invasion in the history of the world, was preceded by an airborne assault on vital inland targets by 24,000 Allied airborne troops.

This vast army of men left behind wives and families, loved ones and hundreds of children who had come to love and admire these strangers who had enriched their lives. *The Silent Day* is based on interviews and the occasional diary entry or letter from those who were left behind when this extraordinary force set forth to Normandy. In the words of the soldiers and civilians, we also hear of the months leading up to D-Day, the day itself as the men approached the beaches and made their first steps ashore under fire and of the returning wounded. The final part gives us the reflections of those involved in that momentous day.

These personal accounts follow wherever possible, the chronology of the events leading up to D-Day, but in the final chapter of the book the reflections of those who were involved have no date, for what they saw and felt would be with them the rest of their lives.

Throughout the book I have retained the American spelling for the personal accounts from servicemen and women from the USA.

Max Arthur
London 2014

Living with War: 1939–44: 'We were not afraid because we didn't understand what was happening.'

Ivor Fairbrother

CIVILIAN

Well, typical English people, most of them seemed to think, we're in this war together and we've got to get on with it. And that was the feeling – we're going to win – there was not ever any question of we were going to lose the war. We will beat the Germans. There was a sort of feeling of being together, more than what you do today; there was more family, more people seemed to look after people in those days because of the war. You could be sure of that.

Phyllis Calow

CIVILIAN

On 16 September 1939, two weeks after war broke out, we were married. Because we thought that bombs would be dropping immediately, we cancelled our honeymoon that was going to be at Brighton. We were managing fairly well, but a year after we were married he was called up. In January he was sent abroad, and I didn't see him for four and a half years.

Tony Clemas

SCHOOLBOY

I was twelve in 1940. My first memory of the war was being sent to the shops with my elder sister, to buy blackout material to cover the windows. I was often woken at night by the air raid sirens. My mother, sister and I would go downstairs and sit behind the piano. My father and older sister were ARP wardens so they donned their steel helmets and arm bands and dashed to the ARP post, checking there were no lights showing in the street. They returned after the 'all clear' sounded but could be called out several times in one night. We could hear the German planes overhead; their engines had a distinctive note.

On another occasion I saw a British plane flying south with a parachutist dangling horizontally from the end of his harness. His parachute had caught on the tail-plane. We heard he was eventually dropped into Poole Harbour but sadly did not survive.

With a few of my school friends, I volunteered to be a Messenger. In the event of a raid, which cut telephone or electricity lines, we were to carry messages from the Town Clerks Office on our bicycles. I remember when we were walking by the river; we spotted a shell partly buried in the grass. We dug it out and took it to the Police Station. They told us we shouldn't have touched it as it was still live.

Living on the edge of Salisbury Plain; surrounded by military camps, the town was always full of servicemen and women: Canadians, Australians, New Zealanders, Poles and, later, large numbers of Americans.

Peter Davies

SCHOOLBOY IN SWANSEA

At our home in Port Talbot, in Wales, when I was about nine years old I used to pile books up in our house and get behind them, make a small gap in the books, and pretend to be a sniper.

All I had was a carved wooden gun. We never did it outside – perhaps we thought we might get arrested.

Caroline Le Maître

YOUNG CHILD

I was the first baby born in Bognor Regis during the war. When I was about five I used to play soldiers with my friend Peter, who was older than me. He had a fort which was full of American and British soldiers. He only allowed me to have German soldiers and every time I attacked his fort he made sure I lost. This happened every time we played. I got confused and when I saw a soldier on the street I became very frightened, because I didn't know if he was an enemy or a friend.

Pat Glasby

SCHOOLGIRL

My mum was just coming along the road when the siren went. As the road was full of military transport she dived under the nearest truck. When the 'all clear' sounded she crawled out and a sergeant said to her, 'Why did you climb under that truck? It is full of ammunition.' She said, 'Well, I had just collected my family's one egg for the week and I wasn't going to lose that!'

John Bowles

SCHOOLBOY

We were there as evacuees from the war's dangerous places – London, Dover, Deal, and many other cities and towns targeted by the Luftwaffe. Sturminster Newton in Dorset was our little haven away from Hell and we loved its rolling hills, the meadows and woodlands.

The London children tended to look down on anyone not from 'The Smoke' and at first referred to most of us, particularly the local children, as 'Swedes', but after a short time we were all good mates and even the streetwise Londoners were beginning to sound like 'Swedes' too, and were developing a Dorset accent.

Brenda Paulding

SCHOOLGIRL

I was born at the end of August 1936. The most unforgettable memory of the Second World War was the telegram boy coming with the news of my only brother's death in the invasion of Sicily. I was six years old at the time and as no one else was at home I went next door to get our neighbour as Mum had let out a tremendous wail of grief and I didn't know what to do. This tragic event coming barely three months after the death of my eldest sister from TB was overwhelming. Dad was injured badly

Around 1.9 million children gathered at rail stations in early September for evacuation, not knowing where they were going nor if they would be split from brothers and sisters.

in the Great War yet despite injuries tried to work and was a sergeant in the Home Guard. I remember peeping under the curtains when his men were doing an exercise in our street, when I was supposed to be asleep.

One morning he came off HG duty and found Mum and I pinned under an iron bedstead caused by an air raid. During the war our back door was blown off three times by bomb blasts and Mum was once caught badly across her back by it; she also cut her arm badly when she slipped getting into our Anderson shelter during a raid.

When my sister was ill in hospital with TB she and other patients were moved from Harold Wood hospital to St Margaret's Hospital at Epping to make room for people injured in the Blitz. Many years later I found that my husband Norman and his mother Winnie were among them following the destruction of their home at Walthamstow by a phosphorus bomb.

My uncle and aunt came south from Sunderland to escape the raids there but only stayed one night because they thought things were worse in the south. When the air raid warning sounded Mum took down the heavy brass candlesticks from the mantel shelf, and picked up a torch and the Fox's glacier mints tin that held all our ration books and other vital paperwork, and shepherded us into the Anderson shelter. Once we had our own shelter in the garden we spent many a sunny day inside it singing songs from our sixpenny songbook.

I was evacuated three times, first aged three with Mum and some neighbours with young children to share a cottage on the east coast. We saw the first lifeboat rescues of the war on 10 September, as we children were having our first taste of seaside behind the barbed wire. Soon home again, as it was safer further from the action, but Mum had to care for Dad because his souvenirs of the Great War were a missing area of thigh and the results of being blinded and gassed. Oh, mustn't forget his 2 per cent pension and care from University College Hospital, London, for the rest of his shortened life. Like most people he expected heavy bombing as practised in Spain earlier and took the crossbar out of the dining table to make a temporary shelter for me and my dolls at bedtime before the shelters arrived.

The second time I was evacuated I went to a Wiltshire village to live on a farm with four adults. I was four and started school there and walked the long way there to and fro alone. On Saturdays my nearest sister in age who lived with a young couple came to play and I cried bitterly when she had to go home again.

For my third evacuation I was billeted with the sister nearest in age with an elderly couple who had never had children. Overall they were very good to us but they would keep our good clothes for best meaning, of course, these were outgrown before outworn, which, especially in a time of shortages, was wasteful. Every lunchtime when we came home for a midday meal we had our hair combed looking for nits. On Fridays we went to the public baths and took our clean clothes in a parcel to be returned with our dirty laundry.

Ken Bowskill

SCHOOLBOY AND UNDERTAKER'S ASSISTANT

As monitor my job was to press a bell push indicating class change. One morning I pressed it and it got stuck; continued ringing meant an air raid was imminent. I was trying to explain to a teacher but was pushed by the rush into the back of the air raid shelter and it wasn't until quite a while that the powers that be realised the bell was ringing and nobody was pushing the button. So we had a nice break from school work. A teacher found out how I'd made it stick and I was relieved of my duties!!

I went to work for an old Jewish undertaker making and carrying coffins. Very busy as the 'blitzes' were providing lots of 'customers'. Employees used to be conned into staying on the premises at night on 'Fire Watch'. One night I was on 'duty' and it was very cold so I found a warm spot, in a coffin. As it was a quiet night I fell asleep, only to be awakened by somebody yelling 'Put that light out' and a door being opened by the local Air Raid Warden. I popped my head up, the guy saw me, complete with shroud, and then he took off leaving a nasty smell. Apparently the curtains weren't closed properly and a chink of light was showing!

Mrs Eager

CIVILIAN

The wireless was the chief mode of entertainment. Kimbells lovely restaurant and ballroom, in Southsea, gave a little luxury in the form of an orchestra, but alas, when the tea came, there were no handles on the cups, and they were very cracked, but it was expected and no one minded in the least. Bombers came over with a great roar, and we knew by the sound whether they were making for London or elsewhere. If they were for us we had little warning, other than the official siren. We then had to leave our supper and bolt for the shelter – a brick and cement building which we shared with the butcher next door. Each evening we tried to get our supper a little earlier to beat the siren, but Jerry beat us every time; and we became worn out, but so thankful to be alive.

The wharf was bombed and the whole width of the High Street at the bottom near the sea was a great wall of fire. We decided to leave, as we considered it to be a target area for more bombs, so we walked a quarter of a mile, to my sister-in-law's house, my husband carrying the baby, and me carrying the bag of necessities including the great comforter – the knitting – but alas, I dropped the ball of wool in the High Street so I trailed it all the way to the house. Realising what I'd done, I stood in the porch and wound and wound and wound, hoping I'd have enough to finish the garment. Meanwhile, my husband had gone to the shelter with the baby, and moments later, he came back looking for me. Needless to say, I was in trouble.

Daniel Cox

SCHOOLBOY

I was awakened by a crash of gunfire, and saw through the

window in the sky to the west a mass of orange-coloured lights, shells from the Bofors guns. With Elsie, I scrambled out in a hurry, called Ted and went outside, saw a plane caught in the searchlights with all the guns in the neighbourhood firing at it. It went out towards the East and, while watching it, I saw a ball of fire appear in the sky, drop slowly behind the trees and houses, and a soft red glow appear across the sky.

Whether it was a plane hit or a flare I know not. Later, another plane came over, this time travelling from east to west. Again, all the Bofors opened up and there was a wonderful pyrotechnic display. The plane could be seen quite clearly in the rays of the searchlights and while the barrage was at its height there was the swish of a bomb or two and the usual dull explosion.

Sea spray breaks over a South Coast seafront wall on to a Bofors anti-aircraft gun crew, 1943.

Doreen Denning

SCHOOLGIRL

At home, we had a Morrison shelter; a table made out of steel, and my youngest sister and I slept underneath it at night. My two older sisters slept on the floor just outside and Mum and Dad in the front room. If the action got really noisy at night, everyone crawled in under the table. The windows were protected with shutters to stop glass breaking inside the room. It was a bit terrifying, but we all went to school next day.

Brian Bailey

ORPHAN

I loved the noise of falling shrapnel through trees. I collected much of the strange-looking material; the lines and markings are fascinating. My collection was my treasure. Sometimes it burnt my hands as I picked it up. When a nurse tipped my treasure out of the case because it was too heavy, I became very upset.

My first Dr Barnardo's home was Babies Castle at Orpington in Kent. I remember being with a group of children and a nurse on a country walk and hearing the noise of aircraft chasing across the sky. We were told to lie down at the side of the road. The puff of exploding anti-aircraft shells in the air was, for us, exciting. When I heard the noise of shrapnel falling through the trees I jumped up and ran to collect it. The nurse chased after me and possibly saved me from injury or worse.

We were not afraid, because we as children did not understand what was happening. Germs and Germans meant the same thing to me. Wash your hands to get rid of them; which didn't help, as we soon learned. The nurses came in the night, wrapped us in red blankets, and rushed us down to the shelters. I hoped that the germs would come more often so that I would be held close again. I used to annoy the nurse by persistently asking her to clip my fingernails for the same reason. One night it was very noisy. We apparently did not have the time to go to the shelters, because we were all told to lie under a row of tables in the dining hall. The thump and crashing of the bombs that night were even making the ground shake, which wasn't very nice of those germs. I never forgot to wash my hands after that. It seems amusing now. I could not quite make the connection between washing my hands and germs in the sky though. Because of the increased intensity of the raids and being just south of London, the children were moved to safer parts of the country.

I was sent to Boy's Garden City north of London, where a different war of sorts was fought. Bullying was never a problem for me personally. Strangely enough, I remember a couple of names, like the Sullivan brothers. The older of the two was the protector of the younger, who had stolen the braces of a boy whose name was Silver, but because Silver was afraid of the older Sullivan he didn't know what to do. The day before, I had already fought him so the bruises were still sore. I challenged him about the braces and, because he was older and bigger, I collected a few more bruises. The braces, with the help of the person in charge, were returned. So I felt that I had won. Other boys, who had names like Frost, or Gold, were made fun of, which got me into more fights. They were my friends so I had no other option. I earned myself a bad name, and was moved to another home, which turned out to be either an administrative mistake or an experiment at my expense.

I found myself at a girls' home, where I was forced to learn ballet dressed up as a girl. After much rehearsing, and feeling terrible pains in my feet because of having to dance on the front of the toes, and being made to wear a ballet dress, I more or less rebelled. One evening we were dancing for some people sitting on gold-coloured chairs. We came in through a door fluttering like swans and going round in circles: doing what all nice little ballerinas do. Then either my toes had had enough or I fluttered in the wrong direction, either accidentally or on purpose. That didn't go down well!

I was one of three children who discovered a door that was not locked and, being curious, we went up into the attic. There was a small window that we opened, which wasn't big enough for us to look out of together. After a bit of a struggle one fell out onto the concrete below. An unfriendly lady came up and was very angry with us. Sometime later a few of us were sliding down the back-stair banisters when a girl fell and broke her back. When the lady saw me standing at the top of the stairs I felt terrible and was punished again for just being there. I had a dormitory to myself and was sometimes locked in a cupboard. When I screamed to be let out, a plaster was put over my mouth. A couple of times I was bound in a women's corset. Anyway, the unfriendly lady decided that she had had enough of me, so I was sent packing.

You can imagine the relief I felt when sent away to a foster home. Most of the grown-ups were kind. The country walks were a nice break from that strict unloving lady. Now I realise that she was probably a very unhappy, lonely person. Only God understands why. He doesn't hate her, so why should I?

Eileen Greedy

SCHOOLGIRL

Growing up in the war was a fast-forward process. When the warning siren sounded and our parents said jump into the shelter, we jumped. Our shelter was an Anderson one. Like all our neighbours, we had them dug deep at the bottom of our gardens, at the backs of our houses. Living on one of the hills looking down into what we called the Cardiff basin, we were very lucky to escape the heavy bombing. When the 'all clear' sirens sounded, we had an excellent view of the aftermath in Cardiff. The fires and the arid stench of the choking smoke caught at our lungs.

It was only our Mama who used to join us in the shelter as Dad was an Air Raid Warden and we worried about him being outside in the night. Often the sight of our big, cuddly, much-loved Mama, struggling through the small opening of our shelter, clutching to her bosom a very old shabby school satchel, was too much.

A young girl emerges safely from her Anderson shelter to face the devastation after a heavy night's bombing.

She would never part with it and in a fit of giggles we would ask, 'What have you got in there Mama?' The stern answer always came, 'Grown-up things, none of your business.' Until one very heavy bombing attack, she answered, 'In here are my marriage and your birth certificates and life insurance policies.' At this we fell about laughing again and with a tear in her eye she joined in with us.

Lawrence Cooper

SCHOOLBOY

I was born and bred in Paignton, and so spent almost the whole of the war in the Torbay area. Looking back on my childhood I can remember a lot of things about the war, but my memories of 1944 are the most enduring. My family lived in a large old house on Huxtable Hill in Torquay – a leafy area between the station and the famous beauty spot of Cockington. There were my parents, myself, aged eight, and my younger brother, who was six. Our rambling old red stone semi was big enough to offer one room for billeting, and this was often taken up.

The year did not start very well for us, and early on we suffered some heavy raids in and around Torquay. I remember one very bad night raid, and we spent what seemed a very long time in the cellar. The party wall was of enormous thickness, and something like a priest hole had been cut out of it, and my mother put my brother and myself into this. One bomb must have just missed the house, as it fell in some open ground just to the east of us, and the blast took out every window in the house. I shall never forget the noise, the sounds of shattering glass, and Mother's voice comforting us. We did not know where Father was at this time, as he was out on duty in both the ARP and the Home Guard!

From the very top of the house we could look out over Torbay towards Berry Head, so in June we had a very good view of part of the gathering Normandy invasion fleet which was to embark the US troops encamped in the surrounding area. At this time we had an American officer, Colonel Storey, billeted with us, and he would often bring colleagues for tea or coffee, and we became great friends. It was wonderful for my brother and I to have such contacts, and led to some spoiling, I suspect. Sweets and tinned foods were sent over by families back in the US, and this even continued long after the war was over.

Mrs Warren

CIVILIAN

I was married on 4 April 1942 at Windmill Hill. There was a raid on while the service took place. I don't have any photographs of the occasion; they couldn't get films then. I'd phoned up the

Bristol Evening World and they promised to come, but an air raid sounded while we were in the church and when we got back home we phoned, but they were still on standby.

Betty Sargent

FACTORY WORKER

I was working at the cigarette factory when somebody came round and said, 'Lingfield's been bombed!' Our forelady lived in Lingfield and told us not to worry, because we all wanted to go home. She phoned her mother, who said it was not too bad. My sister was out and the German planes were shooting – they came across low and they were shooting. One man had his little dog on his bike in a basket and they shot his dog. And my sister was running around a house to shelter and a bullet hit the wall and a piece of brick came out and hit her; she thought she'd been shot, you know. But no, we were very lucky.

The Jewish girls did knitting and we were fascinated because they did it completely differently to the way we did, and they were so quick. I shall never forget the jumpers they wore; they might be red at the front and blue at the back. I think it was so that instead of needing two jumpers they could turn it the other way around so that it appeared to be a different jumper.

Richard MacDonnell

SCHOOLBOY

The war was everywhere around us. Plymouth Airport was a fighter base, Glenholt Woods echoed to the sound of rifle fire, the roads were full of lorries, Jeeps and enormous DUKWs, and, somewhere 'up there' and effectively out of bounds to civilians, there was Dartmoor, which was one massive American Army camp. Long columns of marching soldiers filled the roads, Plymouth Sound swarmed with every type and size of vessel from tiny patrol boats to massive battleships and aircraft carriers, and Devonport was awash with sailors.

I was born in 1937, my brother in 1939, so the curious thing, to our young minds, wasn't the war. War was normal; what was strange to us was this thing called 'Peace', which people talked about. We can't have understood what they meant, though we may have vaguely absorbed that Peace would mean an end to rationing, and to us that meant just the one thing: limitless chocolates and sweets. That, too, was quite an alien thought to take in. We just wanted to live in this Heaven-on-Earth land of limitless sweets. Or so we thought.

Mrs Kelly

NURSE

While I was at Netley, we had lots of air raids. We were supposed to go to the air raid shelter, but we never did. I wasn't scared then. Now, I would probably be under a bed or a shelter. I checked the shelters out and they looked like a tomb or something. I thought that if I'm going to go, I'm going to go. It wasn't very good sense. Instead, we would turn our lights off in our rooms and watch the fireworks. We were surrounded by twin-barrel anti-aircraft guns, which fired at enemy planes, and the place really vibrated when they fired those guns. Of course, it made the patients real nervous. Some of them would get under their beds. But I guess I didn't have sense enough to be afraid.

Anon

AUXILIARY TERRITORIAL SERVICE

The first uniforms did not arrive until six months later, just one hour before our first ceremonial parade. We did not know which was whose, so we quickly used safety pins to make them fit. There was no real time to clean the brass and we had to wear our shirts tucked into the most unbecoming, unfeminine, khaki bloomers, which we called 'The Biggest Bloomers of All Time'. But we made that first parade, even though our feet bled after two hours of marching in the heavy shoes.

Amy

AUXILIARY TERRITORIAL SERVICE

I can remember the shock we had when they first came round with the drink. Washing up water? No, army soup!! That really turned our stomachs. Was this because the camp was still being run by men, we wondered? We were awakened at 6am the next day and lined up outside to be marched off to breakfast outside the barrack square. We then had to go and fetch our uniforms. What confusion. The stores were once again manned by men! The first counter we walked past had a sergeant standing by, sizing us up – literally. Small, medium or large were the only categories and we received a kit bag full of goodies according to the size he had given. When we got back to the barrack room to sort them, what a laugh! We first tried on everything as issued: bra, suspender belt – both in old-fashioned pink cotton and very coarse. Vests, khaki 'silk' locknit knickers with long elasticated legs – we called them jokingly our 'Man Catchers'. The shirts came with separate collars and we were also issued with blue-striped flannelette pyjamas. Then an orgy of swapping started in an endeavour to get a reasonable fit for ourselves.

The incident I recall was after one regular monthly medical inspection that took place in the long Nissen hut with changing benches along one wall. We women were allowed to change in the privacy of the doctor's office, but on one occasion we emerged straight into a line of men, absolutely starkers. We fled, but were ragged about it afterwards. In those days we were fairly innocent; the word sex hadn't entered our vocabulary.

Anon

AUXILIARY TERRITORIAL SERVICE

While in company, women were submissive and accepted the role men expected them to play; in our barracks we were something completely different. We played dangerously and talked dirty. Men were an alien element, yet everything that we women desired. Getting enough sex was all part of the dare that the war represented for us women, because it allowed us to express our liberty and rebelliousness from the male-set archetypes of loving wife and mother that they had always tried to tie us to. This naturally brought women together, and, apart from the prim or religious ones – of which there were quite a few – it enabled women to talk about men.

Yet at the same time, because men were scarce, there was a great deal of competition between us, although we would talk freely about the men we had had. There was one particular working-class girl in our barrack room who always seemed to get as much as she wanted. We regarded her as a little prim, but she was always seen in company with a hulking man who must have weighed at least twenty stone, with such a huge behind that we used to call him 'Elephant Arse'. After she had been going with him regularly for quite a while, the rest of us became increasingly curious as to why she should stick to such a fat-arse! So one night we got her into the barrack room after she had seen him and asked her what was so special about this giant. She replied in her broad northern accent, 'Ooh, ah! You know it takes a big hammer to drive a big nail!'

Rosemary Moonen

FACTORY WORKER

We had to report to a certain diehard foreman. He surveyed us all grimly, gave each one a job to do, with the exception of yours truly. No doubt I looked nervous and scared. He ignored me, and as he turned to walk away, I said, 'What shall I do?' He turned towards me, and sneered. 'Oh yes! We've forgotten sunshine here! What shall *you* do? Here! Take this' – indicating a broom – 'and sod around!' With that he threw the broom at me and walked off. I was stung to humiliation. As time went on I found my niche and they discovered I could work a certain machine and get good results. I was then transferred to another department. Many of the men with whom I worked tried to date me, but as most of them were married, their wives and children evacuated, I declined all invitations. Even the foul language began to flow over my head, and the coarse jokes which prevail in factory life, I ignored.

Mary

CIVILIAN

As soon as my son was a year old I found someone to look after him so that I could do my bit for the war effort again. I became a riveter, using a hydraulic gun to seal the rivets holding the metal skin to the frame of the bomb doors. These were made in sections and joined together when they were put in the planes. There were about ten of us girls and we made the doors for a couple of planes each day. We worked from seven-thirty in the morning to five in the afternoon, with only a half-hour off for lunch. I was up every day at six to get the tram to take my baby boy, half asleep, to his daytime mother. I was too busy and tired to miss my husband much.

Anon

WOMEN'S LAND ARMY

After my boyfriend, who was a Polish pilot, was killed, I joined the Women's Land Army. The life was quite strange at first. Each time I cleaned out the pigs, I brought up my breakfast! But as soon as I got over that, I made up my mind right from the start

A land army girl doing the job of a farmer while the men are away fighting, 1942.

I was going to 'make a go' of this Land Army business, for who was I to grouse? I was lucky to be alive, not too far from home and with kindly country people. That boy just killed had been through hell to get here and he had always been cheerful and never groused. I was not going to let him down. I could take it – and take it I did.

During my service in the WLA I changed jobs several times between milking and general farm work on small and large farms. Then I worked with a gang of four girls going around Wiltshire farms with a steam engine and threshing tackle. It was hard and dirty work. In the spring and summer we did field work, hoeing and 'singling' root crops and spud picking. We were not always treated with respect by farmers, but we learned how to put up with that and throw back the appropriate remarks along with the piles of dung we had to spread over the land.

I worked with all kinds of folks, countrymen and women. Some of the womenfolk thought of the WLA as 'tarts' who were after their farmer husbands, but they got used to us in the end. I worked with gypsies and prisoners of war as well as quite a few younger women who had got out of Hitler's Europe. One cannot forget any of these men and women. But for me it started with that young Polish man who taught me how to stand on my own two feet. Unfortunately he never knew it, but I have never forgotten him.

Connie Mark, born in Kingston, Jamaica

AUXILIARY TERRITORIAL SERVICE

Down in Kingston town, at a place they call Parade, they had two lists put up – a list of men reported missing and a list of men reported dead. And that list would go on and on – sometimes you'd go and you'd see the name of your cousin; you'd go back a few days later and see your friend's brother reported dead.

So we damn well knew there was a war.

What the Americans thought of the War in Europe: 'We had to step in.'

Lewis Bloom

28TH INFANTRY DIVISION

A great number of really fine Americans said, 'Let's not get involved, you know, let's concern ourselves with our problems and besides, you know, the trains are running on time in Italy, and Mr Hitler is just a temporary thing. You know, good German common sense will bring back things.'

Samuel E. Blum

AMERICAN CIVILIAN

Of course what I sensed and felt was that England and France and the countries that could have stopped Hitler never did. You know, Munich is just one example, but there are others. They just never stood up to him; they let him get away with it. I sometimes feel that they said, 'Let him go, the son of a bitch, he's going to take care of Russia next.'

Frederick De Sieghardt

AMERICAN STUDENT

The country was divided. You have to remember that, in grade school, we were singing First World War troop songs, like 'It's A Long Way to Tipperary'. So we weren't that far removed, nor were our parents, but there was a considerable feeling that we should stay out of it. Now, stimulating and encouraging that was the presence of the German-American Bund, an organization of ethnic Germans living in the States who, of course, were seeking to weaken any American resolve to enter the war. They were being fed from Germany with propaganda and seeking to identify themselves with good causes, even as the Klan has done at other times in this country. So, there was a divided attitude. England was not popular in this country, because they'd 'never paid their war debt' from the First World War and that was seen as, really, quite a serious lapse of, if nothing else, courtesy and good judgement on their part, to treat us that way.

William Kenneth Smith

28TH INFANTRY DIVISION

Some people, as in any case, were dead set against it, because we were still a very nationalistic-type country and they just thought it was going to draw us into the war, but other people, I think, realized that, you know, England really wasn't going to survive unless somebody did something. They were an island and there was no way they could get supplies, unless there was some way to augment whatever they could do, and they didn't have a lot of natural resources, through which they could sustain their manufacturing of military equipment.

Sergeant Elaine Bennett

CENTRAL POSTAL DIRECTORY BATTALION

I wanted to prove to myself, and maybe to the world, that we African-Americans would give what we had back to the United States as a confirmation that we were full-fledged citizens.

Lee Eli Barr

EIGHTH AIR FORCE, 306TH BOMB GROUP

I think the news had come through about people being marched into a death house, and that was awful. I tell you, I'm glad I wasn't able to see one. I don't think I would have been able to stand it.

Walter Denise

AMERICAN ARMED FORCES

I thought that we should've been involved, in a way, because we knew that England was going to be overrun. Then we realized this has gone too far. A lot of innocent people were being killed, you know, with the Germans' aggressiveness. And, you know, you look back at the whole thing, at that stage of when they had just taken over France, taken Paris: then they took on England and Russia. They could've taken the whole world on. I mean they were that much of a threat. I think in many respects good wins out. Evil can't succeed forever.

Raymond Bodnar

7TH INFANTRY DIVISION

They felt that if England went, we would be next. The Germans would be powerful enough, even though they didn't have a big navy, to threaten us, or be able to invade Greenland, and, maybe, exercise air activity against us. We heard that kind of discussion.

Robert H. Zeliff

AMERICAN ARMED FORCES

Well, I think everybody here, and I think this was sort of the mood of the country, to a degree, is that we just sort of hoped that we weren't going to get involved. FDR had other thoughts in mind. One way or another, he was going to get us involved in that war.

We had this lend-lease program, before the war started, where we provided a lot of significant help to Britain, but, of course, there were a lot of active pacifists. Charles Lindbergh, essentially, is a classic example of those, but there were a lot of other people who weren't, you know, active, and the common citizenry just sort of hoped that it wasn't going to happen. But just like somebody turned on a switch, we had Pearl Harbor and that was it.

England could not have lasted without our help. We had to step in. The job that this country did in arming itself just boggles the mind. They had the war effort geared up but how in the world did we do it so quickly?

Richard E. McKeeby

AMERICAN SCHOOLBOY

Myself as a child, I remember very well my family sitting around the radio listening to the news about the United States and in those days the Japs and Germans. I remember my father reading V-mail letters to us, saving tin cans and crushing them with a sledgehammer in our basement to be used for guns and tanks, and also gathering scrap iron for the war effort, and going with my father to Route 206 traffic light, to turn it off for blackouts. My father was a civil defence volunteer and wore the CD armband. The top part of the headlights had to be painted black on all cars. We had to turn off all the lights in our house whenever there was a blackout, and us kids had to sit still, make no noise during a blackout. My mother suspected our neighbours, who had a German name, of being spies, and she always thought they had a secret radio in their attic. I remember the state trooper raids on the German Bund camp at Lake Iliff, which is also in Sussex County. I remember seeing all the 'loose talk' signs all over town, and the war bond posters and the 'Uncle Sam Needs You' posters. I remember the army convoys coming up and down Route 206 past our home and going to and from Grand Central Station, after they'd been on furlough. I remember crying and wondering if it would have to be the last time I ever saw them.

After my brother was killed, I saw my mom crying, and it was made worse for me when I saw my father cry because it's tougher than seeing your mother cry. So, by the time of D-Day, when we found out about his death, I was probably nine or ten years old.

If we ever heard a plane we would wonder if bombs were going to drop. As a child, of course, you know your mind really goes wild with that kind of stuff. I just wondered if there was going to come a marching army and take our house away, or shoot us.

I really didn't understand it. I just knew who Hitler was and he was a bad person, and people somehow followed him. I couldn't understand why people like us, with the blond hair and blue eyes, were doing this to each other.

Nancy Potter

AMERICAN HIGH SCHOOL STUDENT

I was living on a farm in eastern Connecticut. I was very aware that the war was going on in England because I had an English pen pal. People grew up early in those days. My pen pal was in an air raid shelter in London, and she would write letters about the war. During two bad winters, she spent almost every other evening in the air raid shelter.

I was standing on the stairs when the Pearl Harbor announcement was made on the particular day, and the declaration of war followed very suddenly. I can remember looking down at the carpet and thinking life would never be the same again.

I was then in high school, and there was a belief that we were all going to be involved. The junior and senior classes were convinced that not only the men would be, but also women, too.

I had several friends in my college class who were in the service. Almost immediately, there were two young men, who were freshmen, who left after a month. Both disappeared. They were shot down on a military flight over the North Atlantic.

I did work as a volunteer in a hospital in Boston to relieve civilian nurses. We were very convinced that everyone ought to be tremendously involved in the war effort. I enjoyed the hospital volunteering, but I found the experience absolutely terrifying. I had been sheltered, and I had not realized that there was as much pain and misery in the world. The hospitals were very short staffed and it seemed to me that there was always too much to do. I think the responsibility was really too much for me at that age.

The war was always portrayed as winnable, but important, popular and fought for a just reason. The newsreels were extremely manipulative. We were taught to be more than scornful of our enemies: the Germans and the Japanese. Our enemies were portrayed as dangerous, inhuman, uncivilized and unworthy of any sympathy. The Americans and Allies were portrayed as radiant, good, decent, honorable and always fighting valiantly. It took me many years to see this manipulation. All of us went to the movies, partially to see these newsreels since there was no television and newsprint was quite censored; we had the belief that if we saw something there that we would see it in a more intense dimension. Since we knew servicemen who were flying or were out on ships, we knew that the newsprint news was not accurate. We received letters from people which were censored and we knew that there was another side. We were all very greedy for the news.

I think all of our patterns of life, particularly our romances, our attitudes towards objects, our attitudes towards the future, and our attitude towards education – all had to do with the war. I cannot imagine a day that I spent from the time I was fourteen until I was nineteen when I wasn't aware of the war for a good part of the day, and it had an impact on everything that I chose to do. There was no point at which, except for being asleep, that I wasn't aware of the war because I had a great number of friends who died.

I had one college classmate whose fraternal twin died. After she got the message, we just simply sat through the entire night trying to think of things to say to her, and we couldn't come up with anything very extraordinary.

I can also remember coming home from lunch one day into my dormitory room; my mother had sent me a letter, and out of it fell an obituary of a young man who died fighting the Japanese. The report of his death had happened a good two weeks before his family heard about it, three weeks before it was in the newspaper, and a month before I heard about it. It was absolutely terrifying. This was happening all the time. It did have a great impact on our lives.

I exchanged mail with several young men who had been in high school classes. Every time you went to a Buddies Club, there would be billboards with names of service men who needed to be written to. We were constantly writing letters. This was considered to be an absolutely essential activity to boost morale.

I never doubted that the war was for a good cause. We talked about the cause a great deal. We believed rather simply that the American involvement in the European theater was an attempt to free those parts of Europe that had been overrun by the Axis forces that had annexed Austria, Poland and France and were busy trying to overrun Russia.

I had actually read *Mein Kampf* and hated it. I saw it as more than distressing – it was dangerous. I didn't see how Nazism could be stopped except by the massive military effort.

Jerry Shuman

SECOND AIR DIVISION OF THE 8TH AIR FORCE
I always thought that everybody was being pushed to learn faster and be faster and get it done. You have to understand the way the country's mentality was. We wanted to get the best possible army overseas fighting, as soon as possible, because the people in England were holding on by a thread.

Gertrude LaVigne

AFRICAN-AMERICAN SOLDIER
We had classes in military organization, how to salute, how to march. 'Take thirty steps,' barked the drill sergeant. 'Fall in! Dress

right! Fall out! Dress right dress! Clean the latrine! Polish the shoes! Make the cot! Police the area! Reveille! Retreat! Mess call! Mail call! Straighten those shoulders! Belly in! Hup two, three! Whatever made you bloody women think you could be soldiers?'

Commanding Officer Barbara Gwynne

WOMEN'S ARMY CORPS DETACHMENT AT STARK GENERAL
HOSPITAL IN CHARLESTON, SOUTH CAROLINA

I had been in England in '37 and was much surprised to see all these factories going day and night, and so I asked someone over there what was going on, and they said, 'We're getting prepared for war.' I was stunned, of course, but I followed what was going on. In September '39, when England declared war on Hitler, I was prepared for it, but this country wasn't really prepared. Once the war had started, I knew that since I lived on the east coast and was near Europe, we would have to go in and help. I think all of us were terrified of Hitler. I mean, he'd gone booming through all of Europe, just doing whatever he wanted to do, attacking and signing agreements that he never lived up to.

Pearl Harbor was attacked on 7 December 1941 and on 8 December 1941 the United States declared war on Japan, then on Germany and Italy on 11 December.

Britain Begins to Get Ready for D-Day: 'Invasion fever is gripping everyone.'

Daniel Cox

CIVILIAN LIVING IN SOUTHAMPTON
Diary entry, 20 May 1944
Rumours in the yard today that after this week the port is to be closed for cargo traffic and the docks are to be taken over by the Admiralty and military, in readiness for the invasion of the continent. How true this is, time will tell. I believe the barges are already being loaded in the docks.

Patricia Cameron

SCHOOLGIRL LIVING IN PORTSMOUTH
It was April or May 1944 and there were lots of troop tents going up on the common, a lot of armoured vehicles coming in, and the common was out of bounds and there were a lot of rumours going round but no one really knew what it was actually going to be. I can remember we were all given a picture of General Montgomery.

The harbour master was very busy with buoys in the channel, and certain signals and beacons, and I can remember having to go down with him one day to take notes about different beacons, buoys and lighted buoys. There was a lot going on but we weren't sure at that stage what it was. There was talk about PLUTO and then there were the Mulberry harbours – we knew about them, but we didn't know what they were for.

Elsie Horton

WREN

In 1944 I was a Wren on the staff of the Commander-in Chief, Portsmouth. We worked at Fort Southwick, an underground complex below the Portsdown hills, behind Portsmouth. I was a watchkeeper in the Signals Distribution Office. All signals coming into the C-in-C, or initiated by one of his staff, had to be recorded and distributed either to officers in the complex or to ships and shore establishments in the Portsmouth command, which stretched from Newhaven to Portland.

In the spring of 1944, increased numbers of personnel appeared; not only Wrens and naval officers and ratings, but army and RAF people and several US soldiers and sailors. We were changed from four watches to three, which meant extra hours. All leave was cancelled: on buses within a few miles of the coast, pay books had to be shown, identity cards for civilians: only those who lived on the Isle of Wight were allowed to visit there.

Portsmouth Harbour was a solid mass of ships and landing-craft of every description. Every little river along the south coast had its share of LCTs and LCAs. Every roadside had its contingent of parked army lorries and tanks, with the soldiers camped along-side. Fareham Common was covered by an army camp. When we were free of an evening, we liked to take a walk and have a chat with these boys, who would often make us a cup of tea.

Daniel Cox

CIVILIAN

Diary entry, 22 April 1944

Southampton is packed with troops. There are camps on every available piece of spare ground. Anti-aircraft guns and search-lights are being placed in various new places in and around the town. Invasion fever is gripping everyone, but somehow I don't think anything will happen just yet.

*A line of army trucks waiting for deployment prior to D-Day. An ATS
mechanic is seen sitting on the wheel arch of one of the vehicles.*

Miss Norah Grocott

CIVILIAN

One late afternoon, early in May 1944, we heard a terrific noise
of traffic coming along the road outside the drive. The road was
full as far as the eye could see of army vehicles of every kind,
shape and size. There were tanks, armoured cars and lorries, and
one or two infernal machines, with huge rolls of chains wrapped

around enormous rollers on the front. These were, of course, for beating over minefields, though their purpose escaped us at that time.

From a leading armoured car, an officer descended, and addressed my brother-in-law. He announced he was sorry to trouble him, but he was taking over the available ground around the house for an 'indefinite period'. My brother-in-law was rather taken aback and, I recall, was bold enough to ask if all this was really necessary. 'Yes sir,' said the officer. I remember I put my oar in by saying, 'In actual fact, we have no choice, have we?' 'No ma'am,' said the officer, with a slight smile.

I think it had dawned on us all by then that this was something bigger than all of us!

The Journey to Britain: 'Our orders came. We went to England.'

Claude V. Bache

SIGNAL OFFICER

This was June 1942, and we didn't know where we were going. I had no idea. They couldn't tell us, of course, and the trip took ten days at sea and we couldn't bathe, couldn't take baths; ten thousand men, and didn't have enough water for us. We wore the same clothes all the time and I was on a bottom bunk and there were three above. We had one porthole that was closed all the time. So there's no fresh air; forty men, unwashed, in this one place, with no fresh air. We ate two meals a day, standing up. At the end of five days, we exchanged places with troops on deck. Troops were all over the ship, and they were even up in the fore-castle and the waves were breaking over them. We slept on the top deck, on the side of the ship. Five of us slept in a row, together, and fully dressed, and we piled our blankets together, so that we were warm enough. We kept asking each other, 'Where are we going?' Obviously, we were in the Atlantic and we thought, 'Maybe it's Iceland,' and then we kept sailing and sailing. We figured, 'It can't be Iceland. It's got to be some other place,' and, I remember, the weather got warmer. The last night at sea, it was quite pleasant and I left the gang and I went up and slept under a lifeboat; just stretched out on the deck, under a lifeboat. When I woke up, it was a beautiful day and we were sailing down a river, somewhere in Scotland. It was the Firth of Forth, and so we docked in Scotland.

Then we got on a train. At that point, we looked sort of ragtag and must have smelled terribly. There was this soldier from one of the Scottish regiments in a kilt standing at the railroad station and he looked at us and shook his head. So, we got on the European-type railroad cars, which we'd never seen before, except in the movies, and we rode the train down to the middle of England to a place called Cheltenham. The first night, they took us to a racetrack and we slept under the stands and took our first shower in ten days. Oh, that was wonderful.

Then, they took us to a place about four miles outside of town and there were some Quonset huts. They were metal-type, temporary houses. While we were there, a German bomber came over one day, very, very low, and dropped a bomb in town, and it flew out over our camp and we were ordered to hide and not shoot at him. Then, we walked into town and inspected the bomb damage and we realized that, you know, this was the first thing of war we had seen.

Carl W. Monn

79TH INFANTRY DIVISION

Well, you got lined up, you got everything that you're going to carry on your back and you walked up to the gangplank, told the guy your name, he crossed you off the list. One sergeant was doing the list; he says, 'I've never seen such a happy bunch of guys so keen to get on a boat to go overseas.' After our training in the States everything was so military, military, military, we were just fed up with it. We all said, 'Get us out of here.' And they did!

Lieutenant George Clafen

INFANTRY DIVISION

While we were on the ship we were up in the expensive area, but all stacked up, eight to a room, but down in the hold were all these young kids. They were airborne replacements, and they were the roughest, toughest young kids you ever saw in your life, and they were rambunctious. They were getting into fights, and, of course, the airborne officers needed relief, so we were sent down at various times to take their place for a while, and we had to keep order. They weren't bad kids but down in that hold was a miserable place to be, and, like anybody else, they got sick and it was really bad, but then it stopped, and they immediately got better. They were in terrific shape and they were great kids.

The first American GIs to travel to the UK arrived in Northern Ireland in January 1942, just seven weeks after the bombing of Pearl Harbor had finally drawn the United States into the war.

Peter Daly Campbell

UNITED STATES NAVY

We left from New England and New York, basically Brooklyn, and there were a lot of Southerners in the navy. There were no problems as far as animosity between the people. The only blacks, as I recall, would do mess duty. They kept very much to themselves and there was no problem between the blacks and whites. At that time, the only sea duties that the blacks would get would be on black ships. They would be totally black, which was wrong. It should've been integrated, but who knew it then? No one really cared to explore the need for that.

I was assigned to a destroyer USS *Moffet* in New York and I was got there late one evening in March 1944 and was admonished by the officer of the deck for not saluting the quarterdeck. I never forgot that. It took us twenty-seven days to get to England, because we were with a very slow convoy of seagoing tugs towing barges.

So, these tugs were towing these gigantically huge barges and it was our purpose to protect them. We had, I guess, about three destroyer escorts along with us and we had some exciting times. We had a couple of submarine attacks. One time a barge broke loose and it rammed into a tug, which was to its stern, and the tug sank in about one minute. We were right on the spot and we were able to rescue the entire crew of thirty-five, plus their dog. So that was sort of exciting.

Then, we returned to the States for another convoy and then another and another. It was a great experience. It was very, very tough.

William Biehler

90TH INFANTRY DIVISION

It was a huge convoy, more than a hundred ships by the time we got out into the ocean and could see everybody, but I was on a British refrigerator ship that was converted to a transport. The food was terrible. The ceiling was very low and there were things sticking out of it, valves and faucets and stuff: so I just kept my steel helmet on all the way over there, and it was very dented by the time I got to England. It was a huge convoy; all we could see were ships and we were happy that an aircraft carrier was in the middle of the group. As far as I know, nobody on that convoy was ever attacked by submarines and we landed at Liverpool.

Boy, the crossing was almost two weeks, because Liberty ships can only go eight miles an hour, eight knots, and they were zigzagging, too. The captain of the ship was British and, just before we got off, he felt he'd better say a word to the Yanks. So he gave a patriotic speech, saying, 'We're glad you're here and we welcome you to England to help us fight the Germans and good hunting, Yanks,' and some guy on the back says, 'Who's hunting?' The Brits were a tough people. I mean, they'd been at war four years already at that time. Then, we were taken by train, all blacked out, for a day-and-a-half and ended up close to Barnstaple in Devon in a big infantry replacement depot.

Herbert Bilius

AMERICAN ARMED FORCES, COASTGUARD

We didn't know where they were going to go. We didn't know if we were going to attack from the Mediterranean in the south of France. Our orders came. We went to England.

We pull into Falmouth and we can't come into the docks. We have to anchor in the Bay of Falmouth. So we drop anchor, and for the first time we are going to wear our blues: we've had khaki uniforms on since I was on this ship. We put on our dress blues and we are going to go ashore. Well, how do you go ashore? You have to row ashore. We get into this row boat and it's not a big thing. The last guy to get in can see that the thing is bobbing up and down; he says, 'I can make it,' and jumps, and hits the side and turns the boat over. We are all thrown into the water in our dress blues, including the executive officer, an old man of twenty-eight, who starts screaming, 'I can't swim.' But the crew is roaring; they're beside themselves that this guy can't swim. Somebody throws him a line. No uniform for days, so no liberty!

Albert B. Meserlin Jr

STAFF PHOTOGRAPHER TO GENERAL DWIGHT D. EISENHOWER
We landed in northern England, and I'll never forget our welcome. Here we were, half dead and seasick, and we had our big duffel bags, and the ramp looked like a hundred miles long going up from the ship. We get to the top, and there was the British Red Cross girl. 'Would you like a cake?' she said. 'My dear,' I replied, 'right now, I'd rather like to die.'

Lyman C. Avery

PERSONNEL CLASSIFICATION SPECIALIST
The ship that we got on was the SS *Alexander*, a German liner that was in dock when we declared war on Germany, and we impounded it and converted it to a troop ship. We had 14,000 troops on board that ship. F deck was the bottom deck and that's where I was, along with most of the 184th. And we hit a north-east storm off the coast and lot of people were just deathly sick. They couldn't even get out of their bunk, they were so ill. We used to hang the helmet liner on the side of the bunk – that's what you used – and they wouldn't allow us on the deck because the weather was so bad. Finally, when the weather cleared up, they allowed us to go outside.

Carol Levin

SECRETARY, WOMEN'S ARMY CORPS
And then, a year to the day after Pearl Harbor, I sent my application in to join the Women's Army Corps. I was stationed in several places in the States, and then I wanted to go overseas, because I felt I was just not accomplishing what I wanted, to end the war all by myself. I went to England, where I stayed for under a year and a half, and it was wonderful.

I went to a place called Burtonwood, which was just about

midway between Manchester and Liverpool. It was interesting. We were repairing or changing the structure of the planes that came in. The planes were made in America and shipped to England. They shipped them over and then made up packets to adjust the planes to a newer style. I didn't win the war on my own but I became a secretary to a lieutenant colonel and a colonel.

Lois Manning

NURSE

Well, we didn't know where we were going. Of course, we had to zigzag and get over there, and I'd never been on a ship before. We landed in Scotland and were put on a train and went down to near Liverpool, where we were billeted in an English home with Mrs Leashman. She would awaken us every morning, pull back the blackout curtains, and bring scones and tea, so that was a nice way to be awakened. I wouldn't mind that now.

*Living Side by Side with the Americans
and Canadians: 'We met often and began
to like each other a lot.'*

Terence C. Cartwright

SCHOOLBOY

At the age of twelve, I had the unforgettable experience of tasting
my first Wrigley's Spearmint Chewing Gum. Tents had appeared
overnight, like mushrooms, and within those miniature Aladdin's
Caves, trestle tables groaned under the weight of 'Camel' cigarettes, chewing gum, tins of exotic meats and foods we had never
seen or tasted before. These 'Treasures' were dispensed by 'Gods'
who spoke like a combination of 'Dead End Kids' and Roy Rogers
to the hordes of grubby, green-candle-nosed, ragged trouser-
bottomed 'Just William' look-alikes, who descended on the camp
like locusts. Yes! The Yanks had arrived!

Naina Cox

TRAINEE NURSE

I was sixteen in 1944 and worked in the accounts department
of a big firm of dry-cleaners in Portsmouth. Due to staff shortages, I was often asked to serve in the shop and saw an amaz-
ingly different number of freshly cleaned uniforms packed up
and handed back to their interesting owners – at least twenty
different services from all over the world. By 1944 the number
of different American uniforms in and out had become very
noticeable.

John Bowles

SCHOOLBOY

Although we missed our parents – most of our dads were away in one of the armed forces and mum was still back at home – we generally enjoyed our lives in the green of Dorset. We continued with our schooling but when that was done for the day we were off to the woods playing hide-and-seek, building camps and leaping into the River Stour from a small railway bridge, much to the horror of the grown-ups.

Then one day something happened that would change the face of sleepy old 'Stur' – the Yanks arrived. Suddenly the roads were crowded with big olive-green lorries, white star on the side, packed with soldiers in strange-looking uniforms and helmets. Many of the soldiers were grinning and waving and, of all things, throwing packets of chewing gum and chocolate bars to the kids. It seemed they were about to take over the town; they certainly took over the vicarage. Hundreds of tents were erected in pastureland on the outskirts of the town and they took over the little elementary school just up the road from Aunt Cissy. In no time, big notice boards were everywhere – '4th Inf Div Pers Only', '4th Inf Div Intell Sec', 'Out of bounds – This means YOU!'

Tall radio aerials appeared on the roof of the school and a generator roared to life and remained roaring day and night. Jeeps and lorries were always screeching to a halt outside the school HQ and officers with silver stars on their jackets would hurry into the building after being smartly saluted by the armed soldiers at the entrance. After some time, they would leave the HQ carrying what appeared to be large rolls of paper under their arms, get back into the Jeep and roar off in clouds of exhaust smoke. We wondered what it was they were carrying and why they always looked so serious. Little did we know.

Eric Barker

COMEDY ACTOR SERVING AT THE ROYAL NAVAL COLLEGE
The Yankees arrived in Dartmouth to take over. It put years on the Royal Navy Officers who had been brought up in the place. I was sorry for the commander. There was a quarterdeck at Dartmouth which was his pride and joy. Any man who failed to salute it was mercilessly dealt with. At the far end was a statue of His Majesty King George V with a telescope under his arm, and every day a fatigue party was detailed to polish him.

The first thing the Yankees did was to use the quarterdeck as a store for dozens of packing cases labelled, 'Lucky Strike Cigarettes'. The final blow for the poor commander came one day on the ruins of the quarterdeck when a huge black sailor put a cigar in his mouth and lit it with a match which he struck on the statue of His Late Britannic Majesty.

Patricia Roach

SCHOOLGIRL
I was fourteen years old at the time and lived with my family in a village called Felpham about two miles east of Bognor Regis in West Sussex. Our home was on the sea front so we were in a grandstand position for any of the wartime activities that occurred. For some months before D-Day, we noticed the build-up of the numbers of troops in the area. We already had for several years been living with the Naval School of Photography as our neighbours. They had taken over many houses on the estate where we lived.

Canadian troops arrived in Bognor Regis followed by a large number of American troops. The latter brought a huge number of vehicles all marked with a white star. The house at the bottom of our garden was taken over by men of the Liverpool Scottish Regiment. They appeared to own only one gramophone record, which they played incessantly!

Canadian troops dressed as cowboys trying to entertain some rather non-plussed British children.

Another hint to us that something big was going to happen shortly was the appearance of objects that looked like concrete blocks which were anchored off Selsey Bill. I could see this from my bedroom window. Two or three blocks would appear each day and it grew to look like a village, which is what we eventually called it. This turned out to be the Mulberry harbour. At low tide, a concrete reminder of the portable harbour that didn't make it across the channel can still be seen on Bognor beach.

Trevor Butler

CHILD

I was nearly four years old. I don't know where they came from. One morning I woke to the sound of strange noises outside our house in Francis Road, Purbrook, near Portsmouth. I was off to see what it was all about; breakfast was unimportant. On reaching the pathway to the front gate I was amazed to see army vehicles parked outside our house. I went into the road through a gap between these vehicles, which were completely covered in camouflage netting, and stood there in complete amazement. On both sides of the road were military vehicles from one end to the other and I later found out that these vehicles were parked in all the nearby streets. There was a smell of oil and petrol and the noises of engines, men talking and laughing, and the clinks of metal as things were moved and checked.

I rushed back into the house to tell my mother. After endless questions from me she told me that they had arrived after I had gone to bed the previous evening and they were preparing to go to war. I went back into the road again, this time with my older sister, Diana, and lots of other children from the neighbourhood.

Most of the soldiers were American. They were very friendly and it was not long before we were having meals with them under the camouflage netting. I remember sitting with other children, cross-legged, eating a wonderful mince stew which they cooked in a huge tin. The insides of the vehicles were kitted out with every kind of storage container fitted into the sides and all the food and equipment was kept tidy and organised. I don't know how they spared the food for us, but after the rationed war years, the food was wonderful. One day a soldier gave me a boiled sweet from a huge bag filled with lovely-coloured sweets. He later came to my house as he realised that, only being small, I might choke on such a large sweet.

One particular morning I had to go to the local shop to collect a newspaper for my mother and as I was passing between two large vehicles, one started its engine, engulfing me in black exhaust. I was petrified and a soldier who saw my plight took my hand and escorted me to the shop. To my surprise, they took me home, a drive of 400 yards in an American Jeep.

Alice Hannah

CIVILIAN

There were lots of girls exploited, and a lot of unmarried girls who were, really, ever so common. Men wouldn't have wanted them if they'd know what they were like. You know, you could see them about around the Tower. That's where the London ones used to be. We always used to meet a friend on the Tower; that was a place we'd arrange to meet – but when they'd come, they'd get their handbags and slosh you one! They thought we were taking their pitch! You daren't go round the Tower after that as it got ever so nasty. They chose where they wanted to stand, you see: some stood outside a shop where it was dark. There were two girls I remember. One was a bonny girl and used to wear a camellia in her hair: ever such a pretty girl was she, prostitutes you see, and the other one was a fair girl, quite attractive, and she'd only just started to appear and of course the Americans all came to her. And they got the disease. The fair one, she ended up in hospital with her disease, you see. 'Course, they came from the slums, you see; they weren't clean! They had ever so dirty habits.

Pat McKee

CIVILIAN

I remember when the first Canadians arrived. They arrived in Liverpool and the billets that were being prepared for them weren't ready and all the Irish ones, or those of Irish descent, got on the ferry and went over to Northern Ireland where we lived in Bangor. My mother and father were the sort that gathered people around them; so we were quite used to having three or four mattresses on the drawing room floor with soldiers sleeping on them! Things like that, you know. I sometimes think I was fairly lucky in the wartime, because I was meeting so many people. Next door was an empty house and soldiers were billeted there; despite the rationing, my mother managed to bake and cook and every night about ten o'clock

45

we'd knock on the door of their house with tea and scones and coffee for the soldiers: trying to make them feel at home. And of course, coming up to D-Day was very exciting in Bangor. We'd people like Clark Gable, General Eisenhower, and a lot of very notable figures of the time. I think Clark Gable came over because the public elementary school, which was quite a big school at that time, was turned into a military hospital, and he came over to visit people there. So, there was quite a lot going on. Great for teenagers. Sometimes I feel a wee bit guilty because I had such a good time!

Anon

NURSE

We met often and began to like each other a lot. One night, as we were all having a drink, Curly said, 'Let's go on our own tonight.' We did – and landed up in a deserted air raid shelter where we made love. We did this several nights. Curly said he loved me and I said I loved him. I was worried, as there was one thing I had not told him: I was already married. I used to take the wedding ring off and put it back on again when I got back to the hospital. I did this every time I met him. Then one night in 'our' shelter, he asked me to marry him. I did not know what to say, being already married. When I told him, he said his mother would understand. I wanted to say 'yes' so much, but somehow I knew that I had to keep putting him off. When the war came to an end, Curly went back to America. We wrote to each other often and he sent me gifts. But then my husband came home, so I stopped writing to him as I was so afraid my husband would find his letters. When I had a son, I kept wishing it was Curly's.

Anon

CIVILIAN

We were half starved and drably clothed, but the GIs said we looked good anyway. A lot was said about them being oversexed, overpaid and over here; maybe it applied to a few. It was just the case that the British women and the American GIs were in the same place at the same time – it was rather pleasant really!

Anon

AUXILIARY TERRITORIAL SERVICE

Along came a Jeep with four yanks in it. They stopped and offered us a ride. Although there were three of us, we just didn't trust them and turned the offer down. When I tell you we had to walk the whole five miles back to camp, and preferred this to the lift, you will appreciate how strongly we felt. I knew quite a few civvy girls who were loved and left – literally holding the baby.

Myra

CIVILIAN

The soldiers used to line up outside a hut by the railway line, near the airfield at Greenham Common, where the local street ladies lurked, while officers and the MPs turned a blind eye to the goings-on. Lorry-loads of GIs would often toss out chocolate bars or VD kits containing contraceptive rubbers as they roared through the Berkshire lanes. They blew them up like balloons and would festoon their lorries with them. Officers kerb-crawled for girls, three to a Jeep. I loved their parties and found Americans such good dancers. There was much jealousy among British men as to what British women were 'supposed to have got up to' while they were serving abroad. The Americans were so very trusting of us, wanting to be liked. The pity of it was that the enemy propaganda blew up the horrific stories of what we were up to 'in bed with GI-Joe' and encouraged the men overseas to think that they were being kept away until the Yanks were safely home again in the States.

non

CIVILIAN

It was all there then, not quite so obvious as now. Whenever young, vital people meet in unusual and unsettling circumstances, there will always be a permissive group. Togetherness in the blackout was the car seat or doorway. We were brought together that way through the pressures of time and shortage of accommodation and a sense of unsettling uncertainty; in fact, nothing was positive. Our generation, through sex education in the forces and all the 'free talk', learned a thing or two about birth control. Few of us lived mentally or physically for tomorrow – or even next week. Many relationships were set for as long as the war lasted – or the posting arrived for elsewhere. A free and easy, in some ways a slightly mad style of living took over. Many girls were married or spoken for, but husbands and boyfriends were not there. Company relieved the tension of what was about to happen. In the background a slight fear hid behind the bravado. The then-current saying – given with a grin – was, 'Don't worry, it may never happen.' It often did! Many girls were left pregnant with no hope of marriage because of death, overseas posting, or rejection. Wartime work was plentiful for us and men were there for the taking. Girls were now able to walk into a public house and order their own drinks and buy cigarettes. We paid for our own cinema ticket and the days of sharing costs had begun. No one would have thought of a date paying her own way before the war.

Doreen Pyne

CIVILIAN

We watched gliders practising in the skies on the Kent outskirts of London. Troops on transporters throwing sweets to the waving children at the kerbside, tanks churning up the surfaces of Westhorn Avenue and Sidcup Road in Lee, south-east London, heading towards assembly points – we knew not where.

Most of the usual air raids had died down – not soon enough for our family though. In a mini blitz on 2 March 1944 my maternal grandmother was killed by a bomb which crashed through the roof of their Anderson shelter, then exploded, killing her and two other adults and a baby; our mother was inconsolable.

Prior to this we did feel that the war was going our way and the worst was over. Three friends and myself all aged seventeen years left our office desks in the shadow of St Paul's Cathedral to spend a week of our holidays helping the war effort working at an agricultural camp in Berkshire. An open lorry met the train at Abingdon; we climbed in, hanging onto the front and sides, then along the winding lanes at speed until we came to a field at Kingston Bagpuize. Our abode was a bell tent sleeping eight, with our feet to the middle. Each of us had a straw mattress and grey blanket: there was a clothes line behind each, deemed to be our wardrobe. After five years of war and rationing we did not have that many clothes anyway. Two wooden shacks were also on site, one for ablutions, the other for meals and recreation. We paid twenty-eight shillings for our bed and board for the week, which was rather a lot as we only earned two pounds a week in our offices, but hopefully we could earn enough to pay our expenses. The food was filling but awful. Entertainment consisted of a dartboard, table tennis, board games and a gramophone plus a few records and the company of a few spotty youths and older men.

We never found a village shop or pub; what were we doing here? One of the girls spotted a notice; we were invited that night to a dance at the US base further along the winding lanes beyond our compound. It was great, Big Band-type music – partners by the dozen. We did all agree to stay together because we had been told what the Americans were like! We were not worldly; our usual recreation was at church youth club level, plus the fact that the bombing curtailed going out a lot anyway. When the interval came we found out that our current partners worked in catering and they asked if we would like some supper. Would we! None of us had seen food like it for years and were absolute pigs. There was ham and eggs, nice rolls and butter, gorgeous chocolate cake and fruit. Back to the dance and goodies to take back for a midnight tuck-in. As the next day was Sunday they asked a dozen of us for a cycle ride and picnic; we all cycled to a field to play baseball or rounders as we called it, paddled in the stream and ate food that you only saw in films. We danced to a radio. As we all lived and worked in London and had endured four years of terrible bombing raids with very little in the way of fun and entertainment, this week we were having a ball.

*A Land Army holiday camp in Cookham, Berkshire, October 1943. The
land girls have invited local troops to a dance.*

During the daytime we went off to the farms in a lorry, mostly weeding, which was back-aching. We were paid one shilling and sixpence an hour. At one farm we were given wheeled hoes with blades at each side, to go up and down the long rows, dipping the blades to clear weeds. I don't think that we helped the war effort very much and, once boredom set in, we had races. Time for lunch, someone boiled a billycan containing tea and condensed milk; we thought that the tea was on its third trip after drying. The sandwiches were two- by one-inch-thick slices of chaff-tasting bread; you could have beef or salmon. Luckily there was the dance and food to look forward to that night. We made sure that we hung on to the cookhouse partners, and who could blame us. We didn't mind the work as we had the dancing and chats with these new colourful visitors to our land to meet at the end of the day.

Frank Rolfe

SCHOOLBOY

The best thing that ever happened to us was when the black Americans took over half of our school. When they went out on exercises, we used to go over and thieve cigarettes or candy out of their kitbags, all manner of things. We had cigarettes under the floorboards at 20 Peterborough Road. Lucky Strike, Old Gold, Chesterfield, Morris chewing tobacco and some chewing gum. My mate would whistle up to the bedroom window, tell us how many cigarettes he wanted and we were selling 'em. Yeah, but I don't know what ever we done with the money. I was a bit worried in case our mum and dad would find out.

One day I went up there by myself and I decided to go in the cookhouse. When I get in, there is a great big chef, a massive man – he was a black man and on the end of the hotplate there was a coil of chipolata sausages. I don't think I ate a sausage in the war, never knew what a sausage was. And I'm looking at them and the first thing he said to me, 'You got a sister?' 'Yes,' I said, 'I've got a sister.' 'She pussy?' 'No,' I said, 'she's not pussy.' The sister of mine, she was a baby in arms. And he said, 'Could you get me a dog?' 'A dog?' I said. 'What do you want a dog for?' He said, 'I want it for a mascot.' So I said, 'Yeah, I can get you a dog.'

I went out the gate and walking up Sevenoaks Road was an old dog that we used to take rabbit catching with us. George, that was his name. I picked him up and put him inside my bomber jacket that I thieved off the Yanks. I was Jack the lad – a zip-up front. So I take the dog into the chef. He just picked the dog up, goes out the back into the cookhouse and as soon as he was out of sight, I grabbed the end of these sausages and I was gone. I run and broke a big length of 'em off and I run through some railings, down the steps across the main road, past The Red Lion, straight down Cosham High Street and I was going past Campions, the baker's, when a foot come out the doorway; it was Detective Popes. He knew all the tricks we was up to. So he snaps half the sausages off and says 'Keep running Frankie.'

I was just a likeable rogue, you know. That's the way we was, so. We didn't see it as really bad 'cause the Yanks had everything, even our women, didn't they?

Mary

CIVILIAN

We lived in a world of uncertainty, wondering if we were going to survive day to day. My husband was away in the RAF as an airgunner, and I'd conditioned myself to the fact that his lifespan was also limited and that our short, happily married life together was over.

I lived in a vacuum of loneliness and fright as service in the army, navy and air force claimed five of our personal friends, whom I mourned as if they were my personal family. When 1942 came in with the hit-and-run air raids, I began to despair that the war was ever going to end. It was while I was in this frame of mind that fate took a hand in my affairs.

The Yanks arrived and set up camps near Manchester, bringing in a wave of glamour, romance and excitement that has never been experienced before or since. They were not welcomed by the British men, but to the English girls they were wonderful. All I knew about Americans was what I'd seen on films, but Field's Hotel, within walking distance from my home, became the meeting place where GIs danced under soft lights. Eating in secluded corners with their girlfriends, the GIs were able to forget the war for a few hours. There I was introduced to an American captain. He was tall with blond hair and blue eyes. I thought at the time what a marvellous German officer he would make on the films. I felt rather embarrassed at his flattering remarks about my long hair and attractive appearance. I felt even more embarrassed when he danced the American way, cheek to cheek. Outside in the blackout, Rick took my hand, clicked his heels together and bowed to me, saying how much he'd enjoyed my company, then he walked down the path towards the waiting Jeep. If I was expecting a goodnight kiss, I was surprised and a little disappointed. 'And they say the English are a cold race,' I thought, and I didn't think I would see Rick again.

One weekend, as I prepared myself for another lonely sit-in, an unexpected phone call from Rick made my heart jump with pleasure. He came around about dusk in a Jeep carrying a holdall and bounced it on the kitchen table. 'There,' he said, 'take a peek.' It was full of tinned goods, butter, sugar, sweets, coffee, sheer nylons, and make-up – not forgetting cartons of cigarettes. He had also thoughtfully brought two bucket-loads of coal.

So began another part of my life on the home front – I shared my extra food with my neighbours and friends. If they wondered where it all came from, they tactfully never asked. It took a couple of weeks before Rick got around to kissing me goodnight. He asked me a lot of questions about my husband and married life, which I had to admit was a very happy one. I did, however, write and tell my husband about Rick. He was delighted I'd found someone to give me a break and that Rick seemed a really decent chap.

So, my mind free of guilt, I began to come alive again. It would be foolish of me to say that physical attraction never entered our lives: it did. With Rick, I knew it was love, but for me it was attraction and the need to hold on to someone. So it happened that we finally made love.

There was nothing cheap about our affair, and if Rick had my body, my heart was with my husband and somehow I didn't feel that I was doing anything wrong. Rick being a single man had fallen in love with a happily married woman, but he knew it was hopeless as far as I was concerned. I loved my husband too much to consider leaving him. Yet Rick and I were together for two years during the final stages of the war, until the evening he was silent and withdrawn after receiving orders to leave for Rome.

We said our goodbyes at the garden gate on 31 May 1945. As I looked at Rick's sad face, I asked myself whether the good times were over because I'd fallen in love and lost him. Then my husband returned and we tried to resume our old way of life.

'John Bull'

BRITISH MAGAZINE

Rudeness to colonial service girls in this country is surprisingly common. A West Indian girl in the A.T.S. (Auxiliary Territorial Service) was refused a new issue of shoes by her officer, who added, 'at home you don't wear shoes anyway'. An army officer to a West Indian A.T.S. stated, 'If I can't get white women, I'll something well do without.'

Sergeant George Self

50TH TYNE AND TEES DIVISION

Montgomery visited us and told us that 50th Tyne and Tees Division would be one of the divisions in the invasion. Morale dropped for a few moments. After he had gone there was a lot of discussion about divisions lying about in the country that had never been on active service, and how it was not right that we should do the invasion. We had already done one D-Day in Sicily, which cost us dearly. People were bitter. We felt we had done plenty of fighting, so let someone else have a go. There were no problems with discipline, but a lot of moaning.

When we moved to camp near Romsey we had battles with the

Yanks nearly every night in Southampton. The main cause of t.
friction was how much money they were paid and their arrogant
behaviour. Eisenhower came to see us and gave us a lecture about
the American soldier. He agreed they were overpaid, oversexed
and over here, but when they got over the other side, they would
show us the road home: how to fight. That was the worst thing
he could have said. That night the blood flowed in Southampton.

Miss Clarke

SCHOOLGIRL

Oh Americans, yes. I was only about fourteen or fifteen, so mother
used to say don't you ever go near them. I can remember running
away from them once. We had been to a dance at the South
Parade Pier and were walking home and there was a crowd behind
us calling out. But we just took to our heels and ran. I mean,
they were probably very nice, but our mothers had so frightened
us that we ran. My brother took me to a dance and this GI
wanted to take me home and I said, 'Well, I'll have to ask my
brother.' Of course, you can imagine what he said. We laugh and
joke now, but I often say to my brother, I could have been a GI
bride if it wasn't for you.

We children loved the black GIs because they used to give us
sweets – candy, they called them – and they were very kind. I
can remember the French sailors too, 'cos they were very good
at dancing the tango.

T.R. Austin

SCHOOLBOY

My pal, Leslie and I had heard that the Yanks were at Frampton-
on-Severn and so that Sunday in June we set off on our bikes to
cover the seven miles or so to the delightful Gloucestershire village
that boasts the largest village green in England. We rounded the final
bend onto the green, normally a flat expanse of grass stretching

Black GIs enjoying a Christmas show with local children, December 1943.

broadly away from a central road, and nearly fell off our bikes in wonder. The entire green was crammed with US military vehicles all decorated with the white recognition star of the invasion force. Between the vehicles, small tents were pitched, and in and around them were the soldiers. We were thirteen years old and some of them were only a few years older. We were soon laden with chewing gum and other goodies such as instant coffee; unknown then in England, and which, truth to tell, was one of our motivations for the trip.

Jean Rouse

WREN

There were loads of troops in the town, mostly Americans; about eight men to every woman so you can well imagine what a wonderful time myself and all the other Wrens had when we went dancing at the Town Hall! We didn't take a bit of notice of the Doodlebugs going over the top. We had better things to do!

Margaret Jackson

CIVILIAN

Girls were brought up on the cinema. They took on many hair-styles and fashions and mannerisms of the stars. Americans black and white on the Home Front, were first perceived, or seen from a distance, as 'glamour fresh from the screen'. They were often generous, handsome, flamboyant and far from being boring, a tag which the British boys at home wore.

John Hobbs

CIVILIAN

I mean, outside our back gate there was a tent where they used to check vehicles and things coming through, and initially it was a Tyneside Division and then, of course, the Americans moved in and all the girls used to come up from the town pestering them for cigarettes. I think they got a lot more than they asked for, from what we noticed on the barbed wire the next day!

Pamela Humphreys

CIVILIAN

Oh yes, yes the Americans had an image. I think the biggest things were the uniforms; they were like silk – just wonderful, silk gabardine – whereas our soldiers had really rough and badly made uniforms.

Well, my Aunt Teresa, she met my Uncle Jim at Blighmont Barracks because they used to hold dances there and she fell in love straight away. She brought him home to meet us and it was very exciting because he used to come and visit and bring tinned food like Spam and fruit salad and salmon that we didn't know about during the war. He made a fuss of us kids, you know, with loads of chocolate and gum. As the Jeep used to come up to our street, all the other kids were quite envious as he came into our house. He was a lovely person and, of course, you know, they decided to marry. It was quite a rushed affair because they knew that something big was coming up.

She married and we had a lovely wedding and I was bridesmaid. It was very difficult to arrange a wedding, you see, because the material was short for dresses and things like that so my mother did that for my auntie. She begged, borrowed and stole to get this wedding together.

Marion Ainsworth

CIVILIAN

An American sailor with the ridiculous name of Everett Englebart, who came from Ohio and was of Norwegian descent, would always make a beeline for Eddy, my sister. Every evening they sat together hand in hand, on the wall, having fallen in love with each other. One evening when his ship was due to sail he refused to leave her. His shipmates desperately tried to get him away but in the end had to leave without him. A couple of hours later two Shore Patrol men at least seven feet tall, with their white belts and white gaiters glistening against their dark-blue uniforms, came and quietly spoke to him. They led him away sobbing. Meanwhile the mothers watching this little episode shouted out to him, 'Go quietly son.' Really he had no choice. Eddy never saw him again. His ship sailed, presumably never to return.

Philip Longland

CIVILIAN

One thing that stands out particularly was, after the pubs had closed you used to get literally hundreds of American soldiers coming back to join their vessels. On one occasion one of our chaps thought he saw a strand of hair poking out the peak cap of one of these sailors. He said, 'Just a minute, take your hat off.' It was a girl; her locks fell out. She was taken into custody and it transpired that she was a prostitute who had made a terrific living out of associating with the Yanks.

From a letter dated 12 April 1944

AN OFFICIAL OF THE SOUTHAMPTON PORT

There occurred last week eleven incidents of assault of US troops by member of the British Armed Forces. Two of these incidents were by personnel of the navy. Of the other nine incidents, knives were used by the British Army assailants in three cases.

In each case the assailants have attacked individual Americans, and the method of approach in all cases is very similar. The American is either asked for a cigarette or for matches, then all his proffered cigarettes or matches are taken and he is asked if he is going to do anything about it. He is then invariably assaulted, and in three cases the American has been badly lacerated with a knife. US forces are forbidden to take weapons of any form out of camp or barracks, and are searched before leaving. It is feared that unless these unwarranted and premeditated assaults are checked, the US forces will secrete weapons outside their camp etc. and recover them on going into the town, and organise retaliation which can only result in serious bloodshed.

I consider it advisable that an order be issued forbidding all British troops from carrying knives of any description when not on duty. This will bring the British Army into line with the present US Army order which, I understand, is universal throughout England.

After diligently weighing all of these assaults, it is my opinion that the only motive is the resentful attitude towards the American soldiers by the British soldiers and sailors. Most of these incidents happen after blackout, and none of the subjects that were attacked could identify any of the perpetrators, except that they were sure the soldiers and sailors they described were British.

Jimmy Mead

CIVILIAN
I think they found coming into the war environment a bit shattering. We'd I suppose gradually developed with it – it wasn't so bad for us. But coming from America straight into a war environment, I think it was a bit much for some of them, and the occasional air raid, if we had the Americans about, gave them their first taste of war.

Anon

REMEMBERING A SERMON BY REVEREND WILSON CARVELL
He described the wonderful relations that existed between the hundreds of thousands of our boys stationed there and the citizenry of Southampton. They were all waiting for D-Day. Tanks were parked along the street everywhere. There were many dress rehearsals. Many a morning, both the boys and the residents all thought that this would be the big day. So Southamptoners staged little farewell parties out of their scant supplies which they had stored away. They drank tea together. On milder days the boys would sleep right out in the open, on the sidewalks, next to their tanks. Colonel Leo J. Meyer, commanding officer of the US Army in that city, once had not slept for three straight nights. He fell asleep in the garden of the home of the Mayor. When he awoke, he found himself in a nice soft bed. He had been carried there by those good people. That happened to many of our soldier boys.

Harry Meacham

BRITISH ARMED FORCES
The American police, we called them Snowdrops because they have white helmets on so they looked like snowdrops. They have great long truncheons and they used to use them too. Often we used to go out as police with them and they didn't mess about. They went

into a pub where there was any trouble and bang, bang, and asked questions afterwards. Just a bit different from us, you see.

Joan Henderson

SCHOOLGIRL

I remember the snared rabbits which were brought into the shop to be taken and sold in Derry. Rabbits were one of the government-identified supplemental food sources, which didn't work out too well, as city dwellers found it difficult to eat furry little creatures!

Then there were the army route marches up the brae which ran alongside our home. We children were generally kept behind barriers till the tanks, lorries and Jeeps passed but we were allowed out for the soldiers. We preferred the Americans to the English because they threw silver, including the occasional half-crown, while the Brits were copper men except for the odd threepenny bit. I remember when a ha'penny, thrown on the ground by a British soldier, lay there until the march was over, despite some other marchers pointing to it. Sometimes we would sneak up the brae well away from the house and stand in our bare feet, as this seemed to bring greater rewards!!

Bert Bragg

CIVILIAN

The Americans and the Free French were very friendly, especially when the sirens went: they were down the shelter before we were. We were immune to it after four years, we didn't worry.

Maeve Kelly

CIVILIAN

The Americans and the Canadians brought in a different way of eating. I mean, we never had popcorn, doughnuts, Coca-Cola or chewing gum.

GIs remained popular with English girls throughout the war.

Once we were standing on the Guildhall steps, spotting the talent going by, and one of my friends said, 'Look at that! Look at those American soldiers! They're fine-looking men!' And I thought, well! Let's take a look at these. And I don't know if it was me or if somebody else said, 'But who's the wee man in the middle with the uniform?' So we looked again, and it was Eisenhower, General Eisenhower!

Ian Roy

CIVILIAN
The first American Army personnel seen in Weymouth was in

the winter of 1942. That's when the build-up of troops began.

The Chapelhay area of Weymouth was heavily bombed leaving streets evacuated because of the damage to the civilian population. It was used at first by British No. 9 and No. 3 Commando to learn the art of street fighting. It was later used by the Americans to hone their skills. The GI's were part of the 1st Army known as The Big Red One.

As Chapelhay boys we had a lot of contact with the troops when they were training in our area. We were often invited to stand in line and to eat their 'chow' as they called their food. In return we helped clean their weapons before they returned to camp.

A. Poskitt

CIVILIAN

A friend of our family, Carol, worked for a dry-cleaners in Hull during the war. One of her jobs was to check the pockets of garments before they were cleaned. A poem was found in the pocket of an American soldier's jacket in 1944.

Carol did not care much for many of the sentiments expressed in this poem, so decided to respond with her own poem. Both poems were carefully returned to the pocket of the American soldier when he came to collect his jacket. We would have loved to have seen his face when he found Carol's poem!

American Soldier's Poem

THAT'S ENGLAND

Where the heavenly breeze whips through the trees,
And you walk through mud right up to your knees,
And the sun doesn't shine, and the rain flows free,
And the fog is so thick you can hardly see – THAT'S
   ENGLAND!

Where you live on Brussels sprouts and Spam
And the powdered eggs aren't worth a damn,
Where in the town you can get fish and spuds
And drown the taste in a must of suds – THAT'S ENGLAND!

You hold your nose and you gulp it down,
It hits your stomach and then you frown,
For it burns your tongue, makes your throat feel queer,
It's rightly named 'bitter' for it sure isn't beer – THAT'S
    ENGLAND!

Where the prices are high and ever so long,
And the poor G.I.'s are always wrong,
Where you get watered-down Scotch at four bits a snort,
And those English dames can't stand a short – THAT'S
    ENGLAND!

And those pitch dark nights when you stay out late,
It's so bloody dark you can't navigate,
There's no transportation, you have to hike
And get your tail knocked with a bloody bike – THAT'S
    ENGLAND!

Where most of the girls are blonde and bold,
And think every Yank's pockets are lined with gold.
There's the Piccadilly Command with painted allure,
Steer clear of them, you'll get burnt for sure – THAT'S
    ENGLAND!

This Isle ain't worth saving, I don't think,
Cut loose the balloons and let the damn thing sink.
I'm not complaining but I'll have you to know,
Life is rougher than HELL in the E.T.O. [European Theatre of
    Operations] THAT'S ENGLAND!

Carol's Reply

THIS ENGLAND!

The rain you are so scornful of, this fog at which you sneer,
Just modify our climate, and we'd rather have it here.
We may not have your sunshine, neither do wild blizzards blow,
No, I guess our weather is like our folk, temperate and slow.
We may not have fried chicken and we miss our roasted ham,
But we would remind you, 'twas America who sent the Spam.
The food may not be good, but we ask you not to forget,
We are living on hard rations for a war we are fighting yet.
And our beer may be too strong for you, it was brewed for
    MEN,
Men with guts, who take hard knocks and get up to fight again.
You scoff at the name of 'Bitter' – we drink a bitter brew,
When we stood alone against the foe . . . where then were YOU?
As for the Piccadilly Command, you have only yourselves to
    blame,
The too wise guy out on the make usually strikes a hard-boiled
    dame.
If a girl is decent you try to make her anew,
You know American soldiers – we owe the 'quads' to you.
There are lots of things YOU do for which we do not care,
But we are too polite to mention them, so we just grin and bear.
Your boastfulness, scorn of our land and somewhat rough
    horseplay,
Intolerance of coloured folk, we say 'It's only just their way.'
This island of ours isn't worth saving you don't think,
You'd cut ballast; let her go, let the damned thing sink.
I wonder, would Russia agree, fighting through mud and snow,
Would Norway, France, Holland and Belgium say 'Let Britain
    Go.'
You may be important in your little sphere,
But you merely look small-minded when you come over here.

You grumble at the petty things we take in our stride,
You're upset by Spam and Blackouts, while our men die by your
    side.
As for your opinion of England, we do not give a damn,
Our concern is for the welfare of every fighting man.
Our pride is in our nation, not in drinking beer,
We accept wartime discomforts of which you openly sneer.
As for the American Soldier, Well, I'm mighty proud to say,
I prefer a British Tommy, To a Yankee ANY DAY!!!!

Stanley H. Jones

CIVILIAN

Trowbridge was one of those towns completely taken over by the military during the war and the area where I lived was one huge 'tank park'. As the war progressed, the army personnel and their equipment varied. The preparation for the many campaigns and return from the battlefields saw many changes. I remember the soldiers training before they left for the continent prior to Dunkirk – and their return. Then there was the build-up of British tanks and our forces defending us with the Germans threatening our shores but now the Americans were taking over. Their large tanks lined Union Street and from our bedroom windows we could almost look down the turrets and watch as the soldiers prepared their equipment for battle. Up Middle Lane large half-tracked vehicles were parked on the wide grass verges – while just over the hedge old Farmer Hancock was still keeping his cows, driving them down to market through the lines of tanks and supplying us with milk. My dad was employed on Ushers transport (our local brewery) and after delivering beer to Bellefield House where many of their officers were stationed, he would come back with tales of the luxurious food they were having! They also had wonderful voices and I still pass the spot where one evening GIs – having formed a choir – were singing just outside their camp.

Bert Bragg

CIVILIAN

My father was working at the time at Marchwood on the concrete Mulberry harbour; that's where a lot of it was made. They didn't know what they were building, they were just building concrete barges, but for what, they had no idea.

Brian Selman

SCHOOLBOY

As a small boy, I was evacuated with my elder brother from Southampton to Poole, just a few miles along the coast, from a place of high danger to one of only marginally less danger. By 1944, we were moving back and forth between the two towns, both crammed full of troops, Poole with British troops and Southampton with American. Southampton, as D-Day neared, seemed under American control. We had to have special passes to enter the city: General Eisenhower was our boss. Southampton Common was a huge transit camp packed with American soldiers. The surrounding barbed wire was hung with 'NO FRATERNIZATION' notices. Yet, through a hole in the wire, numbers of young ladies entered with impunity. American military police patrolled the streets and dealt very severely with any drunken American soldier. They stood no nonsense: any trouble and it was out with their long truncheons, a quick bang on the head, and the offender was loaded horizontally into the back of the truck. I seem to recall that black American police were used to control white soldiers, and white to control the black ones. Local people could do little wrong, even in a fight with Americans.

US troops training in southern England before D-Day.

The streets of Southampton were packed with columns of American and British troops training for the big day. Each night, at 3am, a column would pull out and drive to the docks for loading. At 4am, the next unit would arrive for its twenty-three-hour stop. One day, it was heavy artillery; then infantry; the next tanks, vibrating the bomb-damaged houses and bringing down the loose plaster and the odd brick. The petrol bowsers parked nose-to-tail outside our house were the most worrying even though each house was provided with a couple of large fire extinguishers, in case. All the units were shipped down the coast, to be landed under live fire on Studland Beach. As a small boy, I remember educating American soldiers about pounds, shillings and pence, and that *Queen Mary* was a British ship. In response, I often received unobtainable treasures such as fruit bars, oranges, tins of biscuits and, on lucky days, tins of stewing steak much appreciated by my mother in those days of strict rationing. The contents of American kitbags came up with some surprises –

footballs (I was given a new laceless one once) and even dogs and cats!

In Poole, I went to school half-days in a building shared with a local school, which clearly resented our presence. Such were the realities of war. One day, Poole Park was packed with British Army vehicles parked side by side under the trees. To the soldiers' surprise, that day they were handed buckets of white paint and big stencils and told to paint large white stars on the tops of their vehicles for all to see. All wondered what this portended. Some evenings, as the days lengthened, myself and two or three other boys would secretly cycle down to Sandbanks, where we would slip through the scaffolding coastal defences and the barbed wire for a quick swim. We always posted one of our number to watch the sky over the sea off Bournemouth for German hit-and-run raiders who occasionally flew in low over the sea and swung low along the beach, looking for targets to machine-gun. One evening, after swimming, we stood by the chain ferry in the evening light when, to our astonishment, we saw a long line of ships snaking its way out of Poole Harbour, one close behind the other. Out they came, rocket ships, tank landing-craft, ships of all kinds. We had seen nothing of them before. Now they came from their many hiding places around the vast harbour. We then knew instinctively what all this meant. No one said a word, but each kept his own thoughts. We knew that this was for real and recalled 'Careless talk costs lives'. The ships continued to pass quietly out to sea day after day, a steady and mighty column, covering the sea to the horizon. For many weeks past, we had watched the American paratroops training for battle on the surrounding heaths. We had watched the Dakota troop transports trailing paratroopers, whose parachutes had jammed, flying up and down the harbour, towing the poor men through the water while the aircrew cut the parachutes clear. We were young, but we were familiar with death and the turn of Fate. We had seen men accidentally shoot their best friend when cleaning their rifles, only to break down and be carried away screaming in a straitjacket. Such was life, and we accepted it for what it was and what it had in store for us.

In Southampton, I had watched the great concrete caissons of the Mulberry harbour being built across the estuary, then towed to sea by their attendant tugs; also the great drums of the Pluto petrol lines, each with a gaggle of tugs on either side. Along the town quay, lines of huge landing ships, their bow doors wide open, loaded tanks, guns, lorries, half-tracks and all the vast paraphernalia of war. The centre of Southampton was a rubble-strewn wasteland, lined with American Nissen huts, a veritable American city. The tension increased. The roads were patrolled by American Jeeps with mounted machine-guns and the hours when we could leave our houses were restricted. But still the young ladies went through the gap in the barbed wire at the end of our road!

Jennifer Harper, née Hawkins

SCHOOLGIRL

I was a six-year-old in May 1944, living in Coburg Road, Dorchester, and I can recall Americans or Canadians, parked outside our house in army trucks. We children were given sweets: fruit sweets with a hole in the middle, were a great favourite. One unfortunate little boy was given a packet of sweets, which turned out to be reconstituted army rations to be used in emergencies. Having consumed his 'sweets', he was very ill! Our mother told my sister and me not to accept any more sweets, but I just inspected my gifts with greater care.

Peter Stockton

PAPERBOY

I lived in a small Cheshire village called Tarporley, ten miles from the city of Chester. Aged eleven years I was a newspaper boy delivering papers from the village newsagents managed by my grandmother. One morning I found there was a convoy of US

Army vehicles parked alongside the road full of US troops. I was full of curiosity as this was the first time I had ever seen anyone from another country, more so a coloured person. As I stood staring some of them shouted out, 'Hey paperboy, sell us a paper.' I replied that I couldn't let them have one as they were all ordered by customers and newspapers were in short supply due to 'The War'.

After much pressure from the troops and bribes of sweets and chewing gum I couldn't help but be persuaded to sell them some papers. They told me that they would be billeted close by in a large country house called Bowmere and asked if I could deliver some papers to the 'country house' barracks next morning. On returning to the shop I had to tell my grandmother what I had done, as many customers had no papers that morning. I received a good telling-off. She promised she would order extra for the next day.

The following morning I delivered the papers to the troops at their barracks. This became a regular thing and soon I was recognised by the guards on the main gate, and had free access to come and go as I pleased: going in the evenings after school and at weekends. I was allowed to attend film shows and eat in the mess. My new friends gave me chewing gum, American comics and fresh fruit. These were the first oranges I had seen for years.

That Christmas the troops gave me lots of presents which I took home to my parents and sister, cigarettes for my dad and a huge catering tin of peaches for my mother. She was so excited with this gift. She managed to scrape together enough ingredients to bake a small cake, which I took to some of the troops who had befriended me. They were emotionally very grateful, as this was their first Christmas away from home.

I carried on my paper deliveries and social calls to the barracks during spring 1944. Troops sometimes went away for a few days and would return very tired and dirty but would still pay me for the papers. One morning, sometime in late April, I called at the barracks as usual but no one was there except two or three sentries on the gate. The place was empty and they wouldn't let me into the barracks. When I asked where the troops had gone they just said 'Away'.

Slapton in Devon was one of the villages evacuated by the US military in December 1943 for live ammunition training. Children were happy to tap the generous GIs for sweets and gum.

Jane Pook

SCHOOLGIRL

Dad was stationed at Woking, Surrey, for a short period when he served with the RASC and managed to get away one day to visit home, a few miles away. He arrived in a Duck, a sort of lorry-come-boat-on-wheels. My nan exclaimed, 'Ooh, whatever's that bloody great thing?' The local kids used it as a climbing frame while Dad had a cup of much-missed, bromide-free tea.

My Aunt Phyllis got pregnant by a Canadian soldier. My nan hit him with an umbrella when she found out and told him to stay away. He was only too pleased.

Leonard C. Briggs

AMERICAN ARMED FORCES

In London you could see lots of damage and, of course, at night, it would be totally blacked out and you'd have to find your way around as best you could.

The English were very courageous, although they were taking a terrible beating. I would say that we had a general impression that they actually were following what Churchill was saying, that is, 'Fighting on the beaches, fighting on the fields', and they were ready to do that. I didn't hear any discouragement.

Faith McNulty Martin

US JOURNALIST

At the beginning of 1944, I arranged to join the office of War Information in London, which was the government's propaganda office, where a friend, who was a writer for the *Saturday Evening Post*, was head of a section. I knew him well, and when I told him I wanted to come, he said he would arrange it.

The office put out publications that were to be distributed in Europe to counter Russian propaganda. They sent me to London where I spent nine months on the government payroll working on magazines that would be distributed in Europe. It was terribly interesting. It was fascinating to be in London during the war. I saw it as a very exciting adventure – to be in London in wartime and have an opportunity to advance my career, to do more writing.

It was an experience just to fly across the ocean in those days. It took eighteen hours. I flew in a bomber. It was a wartime, stripped-down plane. It had huge fuel tanks, I think, and very uncomfortable seats. Of course, everything was blacked out, so you landed in total darkness and icy, icy conditions. Because England had no fuel, they didn't heat anything. I've never been so cold in my life. I arrived in London by bus or car of some kind. Driving into this bombed-out city was quite an experience.

When I arrived at my billet in this desolate house, I was told to take a room on the top floor. I climbed up there and I began to unpack, and all the little things that I had packed so lovingly at home seemed really quite useless if they were going to get blown out into the street. They seemed rather pathetic, and I sat there wondering what to do.

Then the siren sound, and I thought, 'Oh my God, I'd better go down to the basement or something.' So I started down the stairs, but on the floor beneath me I heard somebody typing, and they just went right on typing. I thought, 'Well, if they've got enough confidence in the future to go on typing, I'll go back upstairs and unpack.' And I did. I could have gotten hit by a bomb, but I didn't.

Lieutenant Claude V. Bache

AMERICAN ARMED FORCES

We weren't given any instructions on interacting with the British. We decided to go and have a Sunday dinner in town, and so we're walking down a sidewalk and this mother and her daughter were walking along. The mother looked over her shoulder and she saw us coming and she grabbed her daughter and hauled her off the sidewalk until we passed by. We thought, 'Oh, boy.' Well, the reason for that was, just previous to the Americans arriving in town, there had been a Canadian contingent there and, apparently, they were hell-raisers. So, they thought, 'Americans, Canadians, practically the same; the Americans are going to be the same way.' So we walked into a nice, small restaurant, sat down and ordered, and it became very quiet. We started to eat and Gus turns to me and he says, 'You know what?' He says, 'Everyone's watching us,' and I looked around; it was true. No one was eating. They were watching us. We were the only Americans there, and the reason being, it was the way we used our knife and fork. We didn't use the back of the fork, we used the other side, and they had never seen anything like this before. So, that was the reaction of the townspeople.

I had told my friend, Gus, that my mother was English and

she had some family living down in Shoreham near Brighton and Gus says, 'Let's go visit them.' We took a train to London and changed trains for Brighton and travelled down to Shoreham. I found my aunt's address and I knocked on the door. She opened the door and she was wearing one of my mother's green dresses, and they were the same size, same coloring, and it was like my mother standing there. They had clothing problems and my mother had shipped her some of her clothes. We knew that they were short of food and so Gus and I each brought with us a knapsack filled with food, and we dumped it out on their dining room table. They couldn't say a word. They were astounded, and later on we took them to a dinner and to movies in Brighton. When the evening was over we had to get back to camp. When we got off the train we had to walk to camp and, by the time we got to camp, it was about 6am and a guard was patrolling the boundaries. We waited until he went by and ran to the Quonset hut and climbed in bed. I was just in bed about ten minutes when another buddy came over and said, 'Claude, wake up. You and I are being sent to London.' I didn't tell him I had just been there!

We were the advance party for this contingent, this group of eighteen people, and we were assigned to Headquarters, European Theater of Operations. Jimmy Taylor and I were assigned to the motion pictures section. We were to start film distribution and build theaters and, also, organize mobile film units, for this huge army which was in the UK. Hollywood produced a lot of great films in those days and we would get the films before the civilian theaters in the United States got them and it was a job that kept mushrooming and mushrooming all the time.

I had read about the smog in London and they said, 'You can't see your hand in front of your face.' But we got used to it. There were Red Cross clubs and we booked USO (United Service Organizations) shows in there. One of the first USO shows that came over was the blackface singer Al Jolson and the actresses Patricia Morison and Merle Oberon who had played Cathy in *Wuthering Heights* opposite Laurence Olivier. Al Jolson had a sound system with him, with an amplifier and speaker. He comes in our office, and I'm just standing there, watching him, listening to what's going on, and he says, 'You', and he points to me. He says, 'You're going to operate the sound system.' I had never seen a sound system in my life before, and he says, 'You know, you just hook it up and there's a control panel and you control it.' The first show was at the Eagle Club, a club of American flyers in the Royal Air Force, the Eagle Squadron. So we set it up and the first person on is Al Jolson, who starts to sing his signature song, 'Mammy'. Well, it didn't sound right to me. So I'm twiddling the dials and his voice is going up and down and he's shooting me dirty looks. We had no rehearsal. So, I ruined his number. I had his voice going up and down. Then, Patricia Morison got up and she was a soprano and I had her coming out bass. Then we went to an American USO club, and we set the equipment up there and Merle Oberon sat right next to me and showed me what to do. So, with Merle Oberon's help, I got through the second show, but they never asked me to do that again.

Alexander Nazemetz

AMERICAN ARMED FORCES

After all our training they sent us for leave to a rest home for about seven or eight days. The American Army ran it: it was called Walhampton House in Lymington and we were greeted by American Red Cross girls. We ate five times a day; had break-fast, lunch, tea, dinner and a snack before bed, and we were awakened by a butler with a glass of orange juice in the morning. The house was huge with seventy-two rooms and had all this marvellous woodwork in it, and old pictures. I guess, somehow, the US had rented this for the duration. They gave us civilian clothes, sneakers, a sweater, shirt, pants. In fact, I tell ya, it was kind of traumatic at first. After a while, you kind of grow used to it. What they did there, they organized activities for us. We played baseball against a neighboring rest home, and I think it was officers, but you couldn't tell, 'cause they were all dressed in civilian clothes. We brought in from the local area some kids who must have been six or eight years old, and we divided ourselves in half, and half was for one kid, and half for the other, and we cheered 'em on in boxing matches.

We used to hear that they would sell Scotch in the local pub between nine and nine-fifteen, and so we would arrange to get there just in the nick of time. We were in the pub one evening, and we were playing darts and there was a young Englishman and his father. He was in the navy and he had just come back from Boston and they were having a pint together, and we invited them to join us, and we played darts together. We were always taught not to let the English buy us anything, because they didn't have any money. I know they wanted to buy us the Scotch, and we wouldn't permit that. We were gonna buy them, and we did that. You know, we had all kinds of money. I was loaded with pound notes.

Edwin Kolodziej

AMERICAN ARMED FORCES

I took a walk over to where the lions are at Trafalgar Square, where that statue is. So I took a walk out there to look around, and, while I was walking around there, I sat down to have a cigarette, and there was a girl sitting there, reading Shakespeare, and I thought to myself, 'How do you like that? I come to England, and here's a girl reading Shakespeare.' So, I say, 'Excuse me, my name is Edwin and I'm by myself, would you like to talk for a minute?' So we started to talk, and we talked, and we went to lunch, and we talked, and we walked, and we went to dinner, and we talked, and we walked, and we traded addresses, and then, I walked her to the Underground, and she went home, and I went back to my division. We wrote to each other for a long time. She was a very fine woman, but she eventually sent me a 'Dear John Letter'.

Melvin Silverman

AMERICAN ARMED FORCES

I remember in England once, when I was downtown. I was sitting in this bar, and this guy comes up to me and asks me if I'm Jewish. I hesitated a while, but then said, 'Yeah.' He said, 'Can you join the *minyan* [The quorum required for *Jewish* communal worship]?' I said, 'Yeah, sure.' I'm drinking here, and I'm ready to go out, and he wants me to join the *minyan*! You need ten men over the age of thirteen and over, in order to have certain prayers. So he would go to every GI at the bar, and he happened to hit our outfit and in about five minutes he had his *minyan*. So, you know, you went over to where he was, and it took us about a half an hour and when we were finished we went back to the bar. And all the girls were saying, 'Where did you guys go?' We said, 'We went for a *minyan*.' 'Oh, what's that? Is that a kind of a party?' So I replied, 'Yeah, some sort of party.'

John G. Rosta

AMERICAN ARMED FORCES

In England, I found the people friendly. They went out of their way to make us feel welcome, that we were welcome allies, and they wanted to be friendly, but the officers were more aloof, the British officers. We were officers, too, but we were a different class, a lower class. We weren't professionals like they were. That was the impression they gave us.

Pearl Paterson Thompson

AMERICAN CIVILIAN

Well, I'm quite sure that England got a much better king when Edward abdicated. His brother George depended a lot on his wife, who was Scottish, and the Queen Mum was the key influence on his life and she kept him calm and reflective. They stood by in Buckingham Palace when it was bombed instead of skedaddling, so I think that he made a much better king than Edward would have been.

Albert S. Porter Jr

AMERICAN ARMED FORCES

There was a little bit of resentment about how highly paid we were, in relation to English military. I was a sergeant at that time and I got another 50 per cent as flight pay and another 25 per cent because it was overseas in combat. So I had a lot of money and we always went into London, and always went first class.

I had a girl that I met in London and I used to bring things for her family, any food that I could grab, and I remember going to dinner at her house and realizing, for the first time, that this particular house did not have a toilet inside the house. It was outside, it was another room, but it was outside of the house. The English were very, very much behind us in living quarters; at least that's my experience. Refrigeration was unheard of, for crying out loud. You couldn't get a cold beer. I can remember thinking to myself, every once in a while, 'Boy, I'd like an ice-cold beer.' Then a second later, 'Oh, no, no, I'd rather have a milkshake. Oh, boy would I like to have a milkshake.'

Irving Pape

AMERICAN ARMED FORCES

And when I got to London this gal that I knew in New York wrote me. She said to look up Elaine, whose dad was a British colonel. They had everything. They lived in a beautiful apartment on Baker Street. They had another apartment on the same floor, two apartments to a floor. You get the size of how plush this was. It was occupied by a cousin of the Queen of England. So every weekend I would hop on the train from Shrivenham where we were training and go to London. She had contacts all over. We wanted to get into a restaurant or a place to have a few drinks and dance, she got us in. One Sunday morning we were having breakfast and the colonel says to me, 'Well Irv, I don't think we're going to see you after this weekend.' I said, 'What do you mean?' He said, 'Well, you know, in civilian life I'm in the furniture business. Well, we've just got a big order for crosses from the British army. Usually means that there's going be a big push.' So I said, 'Really?' He said, 'Yes, you know what I'm talking about.' I replied, nodding my head slowly, 'Sure, I know what you're talking about.'

Domenic Melso

AMERICAN ARMED FORCES
You never heard the English talk about war. It was amazing. Even when you went to the pub or the movies, you would never hear talk about the war.

Donald E. Lundberg

AMERICAN ARMED FORCES
I met a young lady named Guinevere. She was typically British. Her father was a lieutenant colonel and we had a nice thing going. One evening she said, 'My father would like you to join us for the weekend.' I thought it was all right for us to have an affair, but I didn't want the father to know about it. She said, 'It's all right, he's bringing his girlfriend.' Her mother was back in the town. I said, 'Oh, okay.' We had a lot of fun. She was a very fine young lady, a very pretty, young lady, too. I kept in contact with her for quite a few years and often wondered what happened to her.

Charles W. McDougall

AMERICAN ARMED FORCES
I met Cynthia Hay. Her father was a retired colonel in the British Army, and they lived in Torquay. She worked in London and came

home weekends. So I only met her on weekends and we'd go over to the Imperial Hotel and dance. She was engaged to be married and so was I. Her husband-to-be was way off in the Far East somewhere and had been gone for three years. Anyway, we enjoyed each other's company and I enjoyed her father and mother and ate many dinners at their home. It was a strange time.

American officers at a tea in Winchester, Hampshire, 1944. All levels of society helped to entertain the visiting army.

Joseph Mauro

AMERICAN ARMED FORCES

In London was one of the biggest in England. Oh my God, I went in there and it's so huge; in the center of the hall, there was a rotating platform with a fifteen-piece band. After they played three or four sets, it would revolve, and another band would come on. So it was continuous jitterbugging and dancing. We were having a ball, and we danced with them English girls jitterbugging. I love the jitterbug.

Roy William Reisert

AMERICAN ARMED FORCES
Those uniforms, I tell you, they worked wonders with women. They really did. It was a great way to get somebody to engage in conversation. I met a lot of nice women that way.

George T. Volk

AMERICAN ARMED FORCES
The people were wonderful in Northern Ireland. They hated the British troops based there. They loved us, and, of course, we had the dates. The British troops were mad at us, so you had to watch when you left the dance or something like that, on your way home. You could get jumped on. But in Ireland, the small town, if somebody shouted, 'There's a Yank in trouble,' boy, they came out. You had help all over the place. We were really kings in Ireland.

J. Talbot Smith

AMERICAN ARMED FORCES
If you're invited to dinner, or lunch, or tea in England, you had to bring some butter because they will feed you their month's ration in one sitting.

Theodore K. Robinson

AMERICAN ARMED FORCES
Let's face it, Americans just were all over the place. We used to

say that when we got off the island, it would rise six feet. We were just all over the place.

William H. Epstein

AMERICAN ARMED FORCES

I got sent on my first guard duty. I stood in the bus for maybe twenty minutes and finally the bus stops. The sergeant says, 'Epstein, get out.' So, I get out and I take a look around and I don't see anything. Of course, it's dark; anyway, I don't see anything. So, I said to the sergeant, 'Where am I guarding?' He says, 'Don't ask me, you got here just like I got here.' So, I said, 'What am I supposed to do?' He says, 'Don't ask me,' and he disappears. And I am left there. Besides being dark, it was foggy, very foggy. You hear about these London fogs, well, this was one of those kinds. I couldn't see more than maybe ten feet in front of me and I didn't know what I was guarding. I didn't know what I was doing. The only thing I had was a rifle on my shoulders and a pistol on my gun belt. So I felt my gun and my pistol to make sure at least I had something and so I decided the best thing to do was to try to find something that I could guard. So, what I did was I walked along the road 200 paces. I couldn't find anything but I smelled something and I said to myself, 'I smelled that before. I can't tell what it is right now, but I smelled it.' Then I walked back 200 paces and started again and walked 200 paces in the other direction, but I couldn't find anything. Then I decided to come back and walked 300 paces the other way and the smell became a little stronger and I said to myself, 'Huh, now what is that smell?' I couldn't see anything, so I was afraid to go off the road because I was afraid I couldn't find it again. So, anyway, I walked again, I'm back the 300 paces, walked the other way 300 paces, couldn't find anything. Then all of a sudden I hear footsteps, lots of footsteps. I don't know whose coming or what's coming. 'Could it be Germans?' I said to myself. 'I better, I better hide.' So I went into the bush and listened as the footsteps came closer and closer and then all of a sudden I didn't hear them. I said, 'My God, they've already passed by. I'm going to be court martialled because I didn't do anything and I didn't know what to do. I can't call. I have nothing to call. I don't know what I'm doing here.' So I went back to the road and I decided that I'd walk 400 steps another way. Maybe I could find something. I walked 400 steps, and the strong odour was more distinct. I still didn't know what it was but it smelled really like a chemical of some kind.

Then, again, I hear footsteps. I jump, I run, I dive in the bushes again. I'd read Fenimore Cooper's *Last of the Mohicans* and he could tell by putting his ear to the ground how many people were walking. I tried that. The only thing I got was a lot of weeds in my ear. So, finally, footsteps disappeared. I said to myself, 'I'm certainly in for it. All these men are going by and I haven't done anything: I don't know what I'm doing.' So I got out and I walked again, and still the same thing and I come back and there are the footsteps again. This time, I decided I'm going to do something. I pull out my gun. 'I'm going to, I'm going to fire at it.' I said to myself, 'Why am I firing? If they don't know, if I can't see them, they can't see me.' So, anyway, time passes and finally, about six o'clock in the morning, I don't know what I did, I knew I couldn't fall asleep, because if I fall asleep on duty, I'd get shot. There I am, cold; I'm wet and I'm tired and I'm sleepy and I'm everything, but I can't sleep. I'm walking and I'm pacing. Finally, the sergeant of guard comes and he's shouting. I run up to him and say, 'Shh, we're surrounded, we're surrounded.' He says, 'What's the matter?' I told him. I told him the story about hearing the footsteps. 'Oh,' he says, 'they're rabbits. They're big rabbits.' He said, 'They walk, they make enough noise, you think they're human beings.' I said, 'Rabbits? What am I supposed to be guarding?' 'Oh, didn't I tell you? You're guarding the cesspool.' That was my introduction to army life in England!

I attended a dance and the alert went on and no one moved. The band kept on playing and the performers performed their act, and everything was natural, was like normal, and then when the 'all clear' went out, everybody started cheering. I went to services on Yom Kippur, that's the Jewish holy day, and Hitler had promised they would interrupt the services. The alert went. I was one of three American soldiers there and so I looked to see what the English were doing: they didn't move at all, they continued the service. I wasn't going to run away, because I figured if I ran away that'd look bad for American soldiers so I stood right there and prayed, just like they did. Nobody moved, everybody had confidence that the English would shoot down the German planes. That was a very moving experience. I remember a woman ran, I think rather wisely, with two small children, to a local bomb shelter; nobody else moved.

Herbert Degan

AMERICAN ARMED FORCES

Yes, oh, United Services Organizations, or the USOs as we called them, were everywhere. They were the darlings of the American troops. They were just wonderful. The stars danced, they sang, they fraternized, they ate with us. They were very morale building.

Lee Eli Barr

EIGHTH AIR FORCE, 306TH BOMB GROUP

I used to go to London on a pass but I never did any sightseeing or looking. The idea was to find a young lady and have a good time and it was very easy to find a young lady. A lot of young ladies become prostitutes, and you hear these sounds from all sorts of places because of the blackout. And I wanted to get vulgar. 'Hey, Yank, you want to come home with me?' You didn't have to, but it was a standard procedure. If you said, 'Yes', the next thing you would do is offer this young lady a cigarette. Cigarettes were very tight in those days and she would take a cigarette, then you would light a match and inspect the merchandise.

Frederick A. Almerino

AMERICAN ARMED FORCES

Pahokski was from Pennsylvania and we were talking. I said, 'Well, some of the black people aren't bad. You know, if they get an education, some of them are smart, if they go to school.' Well, he almost tore my head off. He was a tech sergeant, I was only a staff. He wanted to fight me and he was a big guy, I wasn't going to fight him, but he was adamant that no black man was equal to him.

Reid M. Waltman

AMERICAN ARMED FORCES

When we woke up the next morning at this airfield in the north of England, we heard this terrific roar and dashed out to see what this noise was. There was a twin-engine Mosquito bomber buzzing the area below treetop level and he came right in front of us, and then went down the line. We looked and were horrified to see that there was a telephone pole down the line and, being flyers, we knew he wasn't going to make it and, sure enough, he saw it and lifted up, but the tail of this plane hit the crossbars of the telephone pole and spun up in the air, and then it turned and came down and crashed in a big plume of flames and smoke. We realized that there was a casualty of war right there. Of course, he shouldn't have been buzzing, but that's what young pilots do.

That was an introduction to war, right then and there.

Albert B. Meserlin Jr

STAFF PHOTOGRAPHER TO GENERAL DWIGHT D. EISENHOWER

No matter where you looked, hidden in the countryside would be tanks, trucks, ambulances, every piece of equipment you could think of. To this day, I wonder why the Germans didn't see more of this with their air raids.

John H. Cook

AMERICAN ARMED FORCES

We'd had fights in England. We'd lived near Hereford and there were fights between the blacks and the whites because the military was segregated: but we went into the same town. The whites could go into town on certain days and the blacks on the other days, and there was another town nearby, where, if you couldn't go to the one town, you could go to the other town. But there was a lot of fighting against the blacks in England. Later in the war while we were in the south of France, because of this hatred the French had for us GIs, there was more than one occasion where the blacks would fight side by side with the whites against the French, who were after our tank battalion men.

Alfred V. Sloan Jr

AMERICAN ARMED FORCES

We're Reform Jews, you know, no big problem. Just before the invasion, I was in Cambridge at the Red Cross on Trumpington Street, and I grabbed, you know, not a hot dog, must have been what passed for a hamburger, and a cup of coffee, or something. I'm sitting down in the snack bar and the guy opposite me, I noticed, was a Jewish chaplain. I could tell by his collar insignia, the Ten Commandments, which identified a Jewish chaplain. We were having a good chat. He was a nice guy, very informal and pleasant, and so forth, and I said to him, I said, 'Listen, answer for me a question.' I said, 'Because I'm a Reform Jew, if I want to have a ham sandwich – and go up to the bar and order a ham sandwich – is the world going to end?' So, he gave me this answer, and, again, I'm paraphrasing it, because I can't remember the exact words. He says, 'Look,' he says, 'don't make a big fuss over this, because you're Reform, I'm Reform and I don't want to lose my union card, but,' he says, 'frankly, the Lord has got bigger things to worry about than whether Sergeant Sloan eats a ham sandwich or not. But,' he said, 'he'd be very, very upset if you did not share that ham sandwich with a hungry man.' And, I thought, 'Hell, that was a great piece of philosophy.'

Lea Crawley

AMERICAN ARMED FORCES

We used to go up into Neath. I was married, but I was still going to see some of the girls, 'cause you had some black girls there left from fathers who had been in the First World War. Some of those soldiers stayed or left babies there, or whatever, and they were grown women then, but they were some beautiful women.

Well, we worked in that supply depot. We'd go down and get cigarettes. Oh, that was quite a job, too, 'cause you had to keep track of all that. We didn't get cartons; we got the whole case of cigarettes. We even got Kotex towels for the girls: some of them had nerve enough to ask for Modess, which were better quality. We'd just order what they said and we ordered stockings for them and all that stuff.

Carol Levin

AMERICAN ARMED FORCES

You know, when you're far from home, everybody's homesick. So I kept up with everybody at home. All my relatives wrote to me. They were so proud that they had a 'soldier girl' in the family . . . We were all in the army together. We gave up our jobs; we gave up our homes, because we wanted to see the war over. So we all helped each other.

I found out the hard way that one of my officers was a lesbian. I never had any direct problem with that. But a girl that I knew told me that Lieutenant whatever-her-name-was was caught in bed with another girl but wasn't removed from the army because that was the rule at that time. I could never warm to her after that.

Preparations for D-Day 1) The Evacuation of the Slapton Area

By the autumn of 1943 it was decided that Slapton beach, in Devon, would become a major practice area for the D-Day land-ings, using live ammunition and recreating the defences likely to be put up by Germans on any beach to be attacked. The intention was to simulate real battle conditions for troops without any such experience. Since the barrage of artillery from the ships was bound to cause extensive damage to the whole area under attack, the entire population of the area from Torcross to Blackpool Sands, and inland for about ten miles, was to be evacuated.

Sir Hugh Ellis

REGIONAL COMMISSIONER SPEAKING TO THE VILLAGERS IN EAST ALLINGTON ON 12 NOVEMBER 1943

I have never had a task put upon me such as I have now to do. There are 840 households, over 200 farms, and many thousand head of good stock, and we have been asked to do this so that the services may take over and begin practice by 1 January. The case against taking up that area, a case for the valuable agricul-tural property, the case for the upsetting of their lives; all that had been put before the Ministers.

Winston Churchill

PRIME MINISTER

Neither the men, who would have to take part in operations, nor their relations and friends would want them to go in without every possible training, and they had also to try out the weapons and craft they were going to use. They would have to practise every day as long as God gave them fine weather. That was why residents were being asked to surrender their land to permit the practice to take place.

The villagers had to be out by 20 December – five days before Christmas.

Freda Widger

FARMER'S DAUGHTER IN SLAPTON

My mother's cousin lived at the Round House at Slapton – they had army men billeted on them, and when rumours circulated that we were to be evacuated even the army men said, 'Impossible – they could not possibly clear out such a big area.' All of a sudden we had a notice that there was to be a meeting in the village hall, the villagers had to attend and we were told we had six weeks to clear out. I remember the meeting well. I was about twenty-two or twenty-three. Everyone was up in arms. One old man said he wouldn't go. We all thought it was going to be for a month, perhaps six weeks. We did not realise it was going to be for eleven or twelve months.

My mother was very unhappy; she was born in the village and had always lived there. We went out from there a fortnight before Christmas – it was really a traumatic time to go out just before Christmas. We were about the last to leave as we were supplying the village with milk. Everybody depended on us.

Pearl Rogers

SCHOOLGIRL

My father had the butcher's shop in Slapton, which had to close when they left. There was no compensation given for the loss of income from the business for nearly a year. My father got a

Frank Rogers, Slapton's butcher, loading his table into a van during the evacuation of the village, 1943. His daughter Pearl looks on.

job on a farm and was called up as he no longer ran his own business.

I remember going with my mother to look for somewhere to rent. At one house in Brixham the lady took one look at my brother and me and slammed the door in our face – she did not want children! For some, the thought of moving out of the village they had lived in for over eighty years was just too much. One old couple, Mr and Mrs Jarvis, refused to look for anywhere and in the end said, 'We're coming with you Frank.' They were old friends, but not related. So we rented a large house in West Buckland, to have room for the old couple.

However, Mrs Jarvis died before we left, and Mr Jarvis died soon after Christmas. People forget the shock to the old of leaving the village where they had lived all their lives. They could not even be buried in their native village.

Operation Tiger was the code name for one in a series of large-scale rehearsals for the D-Day invasion of Normandy, which took place on Slapton Sands. Communication problems resulted in an Allied convoy of landing-craft being attacked by German E-boats. Torpedoes hit three of the LSTs. One lost its stern but eventually limped into port. Another burst into flames, the fire fed by fuel in the vehicles aboard. A third keeled over and sank within six minutes, resulting in the deaths of 749 American servicemen. This was the most costly training incident involving US forces during the Second World War. The incident was under the strictest secrecy at the time due to the impending invasion, and was only nominally reported afterwards.

Arthur Victor

AMERICAN SOLDIER ON LST 507 OFF SLAPTON

When we were hit, as soon as we heard 'Abandon ship!' guys started over the side in droves. Many landed on top of one another; others, who for some reason were dressed for battle, pitched forward in the water with legs up and faces down. They were top heavy and struggled unsuccessfully to overcome it, even though I could see they were wearing lifebelts. It was unbelievable. Those who survived the jump swam towards the raft.

I threw down my helmet and started to go over the side when I heard someone frantically calling my name. I turned and saw another corpsman standing there shaking with fear. I took his hand and led him to the railing and told him we would jump together, but that he shouldn't grab on to me but should rely on his lifebelt for support. I had to keep reassuring him that we would be okay. Then we slowly climbed over the railing together and before he had time to hesitate I grabbed his hand and jumped.

We hit the water together, our grasp broken as we sank deep into the freezing English Channel. It seemed an eternity before we reached the surface. I stayed were I was, holding on and treading water, getting my breath. After a few minutes I tried heading for the raft, which surprisingly was still in sight, lit up by the burning 507 which was sinking slowly at the stern. I knew there wasn't much time left, and without a lifebelt I wasn't sure I could make it to the raft if I delayed any longer. So I turned and started to move away. Another corpsman screamed at me to come back. I stopped, turned and told him to let go of the landing-craft and work his way to me, but he said he was too scared and couldn't do it. Reluctantly I turned, wished him luck and swam away. I never looked back, even though he kept shrieking at me to return. I was sure he was going to die. I was sick at heart.

I made it to the raft and strangely enough there was only a handful of men clinging to the side. I thought by now it would be overcrowded. I guess a lot of guys floundered and died before they even got started. When I got there, Star was kneeling alone on the top. I found an open space on the side and took hold. It wasn't long before we were swarmed by men who quickly filled the other open spaces along the sides. Those who didn't make it to the open spaces had to hold on to those who did. The extreme cold and hysteria were already taking their toll. Guys without lifebelts and in waterlogged clothing were in a constant struggle to stay afloat, holding on to guys with belts or Mae West's. Men were dying all around in those first few minutes of trying to settle into our perilous predicament. It puzzled me how young healthy men could give up and die so easily. It still does.

As many died, there was still as many to take their place, so we were loading up pretty fast. We spotted another raft about two hundred feet away, but further out to sea, with just a cluster of men clinging to it. I volunteered to swim there to help relieve the load on ours. Some of the others said they would go with me, so I removed my jacket, which had become heavy with water, and let it drift away, but during this intervening time the other raft became full, so I stayed put. However, without my jacket I was left bare from the waist up, which put me at the mercy of the freezing cold water that splashed over us. It was like being naked in a pool of ice water. We were now about a hundred yards out from the landing-craft when I felt a sharp heat strike the back of my neck; then someone started screaming that the water was on fire. I turned quickly and stared at mile-high flames and billowing black smoke making a wide circle, but by some miracle the fire suddenly died out when it was not more than twenty feet away from us.

There were about seventy-five of us now, jammed around and about the raft, holding on to each other as before. Guys came and guys went. It was hard to keep count. Across from me were six other corpsmen clinging to the side, including Rutherford, who had one of them hanging on piggyback. One of the doctors was to the left of me at one end holding up a soldier who kept moaning that his leg was broken. The other doctor was opposite with the corpsmen. We were so packed together that the raft was arm length under water from the sheer weight of us, so we had to extend our arms to keep our heads above water. It was agonising.

Guys were dying off all around us. Those without life preservers just let go, struggled a bit, and then disappeared. Dead weight made it impossible to do much or anything to help them. One of the first to go was a corpsman who was only nineteen years old, married and the father of a four-month-old son. He wasn't wearing a lifebelt and had been holding on next to Rutherford. Suddenly and without warning he was struggling in the water, screaming for help. Star couldn't reach him and Rutherford, who was still holding on to the other corpsman, threw him his leg to grab on to. He managed to get hold of the foot but slid off and sank beneath the surface. We waited for him to pop up, but he never did. He had gone. We were dumbfounded and devastated and prayed for him. That's all we could do. But no sooner was he gone than the boy on Rutherford's back let go and started sliding down. Rutherford reached back to try and hold him up but he was too heavy and wet and kept going straight down. Star tried to help but it was too late. He never said a word and never tried to help himself. Just quietly disappeared beneath the surface and never came up. It happened to be his nineteenth birthday.

The 507 could be seen, still afloat, still aflame, listing at the stern. There were men still running about her decks. Off to our left was the LST 531 and we started kicking in her direction hoping to be picked up. Then we heard two thunderous explosions and great columns of fire and smoke rose from her belly. Ammunition started firing from her bow guns and shot straight up into the sky, making it look like a 4th of July celebration. Bodies hurled from her deck like rag dummies, parts of bodies too. A few guys managed to jump and swim for their lives as the 531 split and went down in a matter of minutes. In a blink of an eye, it blew up and disappeared, taking most of its crew and soldiers with it. When the 531 went down guys started shrieking despairingly that it was the end of the world. They cried because we could be gunned down in the water. Desperate men were praying aloud, begging, pleading to be saved. They started packing in closer and tighter to the raft, pushing it further under. Then a few soldiers banded together and worked their way closer. They threatened to get on the raft and take over. They said that because we were sailors we were better in the water than they were.

I had become almost unbearably cold by now. I had also been swallowing oily-tasting salt water that made me nauseous and I started puking. I pissed my pants to feel warmth. I remember how good it felt pouring over my thighs, but I kept puking my guts. I was numb as we continued drifting and losing men. They seemed to just give up and slip under without much of a struggle, or died in their preservers where they were. The 507 was still in sight but fading from view. Fog was beginning to surround us. We could still hear the cries for help. We called out and flashed our lights to give our position but only a few managed to make it to us. We finally drifted beyond sight of the still-burning 507, shrouded in fog and mist. We could hear the drone of an engine, hoped it wasn't Germans looking for survivors to pick off. But someone said it sounded like one of our small boats, so we took the chance and yelled and shouted and kept signalling with a flashlight that we were able to pull free from the underside of the raft, but the boat never came. Later we learned it was picking up lone swimmers. We continued drifting in a thick fog and heavy swells.

Guys became seasick and threw up, taking in water as they gulped, making them sicker and weaker and hopeless. Guys were dying off in a steady stream. They died and drifted away or died and went under. By losing so many men the raft had been slowly rising to the surface so we could lean on it. The soldier with a broken leg was allowed on top, where he sprawled out. He was a big man and covered almost the entire top of the raft. With him on and us leaning, the raft went under again so we were back to extended arms and heads held high. At some point in time we were joined by Lewis, a bear of a boy who came swimming out of the darkness. I couldn't believe it. After he rested he said 'Bye' and took off. It was even more amazing, as we found out later, that he survived. After about five hours we were down to about twenty of us and the raft had risen to the surface. We were able to lean again. It felt wonderful.

Preparations for D-Day 2) Rehearsals and Dummy Runs

Daniel Cox

CIVILIAN

Diary entry, 31 December 1943

Tonight's news is that Russians have recaptured Zhitomir. Did not stop to see the New Year in, but went to bed at quarter past eleven. As usual, most people are talking of 'Victory in 1944' but I have heard that cry every year since the war started. Certainly things at the moment are in favour, but look how long our Italian campaign has taken.

Marjorie Hirst, *née Crowe*

WREN

From London we were drafted to Weymouth where landing exercises were taking place. We were working very long hours – sometimes from 9am to 1am, with interruptions for air raids when we would have to go up and down to and from the shelters. We were working with manual duplicating machines, making a thousand copies of each page. We realised that the work we were doing was secret and that it was very important. We were never given two pages which followed each other.

My friend and I were sent to Southampton. Here equipment was being assembled under camouflage in the wooded areas outside the town, ready to go on the ships. During this time I saw many important figures, including Churchill, Montgomery and Eisenhower. Six days before D-Day, King George VI came to inspect the fleet, including the Force G HQ ship, HMS *Bulolo*. Sixteen Wrens were wanted on board the ship when the King visited; lots were drawn to choose the lucky sixteen and I was one of them. We were taken down the Solent in small boats and climbed up the ladder on the side of the ship. Our uniform had to be very spick and span – it was a great honour to be there.

A row of Churchill Mark IV tanks, lined up along the Winchester by-pass in Hampshire in readiness for D-Day.

Terence Crowley

WAR WORKER

The effort for the war in this workshop was frantic. The workforce numbered over 1,000 people, men and women, and the great number of locomotives and carriages were built at Brighton. Similar efforts were mirrored at other Southern Railways factories along the south coast. Additionally, the yards had to cope more and more for the build-up to the invasion. Arriving at work in the morning, the yards were choked with tanks, lorries and guns, but at lunchtime the yards were clear and all this war equipment was moved to the South Downs for the troops that were hidden in tented cities awaiting and training for the big day.

Mike Crooks

CHAPLAIN

I attended a conference for chaplains who were going over on the day. This took place at the Combined Operations HQ in Whitehall. There were at least sixty of us present. We were addressed by General Sturges and the Second Sea Lord, Admiral Sir Algernon Willis, and given briefs about what to expect on the beaches and told to draw morphia from the MO. In addition, the naval chaplains were asked to draw a church pennant from stores, which was to be flown by the ship you were visiting if it was standing off-shore.

On the Saturday before D-Day I joined an American LST (Tank Landing Ship) at anchor in the Thames Estuary. This ship was designed to carry tanks in the space below and transport on deck. It was fitted out as a hospital ship, of sorts, for the return journey, with rows of folding bunks on each side of the tank space and an operating table in the Ward Room.

Stan Davison

BRITISH SOLDIER

We kicked our heels around waiting for the big off. Then we did a number of dummy runs like going up the North Sea. Crazy in a way, but we sailed all the way from Portsmouth, which was a dodgy thing to do, and did a landing at Cromarty-Firth. All the way up there for a beach landing. I was so cold. A lovely day, but cold! We had to do a forced march; go up in the hills, and then we had to sleep in our wet clothes. And that was awful. We did two dummy runs. We did another down by the Isle of Wight. So then we were ready for the off.

Major C.K. King

COMMANDING A COMPANY, 2ND BATTALION, EAST
YORKSHIRE REGIMENT

The exercises were spartan, to put it mildly. After embarking, the 'fleet' would drop us around the Moray Firth during the night to simulate the cross-channel journey and then decant us on various beaches on the south side of the Firth, as a very cold bleak winter's dawn was breaking. We would wade ashore catching our breaths at the cold and hopping about trying to keep our vulnerable parts out of the water. More often than not there was a rime of ice along the water's edge. Brigade Headquarters would embark in the HQ ship specially fitted out for Combined Operations including extra wireless communications for the three services and an operations room. When the bridgehead had been secured the brigadier would give the word for Brigade HQ to go ashore and we would clamber down the side of the ship into a small landing-craft. On one celebrated occasion when it was particularly cold and unpleasant the landing-craft grounded rather far out and we had a long waist-deep wade to get ashore. The brigadier stood in the bows and watched us all plunge in and then made the coxswain pull off and go alongside a tank landing-craft discharging nearby, whose vehicles were going into only a foot or so of water. The brigadier transferred to this, walked along to its ramp and, as a vehicle was going out at that moment, didn't step off the end of the ramp, but to one side, right into a hole up to his neck. None of us dared laugh.

Mrs Eager

CIVILIAN

We lived very near the embarkation point, and it was very exciting. We had a front seat for all the traffic that came past. My children were very excited about it. They would get up in the middle of the night to see what fresh convoy was coming along. It might have been the tanks, it might have been the DUKWs, sometimes it was motorbikes and all types of war vehicles, and they were most thrilled.

When things started, we were asked not to talk to the troops, so we did as we were told, but they did say we could give them hot water for their tea. I have one sad recollection of a soldier bringing back his full mug of tea to me and saying, 'You have it love, we shan't need it any more.' And that made me very sad: the full realisation of the whole thing came upon me and I knew how they felt. They were all very quiet and extremely well behaved; there was no noise, no shouting, nothing thrown about, all very tidy. They slept in our front gardens, around the flowerbeds, and spoiled nothing at all. Sometimes we were asked for bowls of water for them to shave in the back garden; we helped where we could.

Bramwell Taylor

CIVILIAN

Of course Woolston was so badly bombed and all the houses were so bad that they used all that area for training the D-Day troops for the house-to-house fighting. It was a lot of ruins anyway, so they just carried on using it as ruins!

Sam Logan

CIVILIAN

The Americans did military exercises on our farm near Coleraine. We were encouraged to stay out of their way, so I didn't get talking to them. Any training with tanks would have been done in their base at Ballykelly. They had vehicles the equivalent of Bren-gun carriers. They practised driving over a ditch, which ruined it for agricultural uses. It climaxed with a three-day exercise that ended in a mock battle around the farm on Sunday evening. There were hundreds of them, firing blank cartridges. This was a couple of months before they shipped out to Normandy.

Hilary McClean

CIVILIAN

They used to march, and they didn't call 'left, right, left, right'; they said, 'Hep, two, three, four. Hep, two, three, four . . .' And we used to imitate them as children you know. Their uniforms, we used to think they were great and they fitted them neatly and nicely. Whereas the British Army uniforms – the sailors' uniforms and all – they didn't look so smart. 'Course, in those days all the young girls thought the American soldiers were film stars, but far from it I think!

Joan Hill

CIVILIAN

Women had a new perspective on life around that time: especially if they were married. It was part of the thing during the war. We had to go to work. And there we learned that we had to stand up for ourselves! We had to be accepted. There were lots and lots of trades in the dockyard and we had to show them that we could do the work of men!

I feel it was an experience I shouldn't ever forget. And of course, the war, you don't forget. You don't forget it. It's always there. And, as I say, we worked very hard; especially at D-Day and that.

Yes it was tremendous, tremendous. We knew it was coming. We could tell. We could tell because of the increased activity everywhere.

Fiona Thomas

CIVILIAN

This policeman said, 'I'm sure you haven't got your gas mask in that case.' I said, 'Well why bother then if you know I haven't got it?' He said, 'Where is it?' I said, 'Well, if it's not in there, then it must be at home.' He said, 'I'm going to have to search it' and he tipped it out and I had two sanitary towels in it. I said, 'I told you, didn't I?' His face was like a beetroot.

Ann Tomlinson

WREN

We were supposed to replace boys. They went onto aircraft carriers. The more Wrens who came, the more boys would be released to go into the war itself. But, scandalously, it was sort of three Wrens to two boys. I thought the Wrens did as good a job as the boys as air mechanics, I really did, and we all felt that, but I don't remember we ever felt militant. We used to laugh about it and look at the boys and think, 'Three of us, lovely us, to replace only two of them, it's ridiculous.' And we laughed about it, but we never made an issue of it or a fuss. No. It was so much taken for granted that women earned less and that women were in some ways considered inferior. It's strange now; the change is so great.

Elizabeth Forster

RADAR OPERATOR, WAAF

Being a radar operator on a GCI station was the next best thing to being in the plane with the pilot (though considerably safer)! You saw the blips getting closer, the pilot then called 'Tally Ho' and the enemy blip broke up. It was very exciting but did not make up for the sadness, for the ones who did not come home.

I was in the WAAF for five and a half years. After the war I found that life as a civilian was rather dull.

A WAAF radar operator plotting aircraft on the Cathode Ray Tube Monitor.

Frank Barrett

DOCK OVERSEER

The labourer I had that night was an American labourer because there weren't enough Southampton dockers to work the ships. The Americans had their own labour force and that particular night they sent me all these men and, all credit to them, they tried hard, but they weren't used to this kind of work. During the night, somewhere around three o'clock in the morning, they were lifting a half-track vehicle up at number four hatch. I could tell by the sounds that things were not going right. I ran as fast as I could towards number four, shouting to the men on the quay 'Run! Run for your life, run!' and they all scattered and then CRASH! – down came this half-track vehicle onto the quay. Had the men not run, and me as well, obviously we'd have been completely crushed.

In the morning some more American staff came along to clear up all this mess and one of the men who was in a bomb disposal squad, who asked what happened, so I told him. He said, 'Wasn't there any sparks?' I said, 'It was like bonfire night; this vehicle came straight down, scraped side of the ship and there were sparks all over the place.' He said, 'You're lucky, that vehicle was packed tight with high explosive and by rights that should have gone off and blown you and the ship to blazes, and half of Southampton as well.

Bernard Turner

FACTORY WORKER

We were overhauling army vehicles. They had to be stripped out and completely overhauled, ready to go back into action. Ford's, at Dagenham, were only producing army vehicles. Ford produced 360,000 vehicles. There were no private vehicles produced.

Daniel Cox

CIVILIAN

Diary entry, 8 August 1943

Heard this morning the Southampton area (extending to Romsey, Winchester, Horndean and Fareham in the east) will be a restricted district from August 17th. Various rumours are circulating as usual. A curfew is to be imposed at once. It is fairly evident that Southampton will be an important port when the invasion of Europe does take place.

Diary entry, 24 August 1943

B.K. has been telling me various things he has heard officially from H.G. headquarters. Heavy bombing raids are expected on the town, with a possibility of airborne troops being landed. I know that the anti-aircraft defences have been strengthened during the last week or two, and there are reports that the fire services have been augmented from other towns. Although this might be a lot of hooey, the signs are that something big is pending, and I can't look into the future with any pleasurable anticipation. Last night we raided Berlin and lost fifty-eight bombers in the process.

The Quebec talks have ended and other news in is that Himmler has been appointed Minister of the Interior in Germany.

Diary entry, 25 August 1943
Heard that by the end of next week all the big boats in the docks must leave. Whether it is true or not remains to be seen. Our vessel must be finished by Tuesday.

Diary entry, 2 September 1943
According to rumours from 'high officials' in the docks the latest date for the invasion of France is between the 10th and 14th of this month. Full moon is on the 14th.

Diary entry, 12 November 1943
B.K. told me today that Len says that all the naval people and bigwigs who came to the yard seem to think that the war with Germany will be over by next March or April.

Diary entry, 11 March 1944
These last few days have been remarkable for the amount of military traffic on the roads. Troops, guns, tanks and vehicles of every description have been going to, and coming from, Southampton. One can't see sense or reason for it all, but I suppose it's part of a plan. But I still do not anticipate an invasion of Europe yet.

Bernard Knowles in Southampton: The English Gateway

AUTHOR
Each of the twenty-five camps that were eventually built in the Area of Southampton was laid out in the form of blocks holding 500 men. Each block was sub-divided into 'villages' holding about 100 men. Fifty pyramidal tents, each accommodating ten men, went to the making of a block, a proportion of tents being set aside for the use of commissioned, and senior non-commissioned, officers.

The basic layout of the camps decided, the real work began.

New camp roads had to be made and old ones improved. Later, tents had to be pitched and numbered; paths had to be 'recced' and marked with posts and wire, or post and sampling, fences; signs, both plain and illuminated, had to be made or erected so that transit troops could find their way about the camp by night or day; slit trenches dug and numbered against bombing attacks; vehicle standings prepared. Above and beyond this, the whole camp organisation had to be set up, including stores, cookhouses, dining tents and entertaining centres.

Certain camps embraced residences housing civilian occupants, which meant giving them the chance of evacuating the camp or becoming bound by military security measures.

Len Bellows

SCHOOLBOY

On one occasion in Hayling Island, I thought I saw a canoe with an engine in it, but it wasn't. It was chugging along and it gradually went under water! I thought it was sinking! I called out the guards: 'Come on! Quick! Rescue them!' Sort of thing. But it was a two-man submarine! We saw all this sort of thing, as a nipper, really, and there's other things. There was a place near Southwark House that had blow-up guns and blow-up tanks. They had all sorts of those dummy things there at that time. And the army were playing with them, sort of thing. So all this we saw, and it was part of life, really.

Mrs Sylvia Kay

SWITCHBOARD OPERATOR

April 1944, we girls were at Bushy Park, Kingston upon Thames, attached to Supreme Headquarters Allied Expeditionary Force manning the chaotic switchboard there. My friend, Private Kay Callaghan, and I were manning General Eisenhower's private switchboard, known as the 'Red Board'. We had a direct line to Winston Churchill on the board.

The weather was very hot, and we dragged our beds out of our huts at night, to sleep outside! The buzz-bombs started coming, and there were gun emplacements all over the camp. But we slept through it. We saw the general a lot – he was always on the go.

About the middle of May, things went very quiet – we sensed that something was imminent. We were told we were moving the next day, but not where. Next day we piled into the lorries, and then arrived at Fort Purbrook, Cosham, near Portsmouth to sleep under canvas! A switchboard had been set up in Cosham Forest. After a few days, the rain started. It went on and on – it was a sea of mud in that forest, and the Americans had to put what I think were 'pontoon roads' down or we might have drowned!

Captain Joe Patterson

MEDICAL OFFICER

The air photographs were very clear, and it would not have taken much enterprise to pick out the place on a map of France. However, we were asked not to do so. The three French troops in the unit nearly all recognised the area at once. Some of them even lived in the area, and had been in the town less than a year before. One used to work the lock gates at the mouth of the canal before the war.

The endless conferences were rather tedious, and to my mind a bit overdone; anyone who had been in action before could feel that such detailed planning was a waste of time. Personally I refused to be tied down to much detail in my plans, knowing full well that things would look very different when the time came. When they tried to pin me down to which house I was to make my Regimental Aid Post, I drew the line completely.

Eve Warwick

LAND ARMY

Land girls, Joyce, Olive, Kath and I, arrived for work one morning to find a soldier carrying a gun, on guard duty. 'What's your business?' he said. 'You can't go down the lane to the shore.' 'We work here, on the farm,' said Kath. He let us pass, saying we mustn't go down to the beach.

Our task that day was potato planting in a large field of about forty acres. Rectangular, it stretched from the lane to the cliff and was bounded either side by low hedges. A tractor and machine had already made the furrows and put out sacks of seed potatoes ready for us. We put on our large hessian aprons, tied around the waist, and, holding the lower edge, we filled them with potatoes. Then we set off along the furrows placing the potatoes at regular intervals. The tractor and machine would return later to cover them. We reached the cliff-top path on each alternate row. Here we paused briefly to straighten our back and have a break. We always enjoyed the view of the Isle of Wight.

Below us, soldiers were unrolling great coils of wire-mesh across the shingle. They didn't notice us on the cliff above; we carried on with our work, wondering what was about to happen.

The next time we came to the cliff a great deal was happening. Several landing-craft were heading for the shore. They drew up the beach as far as they could and let their front ramps down. 'Look,' said Joyce, 'there are three men skimming along on top of the water.' Then the Jeep they rode in emerged from the waves.

We marvelled to see all kinds of vehicles, vans, lorries and Jeeps issuing from the landing-craft and driving through the waves onto the beach. If any stalled or got stuck, big bulldozers were on hand to assist them or tow them up the beach. We couldn't linger too long to see this spectacle as we had to continue our work. We learned later that the vehicles had been treated with special grease to enable them to drive through the sea water.

This exercise was repeated on other days with different troops. Americans were in charge of the bulldozers and these remained at the farm throughout the exercise. It was evident that something important would happen soon and we had to be discreet. The slogan was 'CARELESS TALK COSTS LIVES'.

Some weeks later we saw weird-looking craft assembling in the Solent; like great rafts with a tall pole at each of the four corners. Very strange. Now I know their purpose. They were part of the Mulberry harbour. They were destined for Arromanches in Normandy where they became part of a floating quay, a huge and vital part of the D-Day invasion. This harbour was depended upon to keep the troops supplied with everything necessary to enable the project to be a success.

Winifred Joan Pine

WREN

In January 1944 I was a Wren stationed in Kingswear, South Devon, attached to HMS Cicala, a Coastal Forces Station consisting of Motor Torpedo and Motor Gun Boats used for harrying German E-boats in the waters close to the Channel Islands.

Throughout the previous months a contingent of US Army personnel arrived and took up occupation in HMS Britannia, the Naval College, Dartmouth. They were responsible for smoke screening our ships while they practised landings in Torbay and were known as 'the Smokies'. Some of them came from the Mid-West of America and had never before been close to the sea. For many months we had US Navy ships carrying landing-craft steaming up the River Dart to anchor, and in the early spring the river was so crowded that it would have been possible to walk across from Kingswear to Dartmouth without getting your feet wet. Large contingents of US Army followed in trains which ran day and night and boarded the ships.

Our 'Wrennery' was on a hill overlooking the river, and each morning we would wake up to the sound of Glenn Miller or the Andrews Sisters coming through their loud hailer system. We got to know the words of all the songs and I can recall them all.

On frequent occasions the ships would silently leave for exercises in the early hours.

Sometimes the weather was rough, and on their return we would see white faces over the ships' rails. Slapton Sands, which was nearby, had been chosen for these exercises since it was a good replica of the Normandy beaches where the invasion would take place.

We in the signal station had notice of when and where the exercises would take place and for two or three days the river was empty and quiet until the ships returned. On their arrival the Americans would be allowed ashore and would board the trains to Torquay for rest and relaxation. Often on our leave days we would meet them on the train and they were always curious about us as we were probably the first Englishwomen they had met. We found them to be courteous and well-mannered towards us.

Troops coming ashore in southern England during a D-Day rehearsal.

Mary MacLeod

AUXILIARY TERRITORIAL SERVICE

I volunteered for the Auxiliary Territorial Service, the women's branch of the army, in Stirling in 1943 when I was twenty years old. I trained at New Battle Abbey Army Training Camp and was then posted to the Clerk School in Golders Green, London, to learn shorthand typing using army methods.

After two weeks, eight of us were taken off our course. We presumed it was because we hadn't passed but we were then despatched to part of the War Office in London.

A sergeant approached me ten days into my placement and said I was ready to start work. He knew my whole background and I was instructed to start typing part of the Normandy invasion plans. At the time I was with General Montgomery's Group, the 21st Army. Four of us were then moved to the 2nd Army under General Dempsey and we continued the same job at Fort Southwick in Portsmouth. Our workplace was built into the cliffs and we felt extremely safe.

Ena Howes

WREN

As the Royal Navy is the senior service I was put in charge, although the exchange was manned by an equal number of Wrens and Royal Corps of Signals men of 21st Army Group. I wrote out the Duty Roster and kept them in order. The telephonists worked twenty-four hours, seven days a week, and were divided into three watches to cover the day and night duties. There was a small telephone exchange, which had ten exchanges and fifty extensions, in the War Room and a Royal Marine with a rifle on duty at the door to see that nobody else was allowed in except the top brass and the Wren plotters. As well as a wall map, which had been made by Chad Valley, the jigsaw makers, there was a map of the coasts of Britain and France on a table where the plotters worked moving models of ships and aircraft and men as instructions came through their headphones.

We were always busy answering calls with no time to chat. The switchboard was a mass of small lights that glowed individually when a call came in. The most important people had blue lights when they made a call and the second in importance had red, while the majority had white lights. They also had scramblers and when making a call they would ask, 'Can you scramble?' This meant that the words they were saying were unintelligible without a scrambler device at the other end and sounded like Donald Duck, so were very secret. As D-Day approached, one Wren was heard to say, 'the exchange was lit up like Blackpool illuminations'.

Flight Lieutenant Alec Blythe

RAF

I had recently married and was living in Ashton Keynes, a tiny Gloucester village. A week before D-Day, I rode my bicycle at a leisurely pace through the quiet and peaceful countryside past little places like Cerney Wick, to the airfield at Down Ampney. There I was to prepare for what, I suppose, was to be the largest military operation that had ever taken place.

Lieutenant Colonel Alistair Pearson

8TH PARACHUTE BATTALION

By the beginning of March 1944 I had the battalion very nearly fighting fit and certainly physically fit. We had limited rations, but we were fit. We had a lot of marching, lot of time on our feet. We had a series of tests; the hardest of ten miles in two hours with full equipment, weighing fifty pounds; we had to run to do it. That was hard.

Commanding officers and intelligence officers were briefed about twenty-eight days before D-Day. We weren't told the exact day, but

I knew with the moon and tides that it had to take place within six or seven days of the first week in June. I then had a mental aberration and got engaged. My wife-to-be said that as it was wartime we should have a short engagement and be married on 8 June. This, of course, coincided with D-Day, but I couldn't tell her that, so a lot of surprised officers of the 6th Airborne received invitations to our wedding. Joan had no idea what was happening and was not told until D-Day that she would not be getting married on the Tuesday. I knew that we'd be fighting in woods so I asked my second in command to find me one. He found a scrubby one of about fifty or sixty acres somewhere in Oxfordshire. We shifted the whole battalion up there. I turned night into day so that they would get used to fighting in dense woods, with live ammunition. You have to work down known tracks and keep close together. It gave them confidence because patrolling at night can be very frightening – but it's a great ally, the dark.

About ten days before D-Day we moved to a transit camp, Blakehill Farm, which was alongside an airfield. We had to share this camp with a company of Royal Ulster Rifles. The camp was sealed and the only source of recreation was the NAAFI tent, staffed by about ten NAAFI girls. I told my adjutant that if any man was seen trying to get under the tent to get to the NAAFI girls they were to get a bullet in the arse. One of our chaps took this literally and put a bullet in the left cheek of one of the RUR – beautiful shot too. That stopped their nonsense!

Pat Briggs

BRITISH ARMED FORCES

The weather was bad from the word 'go'. It was terrible. We had absolutely no cover; the waves were breaking over the front of the landing-craft and soaking everyone. The only things that they had covered, of course, were the guns and the ammunition. They were well covered over but not the troops. So we were thoroughly wet, ankle deep in water and seasick.

We spent the last remaining hours of daylight making life rafts. Each of the rounds of 105mm ammunition came in a waterproof and cardboard cylinder, about three foot long. And it was round. Well, we got these together, tied them – the navy let us have some line – and we were making buoyancy aids with these cylinders and we must have had two or three dozen of them and scattered them around the ship. When dawn broke next day they were all gone, they had all been washed away. So it was just as well we didn't need them!

We spent all night getting into odd corners away from the spray. I doubt anyone slept. For breakfast we were given one tin of self-heating soup and a tin of self-heating chocolate. They were extremely good. They were rather like a tin of soup that you get now but it had a fuse running up the middle. You punched a hole in the bottom, ignited the fuse with a cigarette end and within ten seconds you had a lovely hot drink. When dawn broke, which was wild and woolly, nasty, dark, the navy somehow managed to make buckets of tea and we passed around that and plain bread and jam. That was our breakfast.

Joan Dale

WREN

I was a Wren writer for the thirty three Landing-Craft Flotilla, LC Guns, Force G, preparing for D-Day in Southampton. We had the flotilla office and workshop in concrete huts on Southampton Hard. The office was staffed by a flotilla coxswain who had been in the navy; two Wren writers, Kathy and myself; and Stripey, three stripes for long service, no promotion and propped up by rum. Stripey made the tea. This was done by filling a large brown enamel teapot with water, tea, sugar and powdered milk and bringing it to the boil, resulting in a most evil brew.

Every day more and more troops, tanks and guns poured into Southampton. The town was packed, it didn't seem possible to get any more in, but still they came. For entertainment, Kathy and I went to the cinema, or the coxswain took us to the Seamen's Mission to play draughts or watch the film shows; old American serials such as *Custer's Last Stand*.

Corporal Edward Wallace

ROYAL ARTILLERY

Before D-Day we were camped in Avery in Essex. We had been there a week when barbed wire was put up all around the camp and we were surrounded by Red and Blue Capped Military Police and given no opportunity to leave under any circumstances.

We had a number of other regiments in the camp and we were soon to learn the impact a German landmine could have on a human being. A sergeant in a Scottish regiment was demonstrating how to defuse one of these Teller mines when it exploded and blew him to bits as well as injuring men in the class. His remains were placed in a wheelbarrow and paraded around the camp. A lot of those who saw it were instantly sick.

Major John Howard

2ND BATTALION, OXFORD AND BUCKINGHAMSHIRE LIGHT INFANTRY

Central to the 6th Airborne Division's plan to seize the left flank of the area north-east of Caen was the capture of two bridges over the Caen Canal and the River Orne which we knew the enemy had prepared for demolition. Any German attack against the Allied flank would have come along the coastal road between Benouville and Ranville and cross both these bridges.

It was therefore decided that these bridges should be captured intact by a glider-borne *coup de main* party. My company, D Company, 2nd Battalion Ox and Bucks, was selected for this task. We were supplemented by two platoons from another of our companies and thirty Royal Engineers, making a total force of 180 to be carried in six gliders. After my top-secret briefing at the end of April, we had about a month's training. It was very boring initially because for three or four days we just attacked mock bridges, as a battle drill. We exercised every possible permutation of landing and made sure every platoon could do any one of the six tasks that had been allocated. They went over and over this until everyone was very browned off, but they all knew that complete flexibility was essential. For security reasons, I could not breathe a word to anyone about exactly where we would be landing, not even my second-in-command Brian Priday. All I could do was imply that it was for a special exercise somewhere in the UK. But everyone knew full well that the invasion, or D-Day, was imminent and rightly suspected that we were on a special task, and this blew up *esprit de corps* tremendously. As with all 6th Airborne units at the time, ATS girls, dressed in mufti, were going into pubs to try and pick up if anyone off duty was letting anything out of the bag. But as far as information was concerned, they came away with nothing.

Brigadier James Hill

3RD PARACHUTE BRIGADE

I was somehow in the right place at the right time and early in 1943 I was given command of the 3rd Parachute Brigade, which was then in its infancy. I was still having my wounds dressed from my injuries in North Africa and to obtain an A1 certificate I had to agree that I would not get a pension for the wounds I had received up till then. This suited me, because I hadn't joined the army to get a pension.

One day I was summoned to Divisional Headquarters by Richard Gale, who said, 'James, we have been given the one and only Canadian Parachute Battalion to join this division, and I want it to go in your brigade, so you have got to get rid of one of your battalions.'

The arrival of the Canadians brought a new lease of life to the brigade. They were very similar to the 1st Parachute

Battalion inasmuch as they were formed from soldiers who wanted to fight and the sooner the better, soldiers of fortune really. They didn't want to sit in Canada and miss the war, so they'd joined the newly formed Canadian Parachute Battalion. As one parachute battalion is no good to anybody they were very wisely given to us.

Some were very hard men and just what you would expect to come from the Canadian outback. There were forty-nine Red Indians, and about the same number of French-speaking Canadians. I went up to hospital to visit one Red Indian whose parachute hadn't opened. Almost every bone in his body was broken, yet he lived to tell the tale and fathered fourteen children. They could be a bit boisterous and on one occasion, while returning from leave, one of them had crawled along the outside of the train and dropped a hand grenade down the funnel of the engine. I was hopping mad at that because it immobilised our leave train for a month.

I knew it was going to be tough so I insisted on everyone being 250 per cent fit, and they were. I made sure that every officer could do two jobs and this proved absolutely invaluable. Every battalion and company had an A and B Headquarters, so that if one was knocked out, the other could take over. All the soldiers were trained to use other people's weapons and to drive Bren carriers – anything that kept the battle going.

My four rules of battle I rammed home: number one, speed – we had to get across country faster than anyone else; two, control – no good commanding unless you have discipline and control; three, simplicity in thought and action; and four, effective fire power or fire effect.

Staff Sergeant Roy Howard

GLIDER PILOT REGIMENT
In 1942 I was with the Royal Signals and volunteered for the Glider Pilot Regiment. We trained extremely hard; in fact I'd

been training and doing exercises for twenty-one months before D-Day. We had practised a number of precise night landings although we didn't know why. We were only told three days before D-Day what our final destination would be. My objective was a small corner of a particularly tiny field of rough pasture close to the Orne Bridge. If I overshot I would crush us all against a fourteen-foot-high embankment; if I undershot I would destroy my seven tons of powerless aircraft and its human cargo on a belt of fifty-foot-high trees. There was simply no room for error.

Churchill and Eisenhower, Commander-in-Chief of the Allied Expeditionary Force, watching an airborne rehearsal during the preparations for D-Day.

Norma Churchward

SCHOOLGIRL

It must have been one or two weeks before D-Day that the camp suddenly emptied. All day long, convoy after convoy of lorries, tanks and Jeeps swept past our house, full of soldiers, and others walking alongside the vehicles seemingly fully armed and ready for combat, en route for the south coast towns where they would set sail for the beaches. We stood outside on the pavement frantically waving and shouting to all these young men, many of whom had become our friends during the previous weeks. They all waved back and smiled, and as they passed by showered us with goodies – sweets, chocolates and especially wrapped sugar lumps. It was the sugar lumps I remember most of all!

Felix Branham

T COMPANY, 116TH INFANTRY, 29TH DIVISION, US ARMY

We swam through tanks of water with full equipment on. We threw various hand grenades and used enemy weapons in case we misplaced our own weapons. They would show us how to attack pillboxes, what to do if we became separated on a hostile shore. We learned Morse code; we could flip it with a light. If we were abandoned and they had to come and save us, then we would be able to give a signal from a hidden place on shore. We learned how to make various charges. Various people would volunteer and become demolition men. I joined a demolition team and carried a fifty-pound pole charge and a fifty-pound satchel charge made of burlap and TNT. I figured if I make the second front and I get hit with all the explosives on me, then it would all be over real quick; that's the way I wanted it to be.

When we had a chance to sit around barracks, to write letters, clean equipment, or rest up before the next day's gruelling grind, we'd always gab about home and the one's we'd left behind.

Corporal Dan Hartigan

1ST CANADIAN PARACHUTE BATTALION

A few days after arrival, we were quickly mustered and shipped off to Carter Barracks, Bulford, near Stonehenge. There we were met by a tall, thin, youngish Brigadier Hill who possessed a firm jaw and looked like he meant business. Our methods of training changed. Instead of continuous crawling and dog-legging in simulated pincer movements, we turned to long forced marches, ten, twenty, and fifty miles at a crack – with packs, weapons, and other battlefield equipment. Further emphasis was put on weapons' knowledge and handling, anti-tank grenade throwing, mortar firing, and target practice. There were exercises in assault training and preparation of defences. We were worked hard and we bitched regularly, but we enjoyed it.

Amid all the hard work there were good times. Weekend passes came with reasonable frequency. Pay piled up during long periods of training where there was no way to spend it. Ten-day leaves came every three months. The English people were nothing short of marvellous. They took us into their homes, fed us, put up with our cultural differences, and, without saying so, ministered to the need for reassurance that young people, a long way from home and facing danger, required. I will always remember and love them for that.

W. Scott Buist

AMERICAN ARMED FORCES

I spent a lot of time at RAF Tibenham, thirteen miles south-west of Norwich. I go out to the flight line. Everything checks out all right, they're taking off, and the tower shoots the flare up, and the first plane guns it and goes down the runway; the next one swings in, and the next, and all four engines, give it to it. Each is loaded with twenty tons of bombs, full load of gas. This one guy must have blown an engine, just about when he got to pull back. He cartwheeled, and when twenty tons of bombs and thirty-five thousand gallons of gasoline go up in an explosion, that's a dramatic thing. Those guys never knew anything about it, but that was it. The rest of the guys had to take off behind him, almost immediately, through the flames and the debris.

Corporal George Richardson

6TH BATTALION, DURHAM LIGHT INFANTRY

In one major exercise on landing-craft we sailed out into the channel with no idea where we were going. The navy were bombarding and we were diving down and digging in. Everything came in from the sea, including tanks and all we expected. Then, about two o'clock, the firing stopped and we were marched off to find we had invaded Hayling Island.

General Eisenhower inspected us and he stopped at a few men and asked them about themselves, but no one replied. I heard him say, 'Shit, this is not what I've come for.' He went back to the microphone and said to all of us, 'I want you to come forward, as I want to speak to you.' But no one moved. The brigadier told him that we would not take orders from an American general and that he would sort it out.

The brigadier told the battalion commanding officers to call us forward. Eisenhower told us that we were good troops and that we should be proud to wear our African Star, but that there was a bigger job to do yet and that was to clear the Germans out of occupied Europe. It was no good if we are meeting the Yanks in the street in Cambridgeshire and fighting with them; we had to cooperate with them to beat the Germans.

Herbert Bilius

AMERICAN ARMED FORCES

We went out in flotilla, and we were given orders, you know, practice. Drop the anchor, run full speed up on the beach, drop your ladders over the side, let your guys get off, and put the stakes out so the guys would have guidelines to lead by, and then retract. Do the same thing in reverse. Pull yourself off the beach. Each officer had to take his turn, practising at command of the ship, so that he would be proficient in case the senior officer above him was taken out. So we were fairly well trained to do what we had to do.

Leo Garrieppe

CANADIAN SOLDIER

We had known for months what the beach defences were like – what the town was like. We had a photograph of the town – we knew the town – not by a map – we knew the town by photography, where each crew commander had a photograph of the town that had been divided in twelve rectangles. We knew the streets by their names. I knew where there was potatoes – I knew where there was cabbage – I knew where there's turnips. I knew where I was, every inch of the way. We were so well informed about the defences. We had been trained about Juno for a long, long time. The only thing we didn't know about Juno prior to D-Day – Juno could have been in Greece, Italy or Spain. We had no idea where Juno was – we only learned on the night of D-Day.

Eugene Polinsky

AMERICAN AIRMAN

I happened to have been flying the night before D-Day and we weren't told anything. We knew it was imminent. I came back over the coast; I saw all of this activity there. I thought, what the hell is going on? This is important, I better report this. I woke up in the morning and I found out it was D-Day. That was my only connection with D-Day, but I saw it all happening and I didn't know what it was. That's secrecy for you.

Albert S. Porter Jr

AMERICAN AIRMAN

I would say we probably flew three or four practice missions. They wanted to make sure that the pilot and everybody in the crew knows what they are doing. The second mission is our co-pilot's first mission, because, the first mission, they always sent an experienced co-pilot along with you. They want to make sure that our pilot knows what he was doing after all the training. We were over Hamburg and we got hit with flak. I was in the turret and I saw it happen. There's a gigantic hole between number one and two engines where a shell had gone through the wing. The plane started going straight down, straight down. It felt like the plane's going to tear itself apart. I thought that it was going to go any minute. Through the intercom, the pilot is screaming, 'Prepare to bail out, prepare to bail out.' Now, I came out of that turret like I was shot out of a cannon. Well, when the plane started straight down, the chutes took off. So, when I came out of the turret, the chute wasn't there. I didn't have sense enough to try to tie it to the turret in some way. Right now, we're supposed to be a well-trained, well-disciplined crew; forget it. It was absolute chaos and, I mean, seriously, it was chaos. We thought we were goners. We dropped straight down fifteen thousand feet as Lonnie and Bob Cochran, who was a big guy and strong, were trying to pull the plane out of the dive. Finally they got it level and somehow we managed a half-baked landing on some airfield. Now, we're all out of the aeroplane, thanking our lucky stars that we made it, but our bombardier had forgotten to lock his nose guns. We're all around the nose with these .50-calibre machine-guns over our heads. The gunner got back in the nose, lost his balance and fell against the trigger switches of his two .50s, which fired off everywhere as we hit the ground. So when we scrambled out of the plane he was so relieved. He thought he wiped out the whole crew.

Early June, 1944: 'Fear feeds on delay, of course.'

Moreen James

WREN

I was working on a plotter at Southwick House and in that space of time before D-Day I used to write to my mother. Every letter you wrote had to go through a censor. Sometimes I had a right old moan and she'd write back and say, 'I don't know what you wrote, as I only had 'Dear Mother . . . love Moreen'! The rest had been cut out.

We plotters never knew when D-Day would be. We didn't know until we went on duty and saw the table, which had almost became one complete plot, because there was so much shipping going out, they couldn't pick out each individual, but they were going in waves; the plot table was one mass of plots. But, you just carried on. I was only eighteen and didn't realise the significance of what we were actually seeing. You know, you were just still plotting, shipping, plotting, shipping and plotting shipping! But you know, it didn't occur to you until it came over on the messages, exactly what was happening.

Richard J. Mercer

AMERICAN CIVILIAN

In the Golden Ball in Bridgwater we used to play Shove Ha'penny and you play for beer. This old guy, he won. Christ, he won every time. He could be drunk all night just off his winnings at Shove Ha'penny. And I can still hear him now, you know, he spoke with a marvellous Somerset dialect. 'Rainan ineet' – that means 'It's raining out, isn't it?' – 'Rainan ineet'. You know, you get to the point where you can understand all this stuff. But he told us this story of the build-up before D-Day: 'All night and day lad, you should have been here. Night and day they rolled through this town. The windows shook, the building shook, the earth was vibrating. How could they keep it from any spies?' Then he went on, 'What did we know, but we knew it was happening. Here they came, tanks and trucks, men by the thousands: night and day, the din of it, never stopping.' This man was talking poetry. It was beautiful. And he was a common Englishman. Wonderful, Wonderful. Yeah, I think they're great people.

Anon

CIVILIAN

US convoys were parked all along the streets, waiting for the 'off'. One was entirely composed of black men – the USA did not mix races – but after a couple of days they moved on. They were replaced by a convoy of white soldiers, including Julius Ruske, a German who had become a naturalised American. He was short and squat, but my, could he sing! Whenever I hear 'Rose Marie' my mind goes back to D-Day.

My mother took pity on the men, who were desperately tired and had been forced to sleep in their lorries. She invited several into our house where they 'crashed out' on beds and chairs. My mother didn't have much to offer because of rationing, but she made gallons of tea and cut up piles of bread for cucumber sandwiches, which amused them because they thought it so English. In return, they gave us their rations.

Christine Collins, *née Darby*

SCHOOLGIRL

As a child living in a Surrey village not very far from a Battle of

Waiting for the off: British women serve coffee to relaxed looking US troops waiting to cross the channel for the D-Day landings.

Britain fighter station I was very well aware of all that the Second World War meant to everyone, both adults and children. Next door to my own home was a large detached house that had been used at one time to house families who had lost their homes through the bombing. Not long before what turned out to be D-Day the house was again empty and my parents had been wondering, who would be the next occupants?

Playing in the garden one day I was puzzled to see two large army lorries drive slowly down our tree-lined road and finally stop outside the empty house. My mother was also surprised and we waited to see what would happen next. As I watched, several soldiers climbed down from the lorries, checked some papers and then, walking towards the front of the house, took out keys and opened the front door and walked in. To me it was of course a matter of great interest. All that afternoon and evening there had been a great deal of activity, much coming and going, and as anything to do with the war was of concern to us all we awaited events, with perhaps, a little anxiety.

The following morning there was a knock at the front door; on opening it, my mother found two soldiers in battledress standing in the porch. They had come to explain that they were members of a small group of soldiers who were there to 'look after' advance supplies for 'later use'. Their main problem, they explained, was that they had no alarm clock; would it be possible for us to make sure that they were up and about at the correct time? As my father always left very early in the morning for his office in London, where he was a civil servant in a reserved occupation, we assured them that this was possible, telling them that if we saw no lights or activity through the garden hedges at the side of the house, we would rouse them. In those days that did not mean a quick phone call; a house used for the homeless 'bombed out' had no telephone installed. A wake-up call required a visit to the house and a lot of hammering on the front door. However, this only happened on rare occasions.

What did happen was that an invitation for 'the little girl and her mother to come to tea' was issued and I was then initiated into what seemed to me to be an Aladdin's cave of food. In those days virtually every item of food was rationed or almost unobtainable; now, before my eyes, were tins of peaches, fruit salad, jams and meats. Four soldiers were now permanently in residence and their idea of 'tea' was, to a wartime child, an absolute banquet. It included Spam and chips, rarely available since fat or oil was scarce, and this was followed by bowls of fruit and cream and chocolate biscuits. They plied us with all the goodies they had available and obviously took great pleasure in seeing our surprise and especially my enjoyment of all the treats. Three of the soldiers were young privates, the other a sergeant, an older man who was in charge.

We returned home replete, but only after I had been shown

room after room stacked high with tins of food, emergency rations, which included Horlicks tablets and chocolate bars, and, strangest of all, several folding bicycles; these could be divided in the middle and fold into a very neat package.

The following day Eddie, the sergeant, approached my mother. 'We are hopeless cooks,' he said, 'we have all this food but all we can cook are steak and chips and eggs and bacon.' Sure enough they had plenty of meat, despite the lack of freezers in those days, but also they had sugar, dried fruit, golden syrup, butter, suet, dried eggs and margarine; all precious commodities in those days but of little use to the men. We did a swap, my mother made huge trays of spicy bread pudding with lots of fruit, suet and sugar, fruit cakes with more fruit and precious dried eggs. In return we were given what to me looked like a petrol can of golden syrup, dried fruit, dried eggs and sugar, and the much-sought-after butter or margarine.

We became good friends and shared with Eddie his worry over the problems for his wife and child when they were bombed out of their home. I was invited several more times to massive 'teas' and then almost as suddenly as they had arrived they left, only able to tell us at the last minute before they were gone. Within a very short time D-Day was upon us! Then, of course, we realised the significance of the iron rations and, in particular, the folding bicycles!

It is now a small but still-vivid memory.

Marian Haywood

WAAF

My friends and I had been posted to Fareham and I couldn't believe our luck that we were to remain together again. After living in a large house for a short time, we were posted to HMS Collingwood. I thought I was going on a ship! The accommodation was not up to our usual WAAF standards, but one gets used to disappointments.

We had been told that because radar operations were used to bulk plotting, we were taking over the plotting room for the Wrens. That information seemed to boost morale!

Our first visit to Fort Southwick House was, for me, quite a disaster. Special passes were issued to enable our entry to the 'underworld', which lay below many, many steps. The further I went down, the more sick I felt and much to my horror I disgraced myself completely. Everyone was so kind to me and I was led to a point outside on the rocks, looking out to the sea accompanied by the duty guard. The fresh air soon made me feel better and the guard restored my confidence. I was never ill again and the next day found me working at the plotting table with my colleagues.

The plotting room had several cameras located at strategic points around the plotting table in order to record the sequence of plots. One wall was a gigantic map, which was used for plotting aircraft. There were two balconies, one for the controller and officers in charge and one at a higher level for the Teller and the commander and his staff, who often put in an appearance, especially when Allied shipping was being attacked.

After a few days I was fortunate enough to be offered the job as a 'Teller'. I loved it! I had direct telephone contact with 'Sugar King', the HQ for General Eisenhower and also the Admiralty where Mr Churchill was located. It was all so top secret; I had to be taken to 'Sugar King' in a car which had all the windows completely blacked out.

Not only shipping plots were passed, but plots concerning aircraft movement had to be forwarded. We worked thirteen-and-a-half-hour shifts, but it all seemed worthwhile when our efforts contributed to the sinking of an enemy vessel. An enemy ship would be located and our vessels would be directed to intercept. As the two radar plots combined, there would be an awesome silence, which remained until radio details were received giving the result of the action. Much excitement would be created in the plotting room whenever these actions resulted in an Allied success.

The invasion force was plotted twice. On the first occasion, inclement weather prevented the force from proceeding but on the second attempt the multitude of ships set forth and the plotting table was saturated with the massive number of vessels which were taking part. At the end of the shift I had lost my voice. However, when the commander complimented me on my work I was able to glow with pride.

Life certainly was not all work. Off duty, there was dancing, dancing and yet more dancing.

I joined ANC Exec in October 1943, almost exactly at the same time that Admiral Ramsay took up his position there, and early on in the New Year they began having very high-powered conferences at Southwick House, so all the heads of the various forces had to attend. There was Eisenhower, of course, and Tedder, Leigh-Mallory and Montgomery. One day I was on duty at the reception desk and all these heads arrived so I showed them where the conference room was and I thought I'd got them all tucked in there, when suddenly I was aware of someone else standing in front of me. I looked up and there was a sort of small man with a pointed nose and bright blue eyes and he asked for the conference room and I told him where it was, but he didn't move, he just looked at me. So I repeated it, 'Third door on the left, Sir.' Still he didn't move and suddenly it dawned on me that I had seen his face before and of course it was General Montgomery. He wanted to make his presence felt, obviously, by making me recognise who he was before he went into the conference room. And that was my first encounter with him. I think probably my last, except we used to ride in his car when he wasn't there!

One day before D-Day, when they had just made their decision, we had been to get our pay, which was fifteen shillings and a soap coupon. We were walking back when I heard the guard come to attention, and I said, 'Something is happening; let's wait a minute!' And out of the door came Eisenhower and Ramsay and Tedder and Leigh-Mallory, and they saw us gossiping about them. Eisenhower turned towards us and gave the thumbs-up sign and we knew it was on.

Joan Dale

WREN

Then came the day when the flotilla officer came into the office with charts in red covers under his arm. 'Ah,' said the coxswain, 'those are the secret charts. The invasion must be near.' A day or two later he said, 'The invasion will be on 6 June.' This was before General Eisenhower had decided this, but our coxswain had worked out from the Admiralty Tide Tables that this would be the date.

Sheila Duce

CIVILIAN

On the night of 4 June the tanks were nose-to-tail all down Blocks Road leading to Warsash where the Mulberries were. We knew something was going on and the Germans knew, because we just had got to bed when the siren went. They bombed these tanks, which were absolutely stacked with ammunition. It was a terrifying night. All the ammunition was going up, it was ghastly. And as soon as they thought the Germans had gone – the 'all clear' would sound. But of course the ammunition was still smouldering and another lot would go off or another tank would catch fire, so it went on the whole night. Just when you thought of going into the house, something else started to go off, just like lots and lots of fireworks and explosions. Throughout the night it was all clear, sirens and all clear.

The morning of 6 June, I suppose it was about five o'clock, there was this almighty rumble and rumble and rumble. Everything was on the move.

Group Captain J.M. Stagg

BRITISH METEOROLOGIST

When General Eisenhower appeared as Chief Supreme Commander in the early weeks of January 1944, he said, in effect, 'This is all very well, it's very valuable and very necessary – but you know, what I shall really want is an actual forecast for the actual D-Day when it comes to be agreed.' And he as much as said, 'Since I, General Eisenhower, haven't been a forecaster, and I don't know very much about how you forecast in this country, I want to hear, to see, what reliance I can put on your work.' So he instructed that at each of the weekly meetings that he had on Monday mornings with his Commanders in Chief and their chiefs of staff and so on, that I should appear and give a forecast for the Thursday, assumed to be a dummy D-Day, and also for the following days – Friday and Saturday. Now, this was rather a tall order, but it became obvious that it was necessary when I learned how many great fleets of battleships and warships and landing-craft of all kinds were going to be involved in this operation. They were stowed away in harbours all along the south coast and away up the west coast as far as the sea lochs of Scotland, so that the more slow moving of them, you see, would have to start about three days in advance of the actual landings in order that they could converge with all the other forces on the actual morning. In effect, then, General Eisenhower would have to give his decision three days before the actual landing. He also wanted to know whether the weather on the two days succeeding D-Day was also going to be reasonably good for all the important follow-up operations to the initial landing forces.

Private Joe Minogue

7TH ARMOURED DIVISION

Before the invasion we went down to Beaulieu, Lord Montagu's estate. It was really like a concentration camp, because we had to be checked in and out all the time, and I think this is when the army began this business of bleating like sheep, which was to stick with us for several months. So whenever an officer gave us a roll call for his men, we began to bleat like sheep. It was a bit of light relief, I suppose.

During this period we were all thinking about the invasion, and we used to get the odd briefing – as much information as the army could provide about the kind of conditions we were likely to meet. And fear feeds on delay, of course, and we didn't really know just when we were going, and we used to have these long conversations with each other about the kind of things that might happen – you know, whether we'd ever get off the beach alive, and all the rest of it. And the great things that worried tank men are – I think there are two main fears: one is the danger of being trapped inside a tank that is on fire, and the second one, because we were soldiers and because we were used to being on the land all the time, was our fear of water. And really, I would think, you know, we were more terrified of being drowned in that damn tank than anything else. During this period, the fears were mounting; I think everybody who was involved in the invasion was afraid – and later one learned to realise that basically this is what war is about, and it's really two groups of very frightened men, facing each other.

Group Captain J.M. Stagg

BRITISH METEOROLOGIST

The date for the actual invasion was of course fixed for the 5 June and during that time, during those last days in May, just as the whole of General Eisenhower's forces were assembling round the south coast and up the west coast of these islands, so also, and most unfortunately, did the depressions in the Atlantic. So that by the end of May, by the 30th, 31st – there seemed on our weather charts to be nothing but a series of great depressions with almost winter-like intensity. On the evening of that Wednesday, 31 May, even then, I advised General Eisenhower that conditions for the oncoming weekend – especially over Sunday night and Monday morning, the crucial times for Overlord – were going to be stormy. But we went on with the meetings. I had to go before General Eisenhower and his commanders, who met for

Group Captain James Stagg played a vital role in Operation Overlord.
As senior meteorological officer he found the critical window of
opportunity for the Normandy landings on June 6, 1944.

nothing else, twice a day, during those fateful days – 1st, 2nd, 3rd June – down in Southwark House, behind Portsmouth. But as the time went on, the seriousness – the ominousness – of the whole situation got worse, until by Saturday night it became obvious that there would certainly be a storm in the Channel area on the Sunday night and Monday. General Eisenhower at that meeting, decided to hold the operation. The next morning, he suspended and stopped the remaining forces. He stopped them from sailing and the others had to come back. Well then, on that Sunday morning, 4 June, after the three days of tremendous tension, we were completely uncertain what could happen. Here was the whole business completely suspended. The naval craft all returning to what bases they could get to in England, and no suggestion on our charts that the weather situation would or could improve for many days ahead. It was a day of dreadful tension. Then, miraculously – mercifully and miraculously – the almost unbelievable happened. During that Sunday we spotted from two reports from the Atlantic that there might just be a slight interlude between two depressions off West Ireland.

Waiting to Depart: 'A solemn and strenuous day.'

Brigadier James Hill

3RD PARACHUTE BRIGADE

Well, the great day was arriving and all my battalions were penned in their camps, which they weren't allowed to leave. This period was very interesting to me. All day long the Canadians, with whom I'd pitched my tent, were playing games – baseball, throwing balls about – and I thought what tremendous vitality these Canadians had got. Then in the afternoon I would visit my English battalions and find half a dozen chaps desultorily kicking a football, and the rest asleep. I thought to myself, here is the difference between the Old World and the New; the *élan* and *joie de vivre* of the New World of the Canadian, and the maturity and the not worrying, not bothering and having a good nap while you can of the British.

Attached to my Brigade HQ was my commando liaison officer, Peter Haig Thomas, who before the war had been stroke of the Cambridge boat and the British boat in the Berlin Olympic Games. He was a very great naturalist who had gone to live with the Eskimos for two years in Greenland in order to study the Greater Snow Goose. I went out for a walk with him and we found three quarter-grown hares running about. He said he could talk to them so he left me and walked up very close to them, squatted down, and talked to them. As he walked back I had an intuition that I shouldn't see him again after D-Day. He was one of the most remarkable characters I'd met in my life. And, of course, shortly after the sun rose on that first morning in Normandy, he was dead – what a loss!

The evening before D-Day arrived, I went round to brief all the officers in every battalion and a lot of chaps as well. My final words to them were, 'Gentlemen, in spite of your excellent training and your splendid briefing, you must not be daunted if chaos reigns. It undoubtedly will!' Chaos certainly did reign, and what I had said stuck in so many people's minds that they were not daunted.

Staff Sergeant Roy Howard

GLIDER PILOT REGIMENT

We got out onto the airfield about 9.30pm on 5 June. I think everyone knew on the airfield what was happening except one of the ground staff from the Air Force, who came up to me and said, 'Are you bringing this one back tonight, Staff?' I said, 'No. I don't think so.' He walked away looking dazed.

Petty Officer Frank Coombes

55TH MOTOR TORPEDO BOAT FLOTILLA

On Sunday 4 June, we paraded to attend a flotilla church service. It was obvious from the shipping and assault craft in and around Portsmouth that the attempt to assault 'fortress Europe' was imminent and that coastal forces were to play an important part. The church service only confirmed that our flotilla, the 55th, was allocated an especially prominent role. The parson did not help one little bit when he exhorted us to be 'valiant unto death'; we wanted to get it over with. Everybody knew that this was it. That church service was better than any enema.

Three Horsa gliders were allocated to each bridge. Each glider to be loaded with identical equipment and each to include Royal Engineers to deal with the demolition charges on the bridges. We spent the entire afternoon being briefed in the different tasks of each twenty-five-man platoon. Then the tasks of each seven-man section were considered and in cases where individuals had special tasks, these were also looked at in detail since, working in darkness, it was essential that everyone knew what everyone else was doing at any given time, and to be in a position to carry out their job if the appointed individual was not available for any reason. Nothing could be left to chance, and split-second accuracy was vital for the success of the mission. My platoon was to fly in the first of the three to go down onto the canal bridge.

At around 22.00 hours we turned in for the night. It was hot in the small tent and I didn't feel much like sleeping. The task that had been allocated to us seemed so great and our force so small, and although it would hopefully only be for a short time, the prospect of initially being the only unit actually in France, and facing the might of the German army, seemed to me to be a daunting proposition.

Glancing around our seven-man-section tent, dimly lit by a hurricane lamp, I noted that although it was after 22.30 hours and in the normal way we would all be asleep, several, if not all, were still awake. It was well into a restless night, and the best part of a packet of twenty cigarettes later, that I finally dropped off into a shallow sleep.

Patricia Cameron

HARBOUR OFFICE WORKER

Shortly before the embarkation of troops when there was an armed naval guard actually stationed beside the Harbour Board offices – we realised something important was imminent.

I can remember that nothing was explained – it was what you picked up all the time and all you were told was TOP SECRET and you knew you read it and to all intents and purposes forgot it. Every secret letter had to go in double envelopes – the internal envelope was marked TOP SECRET and the outside envelope was just addressed to The Admiralty, Bugle Street.

There was all this with the building of the ramps – we knew what the ramps were for – there was also talk about PLUTO, which was the Pipe-Line-Under-The-Ocean. We knew the big day was fairly imminent because they whitewashed all the windows on the sea side of the Harbour Offices so that we couldn't see what was going on. But we had a jolly good idea!

Marjorie Hirst, née Crowe

WREN

We heard aircraft during the night of the 5th and 6th and realised that the invasion had started. There was a sense of anti-climax; we had worked so hard up till then but we were at a loose end once D-Day started – we went to the cinema about four times in two days!

Pat Briggs

BRITISH SOLDIER

Once we were in the camp at Bolney, Sussex, behind the wire, we were extremely well briefed. They had tents set up with map boards, sand displays of a particular stretch of beach that we would land on. We knew the code name of every town, village, and strong point. The only thing we didn't know was which country it was in. So speculation was rife. We were suddenly issued with Francs, and a French phrase book. Right, we thought, this is part of a big deception. They wouldn't give us French money and phrase books, so it's not France. So everybody started talking about Holland, Belgium. When we did find out, our morale was very high. We knew what we had to do, basically.

We moved down to Portsmouth and, towards the end of May, we were told that we were going to be inspected by the King and General Montgomery, so we had to prepare ourselves. We were loaded onto three tonners with a very strong police escort and we ended up in Rowlands Castle. We were dismounted, and found the whole of the 185 Brigade assembled there. That is the Warwicks, the Norfolks, the KSLI and ourselves. The King and Montgomery turned up, walked through the ranks, then disappeared, and we got into our vehicles and went back home again! I don't think it went down very well. I didn't see the King speak to anyone. But he was heavily made up. That was the impression we all got. We were all talking about it. He was very, very heavily made up. Grotesque, in fact, we thought.

Well, people had different opinions of this. We had been living out in the open a lot – over two years. So we were pretty brown and healthy looking. Whereas he looked dreadful alongside the troops. So they made him up for the camera. But it really was quite an eye-opener. Monty, though, was great. We knew he would never start anything until he was absolutely sure we had the equipment to do it with. Everybody thought a lot of him.

Three British troops on a landing craft waiting to be launched into the channel pass the time by reading an army-issue booklet on France.

We spent our last night in a naval barracks, in a barrack block, where we were confined. Our meals were brought to us. There were no beds, no bedding, so we slept on the floor with our blanket. Next morning, we marched from the naval barracks down to the Gosport pontoon; there were dozens of kids waiting for us outside the gates. 'Can we have your spare English money?' – these kids knew, you know. We gave them all our loose change and cap badges. We got on the launches and were taken out to our boats, and by mid-afternoon we sailed. There were hundreds of people on the foreshore of course.

The harbour was full of landing-craft, all of which had the 3rd Division sign up on their funnels. They were forming up, milling around, and getting into the formation, which takes some doing, and eventually we pulled out through the harbour, past the Round Tower on our left and then veered off towards Nab Tower where they had a big sign: 'VICTORY'.

This particular time, as we pulled out of the harbour, before it got too rough, a troop commander called us all forward to the ramp, where he had set up his map board. 'Right, now we will tell you where you are landing,' he said. 'You are landing in Normandy, your city is Caen, Le Havre is on to your left, and you're landing at a place called La Brèche: a very appropriate name. You will be landing there, your first gun position will be at a village called Hermanville' – and then he proceeded to tell us all the place names. So now we knew.

Mrs Mary Thomas

CIVILIAN

In May–June 1944, when I was about fifteen, I used to cycle to Northgate Grammar School along Heath Road and Colchester Road. For a week I cycled beside army lorries, tanks and guns which were travelling to Nacton Shores. They drove straight across the roundabouts, churning them up. They stayed there at a standstill for days – everyone was taking out cups of tea for the soldiers.

This was a decoy to make the Germans believe that the invasion was going to come from East Anglia.

Mike Crooks

CHAPLAIN

On boarding the ship I found that the troops were feeling the strain of waiting. All ships had been loaded and 'sealed' a week previously with nobody allowed to leave – it was stressful. The following Sunday morning, I held a Holy Communion Service at the intersection of two passages. Difficult! Like catacombs. This was a momentous occasion, for those communicants were all aware that in a few days' time they might be dead – and some of them were. The Holy Mysteries of Christian Communion probably meant more to them that day in those overcrowded passages than at any other time in their lives. I shall never forget the look in the eyes of some. We were all trimmed down to size at that moment. At the end of the service the 'sealed' ship rule was broken for I was given a launch and allowed to go and take prayers and Holy Communion in several other ships. It was a solemn and strenuous day ending with a service that I conducted on the ramp in the tank space.

The following morning, the long wait ended. The engines came alive, the rumble of the anchor chain, the engine room telegraphs and we were off. It is impossible to describe the feeling of relief. It was strangely exhilarating. The sense of brooding suddenly evaporated and gave way to smiling faces, jokes, light-heartedness and rudery.

Private Tom Tateson

7TH BATTALION, GREEN HOWARDS

To my astonishment I was told that I was to go on immediate leave for forty-eight hours. While elated at the news, I was baffled as to why I had been given preference over the other, much longer-serving men. For a short time previously, letters home had been censored, with the exception of a limited number of 'green envelopes'. These could not be censored in the writer's unit, but could be opened further up the line. I had already used my limited quota when I received a letter from Olive telling me she was pregnant again and was very upset and worried. I had to use an ordinary envelope and just hoped it would not be opened. My letter was very tender and emotional, which I would not have sent through the 'open' post except for the urgency. Lieutenant Wilson never mentioned it to me, nor did the NCOs, who must surely have enquired why I should be so favoured. But I feel it was because Lieutenant Wilson had read that letter that he gave me a last chance to see Olive. The army was not totally without sensitivity. I was very conscious that there was a real possibility of being killed. This meant leaving Olive widowed with a child not yet a year old and another on the way. Olive was to hear no more of me from that time until October, when she received my printed postcard informing her that I was alive and a POW. This was one week before Robert was born.

Diana Holdsworth

CIVILIAN

We were startled by the familiar roar of an army motor bike. The front door, which was never locked, was opened noisily and my husband's twin brother came banging up the stairs to the flat. He stood in the doorway looking embarrassed. He looked so comic in his blue-striped pyjamas over which he had thrown a battledress blouse and a pair of army boots. He spoke hesitantly, without his usual assurance. 'This is it; we've got to get back to camp pretty damn quick.' David told his twin to wait for him downstairs. Michael turned on his heels without a word of farewell and clattered down the stairs again. David kissed me. Then, using the same words as Michael, he said, 'This is it my darling, I have to go.' He went quietly and quickly down the stairs, the front door banged. I looked out of the window and watched them ride off together into the night on the swaying motor bike. The next ten days seemed like an eternity. Suddenly, one night the sky was full of aircraft and I knew the invasion had begun. It was almost a relief.

Edgar Peara

AMERICAN ARMED FORCES

I saw some men vomiting with fear; some men, their palms were wet with perspiration and they were wiping them on their combat jackets. Another man I could see would light a cigarette, take a puff, then throw it overboard and light another.

Trooper Austin Baker

4TH/7TH DRAGOON GUARDS

Major B read out messages from Eisenhower and Montgomery, and told us that he personally thought we should all be very honoured to be in on this affair. I think most of us felt that we could have stood the disgrace of being left out of it.

Able Seaman Ken Oakley

ROYAL NAVAL COMMANDO

On the evening prior to the D-Day landings, the Senior Arms Officer gave us a briefing and I will always remember his final words: 'Don't worry if all the first wave of you are killed,' he said. 'We shall simply pass over your bodies with more and more men.' What a confident thought to go to bed on.

Private Gordon Duffin

2ND BATTALION GLOUCESTERSHIRE REGIMENT

A week or so before D-Day I was a nineteen-and-three-quarter-year-old Bren gunner in A Company, with one and a half years' service. We moved from our sealed camp at Brockenhurst to Lymington, where we boarded our Landing-Craft Infantry, and sailed to Southampton New Docks. There were so many craft filling the dock that we had to tie up seven or eight abreast throughout the whole length of the dock. From end to end of the dock were hundreds of landing-craft of all types, waiting.

Landing craft assembled along the quayside at Southampton, waiting for D-Day.

Once tied up we disembarked, which involved crossing the decks of other craft to get to the large warehouses where we could relax and stretch our legs. On the floor of the warehouses were hundreds of mattresses on which we could sleep until it was time to embark again for the OFF. As one can imagine, the whole dockside area and warehouses were packed with troops and admin types, handing out cigarettes, food and tea like there was no tomorrow. Canadian Sweet Caporal cigarettes in boxes of 100 were issued free, a gift of the people of Canada.

As everyone now knows, D-Day was postponed by twenty-four

hours, which meant we loaded up twice before sailing on the night of 5 June. We embarked for the second time on the afternoon of 5 June. Touching the dockside as I embarked, I wondered if I should ever touch 'English soil' again.

Captain Peter Goddin

151 INFANTRY BRIGADE

Then, out of the blue at the end of April 1944, I received a notification from the Military Secretary's department that Temporary Captain P.R. Goddin was to report forthwith as Staff Captain to 151 Infantry Brigade. The brigade was under canvas in a camp in Nightingale Woods outside Southampton and was due to land on Gold Beach on D-Day. I found that my predecessor had succumbed to nervous exhaustion and had been hospitalised three days previously. In the six weeks prior to D-Day I wondered at times if I too would succumb. To me, D-Day was an enormous relief and I was told it showed too.

My brigade was due to cross the Channel in infantry landing-craft, which could carry 240 men, most of whom just sat on the deck – not exactly luxurious accommodation. Brigade HQ staff were spread across a number of such landing-craft as a wise precautionary measure. We received orders to embark on our landing-craft on Saturday morning, 3 June. The intention was to sail that evening. Various dignitaries came to wish us 'bon voyage', some no doubt thinking 'rather them than us'! We were provided with excellent pre-packed rations, which included pure white bread, something we hadn't seen for years; the white flour had been especially shipped from Canada.

Boyd Rigby

CIVILIAN

I recently came across a poem written by my father in pencil on a piece of scrap paper. The poem, entitled 'Sunset and Sunrise', was apparently written on 5 June 1944, on the battlements of Dover Castle, where he was waiting with his regiment to cross for the D-Day invasion. The paper was sent with a letter to my mother.

SUNSET AND SUNRISE

I watched the sun go down last night; I saw him sink to rest:
I watched him shine with glowing light, then vanish in the west.
His awful face was fiery red;
He touched the earth with eerie glow.
The life-blood of a million dead
O'er England's landscape seemed to flow.
To south, across the Dover Strait, a bloody pathway shone,
As if, from France the Nazi hate had caused the sea to don
The hue of all their victims' blood.
The clouds above were livid too;
My mind weaved pictures as I stood,
I shuddered at their gloomy view.
The evil hosts of Nazi-dom, fanatics in their hate,
Across the narrow sea did come; and in a fearful spate
A sea of blood flowed o'er our land,
All conq'ring Hun! And yet my mind
Groped upward to th'unfault'ring Hand:
Surely His strength and help we'd find?
I watched the sun come up today, and I am glad I did!
I watched him loose his quick'ning ray and all my fears were
    hid.
Fair England smiled; her sweet face shone;
The landscape beamed; the sea seemed glad:
The doubts of yesterday were gone,
To harbour doubting thoughts was mad.
To south, the Nazi lands shrouded in gloomy haze
That must engulf them – lands and men; so seemed it to my
    gaze.

For, in the morning's cheery light
My fears were gone, my heart was sure;
The fear beget by coming night
Had vanished – Britain would endure!
The War had dragged the earth in gloom, and fettered many a
    land,
And broken millions; yet the doom of Hitler is at hand.
For, sure as morning follows night,
So sure will chaos end in peace.
Sure as the darkness heralds light,
Peace heralds victory – and release.

Boyd Rigby, Dover, 5 June 1944

Private Joe Minogue

7TH ARMOURED DIVISION

We loaded up on a Saturday afternoon and we tied up against an American tank landing ship and the Americans, so very generous, invited us aboard for a meal and we had more meat than we'd seen for several years, as much ice cream as we could manage – and then finished off with slabs of angel cake – and this was one moment of high relief. We got back aboard the tank landing-craft and, you know, we read this great message from Monty about 'good hunting in the fields of Europe' and all this rubbish – and naturally being a soldier, thought what a load of old cod's it was. Anyway, we settled down for the night, and then suddenly, in the early morning – this would be the Sunday – we set off down Southampton Water, and we thought, 'Hello, this is it.' And not being used to water and not liking it, we were all beginning to feel a bit lousy, when suddenly the whole group of landing-craft we were with turned back and we finished up, tied up for the rest of the Sunday afternoon against this American ship again. Unfortunately they didn't invite us to dinner for a second night.

Rifleman Patrick Devlin

18 PLATOON, C COMPANY, 1ST BATTALION, THE ROYAL
ULSTER RIFLES

In the transit camp behind the barbed wire, where we were kept locked in after being briefed on the D-Day operation, we had a special pay parade. The table was covered by an army blanket; sitting behind it was the company commander, the CQMS and the orderly-room corporal.

When my name was called I marched to the table, saluted and was asked to sign for a military 200 French francs, about two pounds sterling. I was also asked to take three condoms. We had never been given these before. I was RC and refused them. I said to the major, 'I thought we were going to France to fight sir.' I could see he was embarrassed. The colour sergeant saved the day by telling me it was orders from high. He said, 'Take them, wee Joe, and give them away.' To prevent further embarrassment I took them and gave them away. I often wondered if we would have been issued with condoms if we had been invading any other country than France.

Group Captain J.M. Stagg

BRITISH METEOROLOGIST

By the evening, my own confidence in the forecast for this quieter period had so increased from further reports that had come in, that I convinced General Eisenhower and his commanders that it would indeed arrive later on Monday after the storm of Sunday night and Monday morning. It would, indeed, arrive late on Monday and continue through Tuesday and probably into Wednesday. The next morning, early on 5 June, they met again to confirm this decision, and when I could tell them that we were even more confident than we had been the previous night that the fine or improved quieter interlude would indeed come along, the joy on the faces of the Supreme Commander and his commanders after the deep gloom of the preceding days was a marvel to behold.

Sergeant Hyman Haas

A BATTERY, 467TH ANTI-AIRCRAFT ARTILLERY BATTALION
There were religious services with a Catholic priest holding mass on one side and a minister holding a service for the Protestant boys on the other. It was really strange – everyone praying in different religions and denominations, each watching the other. At the same time we had a Jewish religious service. When a Jew is praying he wraps himself in a prayer shawl and wears phylacteries. We had a rabbi who was fully equipped, wearing a prayer shawl which completely covered him. I felt very strange, as though somebody was saying a prayer for the dead. This has always stuck in my mind.

Vernon L. Paul

US NAVY
I was on watch on the night of the 4th as a radio operator. We had these frequencies we were supposed to guard. One of the voice frequencies was supposed to be strictly monitored and we were not allowed to transmit on that frequency under any circumstances.

I was in this shack by myself, tired and looking forward to being relieved so I could hit the sack, when I heard what sounded like a transmitter coming on the line. I said to myself, 'It can't be. No one would dare transmit or break radio silence on that channel.' I then heard a voice say, very softly, 'Who dat?' Next, another transmitter coming up to power and a voice, a bit louder, saying, 'Who dat saying who dat, when I say who dat?' Very soon the whole channel opened up with everyone saying, 'Who dat?' and 'Who dat saying who dat?' and the whole thing went crazy. It sure broke the tension.

Frank Lawson

CANADIAN FIELD REGIMENT ARTILLERY
About two weeks before the big push, the entire regiment was put behind a barbed wire cage so that we were completely cut off from all contact with the outside world; this was at Park Gate, near Southampton.

John T. Waters

AMERICAN ARMED FORCES
I know we had lunch on the LCT, and they gave us the British rations, and that's the first time we ever saw them, but they had this gadget with the soup. You twisted this thing and let the chemical out, and the soup got hot, and we didn't have anything like that. All we had was the five-in-one rations and the K rations for an emergency. So, everybody got a big kick out of that, how they got that soup hot.

Robert Macpherson

AMERICAN CRYPTOGRAPHER
As we got closer to it, we had one kind of interesting incident in Plymouth, in that some of us decided to take liberty on the beach, and, of course, being on the navy ship, we had no knowledge of the fact that over the previous few days all of England had been locked down. On land what we didn't know was that the army was trying to find people who were AWOL or who were, maybe, dressed in American uniforms and weren't Americans. This group, four or five of us, got about a hundred yards up from the landing, and this MP vehicle screams up alongside of us and we get, 'Who the hell are you guys?' We were very limited in what we could say, but we offered our IDs. Finally we were taken to an officer, who looked at us and started laughing. 'Look, do me a favour, will you?' he said. 'Give up the liberty for today. Go back to the ship. You're gonna louse up the whole operation.' So, naturally, we did.

The Signal to Depart is Received: 'Would I be alive tommorow?'

Staff Sergeant Bernard Krein

AMERICAN ARMED FORCES

We left Dartmouth aboard an LSI (landing ship infantry). These large LSIs carried smaller landing-craft which were to be launched near to the landing beach. Our dry runs had taken us on the LSIs many times. We knew its gangways, decks fore and aft. There would be no more room for error when the red light went on in the dark hold. We could do it with our eyes closed. Up to the twenty-two steel steps, count them, to the top of the iron grated platform, then step high to clear the murderous door jamb; a fall here could mean a rupture, a broken leg, or worse.

Now bend low to avoid the overhanging plates of steel that were put there just to smash our heads in, squeeze through the narrow oblong unbolted hatchway, don't snag your harness on the flywheel of the door. Now, some to the right, some to the left: KNOW YOUR ROUTE TO YOUR LCI, DON'T FUCK IT UP NOW. We had to know where our LCI was moored to the mother ship, where the rope ladder was, so as to scramble thirty feet down the side of the ship. UNBUCKLE YOUR HELMET STRAPS. A fall from this height into the sea feet first and the impact of the water into your helmet could break your neck. All our murderous equipment had been prepared and stored in our LCI, all ready for the killing game.

Once on board we were hurried along the deck to the steel hatch and down into the hold. Every man takes his place and falls into a sitting position, his seventy-pound pack eased on his shoulders. The loud hollow clang of the steel doors being shut echoes off the walls of the hull. It is pitch black, not the ghost of a light, the purpose being to accustom our eyes to darkness when we go topside.

In the darkness I pondered my fate. Would I be alive tomorrow at this time? We must have been down in the hold an eternity when the tension began to ooze from our pores. You could feel it from the sounds of hot breath being expelled and sucked back in. We were all waiting for the first weak link to break and blow his stack, setting us all off, and then it happened, the miracle. From the far dark reaches of the hull came a call, 'caw-caw', then somewhere from the right, 'cock-a-doodle-do', over there, 'moo-moo', and then a wild burst of all the barnyard animals imaginable and some not yet invented. Suddenly a commotion from above, and the heavy beam of a flashlight piercing the darkness. 'What the hell is going on down there?' The animal calls stop, a five-second pause and then laughter – uncontrollable laughter from one end of the hull to the other. The tension was over, the laughter stopped, we could feel each other's presence, we were going to make it over to the other side, and after that, who knows?

Frank Lawson

CANADIAN FIELD REGIMENT ARTILLERY

When orders eventually came through for us to leave the compound, we knew that things were on the move. All the tanks loaded with ammunition were parked nose-to-tail for miles along the roadside waiting to head for the landing barges. Then, without warning, at about midnight, a lone German bomber flew over the convoy and dropped its load, hitting the tank in front of me and others. Ammunition was soon exploding everywhere. Tank drivers who could move their tanks did so to a safer place, even though some were on fire. A large amount of armoured equipment was thrown a considerable distance by the explosion and a motorcycle was blown some 800 yards away. Also, a number of houses were destroyed but no one was killed. The toll for the night was two Sherman tanks, four SPs, a Jeep and three motorcycles, all of which had to be replaced and waterproofed before we could load.

We loaded onto the barges at Gosport on 1 June, packed tightly together, and then moved into Stokes Bay where the navy put a camouflage net over the tank landing-craft, which were flat-bottomed and open to the weather. There was little room to move and everyone was stiff. We stayed there until 5 June and the weather was appalling during this time but I learned to play chess to keep my mind from what lay ahead.

Ena Howes

WREN

We had been called to a meeting the day before D-Day when the weather was too bad to sail, and Admiral Ramsay arranged a cricket match between the officers and Wrens. When one Wren had difficulty batting, he changed from bowling overarm to underarm to give her more chance of hitting the ball. It reminded Rear Admiral Creasy of the Armada before which Drake played bowls on Plymouth Hoe.

The weather was not ideal on 4/5 June 1944 but at the meeting in the War Room on the eve of D-Day, the Met officers advised that it would be two more weeks if the invasion was cancelled before the tides and moon were right for the landings. So General Dwight Eisenhower famously said 'let's go' and the invasion of France was on.

Carl W. Monn

AMERICAN ARMED FORCES

All night long and all day long on the 6th, you could almost walk on the aeroplanes going overhead. They were just one after the other, flights going over to bomb this, that and the other targets, you know, to make the Germans believe that we were going to land at the Pas-de-Calais. I will always remember the constant roar of those aeroplanes. It was unbelievable, really.

Robert Billian

AMERICAN ARMED FORCES

When I first got to London this gal walked by, she turned around and came back, and she made some kind of excuse to get talking and, of course, I didn't know what to say to this stranger. She said, 'Well, I'm going to be back in town' – I think this must have been a Wednesday – 'on Friday night.' Then she added, 'If you're gonna be in town, I'd like to meet you here.' I said, 'Jeez, that's kinda of nice.'

Well, on Thursday, we shipped out. So I think to this day there is a girl in England who hiked five miles into town on the 5 June, only to have a very disappointing wait.

Captain Joe Patterson

MEDICAL OFFICER

It was clearly impossible to start in such weather, and we got more and more depressed. The prospect of postponement for fourteen days really appalled us, as it would mean returning to imprisonment in camp again. On Sunday 4 June the spindrift was flying in scuds across the roadstead and people were coming in on duty craft soaked to the skin. It was during the small hours in the blackness of the nights that I felt really chicken-hearted at times, but the foul weather always made me feel that 'it couldn't be today'.

It was teatime on Monday 5 June when, noticing the mine-sweepers beginning to creep out, I realised the show was on. I had been offering heavy odds that it would be cancelled again at lunchtime. I felt rather appalled when I looked at the sea. It was blowing half a gale from the south-west, and banking up black and beastly for what promised to be a thoroughly dirty night.

Vehicles and troops on board a landing craft head for the enemy coast.

Now all the shipping was quietly and slowly out through the booms, the LCTs with their camouflaged loads of tanks and ammunition, the big LSTs packed with vehicles, the LSIs, all slung around with their LCAs and the little LCIs with their troops sardined aboard. All the rest of the brigade was in LCIs, and the French troops ranged up alongside us. Besides all these hundreds of craft, were countless corvettes, and frigates, rows of destroyers, some cruisers and the monitor, Roberts. It was wonderful to watch the quiet steady stream of craft slipping out past the Portsmouth forts, so silently and orderly, with no sirens or fuss, their balloons marking those already hidden by swarms of inter-vening craft.

Feeling rather small and chicken-hearted, I set about my final packing. I spliced my identity discs on string and gloomily hung them round my neck. I dished out anti-seasickness tablets and morphine and talked to all the troops about my final medical plans. I had a heated tussle with the brigade major on the subject of the rum issue, finally settling that troops could only have it thirty minutes before landing. To issue it as intended, before embarking in the LCAs, with two hours of cold and seasickness ahead would have been folly.

The wind howled and it rained in vicious scuds. As the skipper said in his speech to the ship's company: 'the high command must be counting heavily on surprise, for the Germans must surely think that not even Englishmen could be such fools as to start an invasion on a night like this'.

Captain Kay Summersby

BRITISH MECHANISED TRANSPORT CORPS

We dropped everything to make the long drive to Newbury and visit the 101st Airborne. They would be the first troops to land in Normandy behind the enemy lines. Some would be towed over in huge gliders that would settle down quietly in the darkness with their cargoes of young fighting men. Others would parachute down into this heavily fortified area. Ike's last task on the eve of D-Day was to wish these men well.

His flag was not flying from the radiator of the car, and he had told me to cover the four stars on the red plate. We drove up to each of the airfields, and Ike got out and just started walking among men. When they realised who it was, the word went from group to group like the wind blowing across a meadow, and then everyone went crazy. The roar was unbelievable. They cheered and whistled and shouted, 'Good old Ike!' There they were, these young paratroopers in their bulky combat kits with their faces blackened so that they would be invisible in the dark of the French midnight. Anything that could not be carried in their pockets was strapped on their backs or to their arms and legs. Many of them had packages of cigarettes strapped to their thighs.

They looked so young and so brave, I stood by the car and watched as the general walked among them with his military aide a few paces behind him. He went from group to group and shook hands with as many men as he could. He spoke a few words to every man as he shook his hand, and he looked the man in the eye as he wished him success.

He told me later it's very hard really to look a soldier in the eye when you fear that you are sending him to his death. On the drive back he said, 'I hope to God I know what I am doing.'

General Dwight Eisenhower giving a morale-boosting talk to the US 101st Airborne Division on the eve of D-Day.

Private Gordon Duffin

2ND BATTALION GLOUCESTERSHIRE REGIMENT

Crossing the deck of other craft we reached ours and started the slow process of 'racking up'. By this method 100 or so men could be crammed into this type of landing-craft. The landing-craft was divided up into a number of compartments, the walls of which were fitted with racks reaching from floor to ceiling. Each rack consisted of six hinged metal-and-canvas frames. As the distance between each frame was only about twenty inches, all equipment and weapons had to be left on the floor between the racks, which was also the main exit and entry, about three feet wide! The first soldier in would remove his equipment and place it on the floor, hinge down the bottom frame, and slide himself edgeways onto it. The next soldier would do the same with the next frame and so on, until all frames and racks were full.

Thus stowed we felt our craft moving down Southampton Water and towards the Channel. Shortly the loudspeaker in our compartment announced that troops in small numbers could take turns to go up on deck for a few minutes each. I thought I would like to get a better look at this great event and went up first from our compartment. On deck, I was very surprised to see only one other soldier there, an officer of our unit. He remarked that on this great occasion he thought that the deck would be crowded, but it was not so.

Private Tom Tateson

7TH BATTALION, GREEN HOWARDS

Montgomery's inspection over, he took up his familiar position on the top of some army vehicle and called us to gather round in an informal manner. He then told us in his characteristic way that we were going to land in France, knock jerry for six, and finish the war off. There was absolutely no doubt about it – it was all planned and organised. We would just go in, do the job, and that was that. There was something so tremendously impressive, almost hypnotic in his performance, that it did inspire us with a confidence which in retrospect was not at all justified. It was the sheer matter-of-fact certainty of his message that was so much more effective than a high-flown Henry V's Harfleur-type effort.

Margaret

WREN

I was working as a teleprinter operator at Southwick Fort on Portsdown Hill above Portsmouth taking down the coded messages and passing them on. I worked underground for two years for the Commander-in-Chief, Portsmouth, HMS *Victory*. We worked in three shifts, but there must have been about 200–300 of us working there on combined ops at any one time.

I remember I was just coming on for night shift when I saw the smokescreen all over the town, so I knew it was 'on', because of course it had been postponed a couple of times. We'd been training for it and we were waiting for it, so we were all prepared. I suppose we all felt relief really, that it was finally happening, that it had actually come. It didn't change anything about what we were doing: we were always busy anyway and didn't know what the messages were that we dealt with, as they were all in five-letter codes.

Funny, I never thought how important that smokescreen was, but it would have acted like a fog so that any enemy aircraft couldn't see what was happening. But that's the first thing I think about when I think about D-Day: that smoke.

Elsie Horton

WREN

Night watch on Saturday 3 June: the first couple of hours passed in the usual busy way, ships passing to and fro. Then at about 22.00

hours a signal gave news of a convoy sailing from the West Country, its destination 'Far Shore' – a nomenclature soon to be familiar, and translated as the coast of Normandy. This was followed throughout the night by similar ship movements; it was obvious that the 'Second Front', so long awaited, was at last taking place.

On the Monday I was on late watch, approximately 14.00–22.00. As all the signals relating to D-Day were secret, only a few were aware of impending events. We were relieved by the night watch and returned to our quarters in Fort Wallington in the liberty boat, which was a battered old bus. We had eaten at Fort Southwick so it was straight to bed. While everyone else slept, I had a sleepless night, listening to the roar of planes over-head, and thinking of all the men, soldiers, sailors and airmen on their way to battle, and what they might face.

The next morning, on arriving at Fort Southwick for the early watch, it was strange to look down over Portsmouth and see the harbour, which had been so full, now empty of all shipping. Only HMS *Victory* was still there – was it a hopeful signal? It was quite a relief when it was announced on the BBC news that troops had landed on the coast of Normandy, and I was free to talk about it. That first week or so was extremely hectic, as we were the only UK base in wireless transmission contact with the inva-sion fleet. We had to learn a whole new language: code names.

Ralph Rayner

ROYAL ENGINEER

We were due to land on Gold Beach at 7.30am and as dawn broke we could just see the French coast on the horizon and the view of the convoy was a sight to behold, one that I shall never forget. There were ships and landing-craft in all directions as far as we could see, but as we approached closer to the coast the convoy split directions, each group heading for their respective landing beaches. As this manoeuvre progressed, we eventually found ourselves at the front of the column heading for Gold Beach. Many of the troops were suffering from seasickness and lack of sleep due to the pitching of the craft; it was at about this time we were each provided with a very generous tot of 100 per cent navy rum.

Jack Close

BRITISH ARMED FORCES

We set off in our tug down one of the allocated mine-swept channels towing six lengths of floating roadway; a hospital ship passed us going northward in an adjoining channel – her bows had been blown away and she was being towed stern first back to England, having probably struck a mine. A number of landing-craft also passed us in the same channel; most were empty but some had wounded lying on their decks. Everyone managed a wave. Struggling at around four knots, we were passed by two battleships going south at great speed. A corvette that we worked closely with on the south coast also passed us; its Aldis lamp flickered: the message said, 'Come back safe.'

First Lieutenant Peter Meryon

ROYAL NAVY

I feel I was a fairly hardened naval officer, but, of course, the uncertainty and fear of what lay ahead had not to affect my continual contact with all those in the ship's company. Added to which, I had become engaged to be married early in 1944, a very personal worry for my private life – Daphne was a Wren Officer serving in the Admiralty in Whitehall which was regularly being bombed.

Mrs Ramsey

ROYAL NAVY NURSE

One day it seemed like the whole area was full of ships and the next morning there was not a single one. We knew the invasion had begun. We were on alert. We could not leave and were on duty twenty-four hours a day. And we didn't know what we were waiting for.

Lieutenant William H. Pugsley

RCNVR ON HMCS *GEORGIAN*

By sundown our little flotilla of sweepers was hurrying south-east for the rendezvous from which the whole invasion fleet would head for France. From far away downwind on our portside came the steady drone of hundreds and hundreds of landing-craft heading in the same direction, white water flashing from their blunt bows in the last of the daylight.

That night we fixed bayonets on our rifles. We were perhaps a little disturbed as we sailed towards Normandy. Only a fool wouldn't be. We'd be right out in front, sweeping a path for the armada that followed. With the dragging weight of a sweep out astern, our manoeuvrability would be almost nil. Thus would we be expected to meet the Luftwaffe, out in force surely to protect the Atlantic West Wall, since surely the easiest time to stop us would be before we got a footing on the land.

No one spoke about it, but every one of us expected bombs, torpedoes, gunfire, mines, E-boats, destroyers, secret weapons of new and horrible types, and gas. Besides our ordinary respirators we were issued with transparent visors against liquid gas. Each was good for only fifteen minutes. Then you tore it off and put on a fresh one – very quickly.

Fellows went about quietly making their own arrangements for the coming fray. Silently they adjusted the bands of their tin hats, checked their identification tags, made sure their life-jacket's flashlight worked or tied their most precious possessions in a small bag at the waist. One lad was practically draped in razor-sharp sheath knives. 'Figurin' on some hand-to-hand fightin'?' I asked. 'You never know,' he answered vaguely.

The boys were very keen on the new RCN life-jackets. We were practically living in them now. They'd been issued on board the 'tribal' destroyer HMCS *Athabaskan* just before she went out on her last patrol before she was sunk, and they saved many lives then. We liked them and were preparing to float around in them indefinitely as survivors.

Choice edibles the fellows had been hoarding in their lockers now came to light. Nothing could have shown more clearly what they thought was ahead than the way in which they now brought out those titbits from home and insisted we eat them – right away, while we still could! No use going into the water on an empty stomach! Even the canteen manager had let us buy all the chocolate bars we wanted.

I'd never seen ratings taking things so seriously. They tested the escape hatch in the mess-deck to see that it worked, and the ladder to be sure it came free easily. One of the 'Killicks' checked and double-checked the 'bottom-line' that ran around the bow to take a collision mat in case we got holed. At night, without any orders whatsoever, guys went round checking up on the ship's blackout, so no chink of light showed to a prowling E-Boat. I even went and hacked off my lovely beard, after reading in an old newspaper how bearded survivors from a torpedoed frigate nearly choked to death in fuel oil.

Our ships, all twelve, would take up a sort of arrowhead formation. The leading ship would then put out a sweep on both sides, and the next ship behind her on each flank would put a sweep in the direction of that flank. With each ship keeping her bow inside the end of the next ahead's sweep, we'd clear a wide channel and no one would hit anything. At least that was the theory!

There were two small Yankee MLS (mine laying ships) to sweep ahead of the flotilla and so protecting the leading ship. The senior officer in the MLS was the man who'd spirited General MacArthur away from the Philippines. So we had faith in him.

Next morning we were having breakfast in the mess-deck when the whole ship shook like a piece of sheet tin. There was a dead silence in the mess. Then it came again and much louder than before, BOOM! This time everything on the table leaped into the air. A voice yelled down through the for'ard hatchway, 'Hello, below! In case you're interested, we're cutting mines out here.' As if we didn't know!

Well, we rose from that table as one man. The first bloke took off with the coffee-pot in one hand, his plate in the other, and his mouth so full of toast he couldn't speak. Another chap came flying out of the washroom in such a hurry he left his false teeth behind.

Several mines were cut by the ships ahead of us, and we opened up at them with all our small arms, but couldn't hit the horns. Then, as their outer casings became pierced with bullets, they filled and sank. One popped up much too close for comfort, which had us pretty excited, until it turned out to be an old bucket dropped overboard by a ship up ahead.

By the middle of the afternoon one spearhead of the armada was right behind us. The landings were set to begin early the following morning. Besides the infantry and tank-carrying vessels, there were ocean-going tugs, landing-craft towing barges laden with more landing-craft, barges with heavy guns and raft-like somethings, barely awash, with people walking about on them. There were also the rocket ships, looking like a direct steal from *Popular Science* or *Amazing Stories* magazines.

We hadn't met any opposition at all so far. We couldn't understand it. Why hadn't there been any German planes? Lordy! Maybe they were waiting to trap us close in by the coast.

But whatever the Germans did about the invasion fleet, obviously we'd catch it first, and the boys kept chattering contently about the awful time we'd be having in just a few hours. They weren't exactly measuring themselves mentally for harp and halo; rather just groping for a few quotable last words. The situation was growing more tense by the minute and they frankly revelled in it.

Lieutenant-Commander Roger Hill

ROYAL NAVY

At 19.00 on 5 June we were in position convoying group G9, which carried the assault troops for Gold Beach – the 50th Division. It was a great moment – at last we were under way and off for France to finish the war. Even if ships were sunk all round us, we were going on to the beaches with anything that stayed afloat. I felt a sense of relief that our object was crystal clear and there were no difficult decisions to make when casualties started.

All through the night we overhauled the line of shipping, which was now an endless stream. 'We have built a bridge of ships from England to France,' Admiral Cunningham had said, and we passed it all keyed up for explosions and losses, ships on fire and everything that goes bump in the night, but nothing happened.

The minesweepers had done their job and the coastal batteries and the mined beaches had been plastered by Bomber Command during the night. At daylight 900 Flying Fortresses came over high and dropped their bombs in the same area. As the roar of their engines and noise of the exploding bombs died away, there was a sudden pause and quiet.

Rhoda Brown

WREN

On the eve of D-Day we were stationed at Ventnor on the Isle of Wight and had been to a dance – we were walking back about 11pm and took the path along the coast. I shall never forget the sight – the whole sea was completely covered by craft of all shapes and sizes all travelling to the French coast. It was a bright night so we could see very well and it was a most impressive and rather frightening sight. When we got back to the 'Wrennery' – which was high up on the cliff road – our officer told us that we had to sleep in our clothes that night as we didn't know what repercussions there would be.

Aerial photograph of ships of the Royal Navy massing off the Isle of Wight before setting off for the Normandy beaches.

To us it was terribly exciting, and I must say that we felt very flat when nothing at all happened that day. It was, however, very exciting to be on watch with our operators, as they could tell the progress of our troops, and when our people took over an enemy position the Germans' transmitter was put out of action and afterwards taken over by our people, so we were able to monitor how the battles were going.

Ralph Rayner

ROYAL ENGINEER

I remember on the Monday evening of 5 June, before going home in the evening, looking across to the Isle of Wight and a thought struck me that I could have walked across the Solent to the Isle of Wight on the armada of vessels that were present.

Hugh Spensley

BRITISH ARMED FORCES

My vivid memory of that final day was the sound of hymns, like 'For those in peril on the sea', being sung with fervour from ship after ship as a padre made his way around the anchorage. However, on the evening of 5 June we weighed anchor and set sail, forming up in convoy – it was on.

In the early hours of the morning of 6 June, before it was light, we heard the reassuring drone of hundreds of Lancasters and Halifaxes as they flew over to hammer the German defences and I remember saying to myself those lines of Shakespeare from *Henry V*: 'He that outlives this day, and comes safe home, Will stand a tiptoe when this day is nam'd . . . And gentlemen in England now abed shall think themselves accursed they were not here.'

Rozelle Raynes

WREN

I awoke from a dreamless sleep to find that someone was squeezing a sponge full of ice-cold water over my face. A signal had just come through to say that all of us were wanted at Town Quay, Southampton, immediately. I had not bothered to undress that night, so it took no more than a couple of minutes to pull on my sea-boots and duffel coat, brush my hair and ram a cap down on top of it. Ten minutes later we were lined up in front of an officer listening to what he had in store for us. 'There are three personnel landing-craft which have broken down somewhere near the Needles,' he told us, 'and I'm sending you girls down there on a tug to bring them back. I know some of you would rather stow away on a ship that's bound for

France, but the navy won't allow that and this is the best I can do for you!'

At 10am we were all aboard steaming down the River Test towards Southampton Water. Although the wind was no longer blowing gale force there was plenty of it, and we were soaked to the skin before we had gone very far. Presently the sun came out and the coxswain let Joan Preece and I and some of the others steer the tugs in turn. Bryn was down in the galley making cocoa, and from the open hatch cover above the engine room came the clear beautiful notes of a sailor's voice, singing 'Roses of Picardy' and a thin spiral of pungent smoke from the PO's pipe.

All around us the great armada was on the move. There were all the ships we knew so well; the Force Pluto ships from Abatos, the infantry landing-craft from Tormentor, all the hundreds of tank landing-craft from Southampton; so many of our favourite ships, all flying barrage balloons, like silver bumble-bees sailing among the fast-moving clouds. Then there were the armed merchant cruisers, destroyers, minesweepers, corvettes, trawlers and ocean tugs, every one of them moving southwards towards Normandy and a fate unknown.

At last the great day had come; the tension was broken and the soldiers and sailors laughed and cheered as our little tug kept pace with them, clouds of rainbow-tinted spray breaking over her stubborn black bows. One man leaned over the stern of his landing-craft and called out to us: 'You're the last bit of Old England we'll see for a while, girls, and you sure look worth fighting for!'

Dennis McLarin

BRITISH ARMED FORCES

It was a day like no other. We were all moving out of Plymouth Harbour and it took on a sort of circus atmosphere, not a happy thing but one in which the adrenaline was running high.

Charles Jones

BRITISH ARMED FORCES

We sailed on the evening of 5 June for a point south of the Isle of Wight, marked famously as Z Buoy. There we all turned south in the darkness towards Normandy, through cleared minefields marked by dimly lit buoys. Some COs were high on Benzedrine tablets to ensure that they stayed awake and alert. My twentieth birthday – 6 June 1944 – arrived in style.

Private Gordon Duffin

2ND BATTALION GLOUCESTERSHIRE REGIMENT

We were still in Southampton Water and moving at good speed, and we were near enough to wave back to hundreds of 'civvies' who lined the shore to cheer us on our way. Pointing to the stack of 'compo' ration boxes on deck, the officer told me that there were enough rations there for a week, so if I needed any extra, to help myself. I knew that some of the 'compo' boxes contained two-pound tins of peaches, so I opened one and 'bingo' I was lucky first time. The officer looked on with amusement as I ate all the peaches and explained that, as I was the champion 'sea sicker' in the unit, they would slide up just as easily as they had slid down!

By now it was quite chilly, so I shook hands with the officer and we wished each other the best of luck tomorrow, and went below to the warm fug of the 'racking area'. With a good supply of 'bags vomit' in my possession, I slid onto my frame and went to sleep. Sometime in the night I woke up feeling terrible. The craft was rocking something awful, I saw my peaches again immediately and that was the start of seasickness that lasted until long after we had landed on Gold Beach. I did a sickly grin at the usual remarks about greasy bully sandwiches and fat pork chops, which the iron-gutted lads always made, but it showed that they were in good spirits.

When it was time to get ready to land, we 'de-racked' ourselves, put on our equipment, checked our weapons and stood waiting in the space made by folding up our frames. Our full 'bags vomit' were left behind, dozens of them. We always had a thought for the poor sailors who had to clean up behind us, but with luck this time it could be done by Jerry prisoners!

Sub-Lieutenant Jim Booth

ROYAL NAVY

When we were under way beneath the water, I was either on the steering wheel or the periscope aboard X-23, a midget submarine marking a specific beach for the invasion. In those days we had to do navigation the old-fashioned way to find our destination. We took charts, pictures, anything we could lay our hands on. When we arrived we went up the beach a couple of times to take bearings. All the technical stuff like radar was turned off. Finally we got the position dead right and at that point we bottomed fairly fast to about six fathoms, or thirty feet, and dropped anchor. And there we sat making tea and eating baked beans or soup and waited. We talked mostly about beer and women. That was the case with most of men that age. We were a close team and knew each other very well. Unfortunately the first message meant it was all postponed for twenty-four hours. We were a bit worried because we were short of oxygen. There was an oxygen tank aboard but we knew it wouldn't last forever. At times like this we were expected to take a nap to use less oxygen. At night when the boat surfaced we could walk about on deck a bit to get some fresh air. The day before the invasion we had the little periscope up. We could see the Germans playing football on the beach. We came up at night and got the message to stand by. Afterwards we sat on the bottom for a bit and surfaced at 4am. Then we had this spectacular experience as this incredible mass of planes arrived, which bombed the beach in advance. After the beach was pulverised, the planes suddenly stopped coming. Along came the first wave of landing-craft. It was dawn by then. They passed us, knowing they were going to hit the right beach, at the right depth. That was critical. If they had gone east it would have been disastrous.

Captain Peter Goddin

ROYAL WEST KENT REGIMENT

We sailed that Sunday evening with a solitary Wren waving farewell from the quayside that in peacetime catered for the transatlantic luxury liners. The seas around us were an incredible sight with countless craft of all shapes and sizes. I think it was by being part of that mass of shipping that supreme confidence outweighed the big negative of 'What if we, or I, don't make it?'

Margaret Blackwell

WREN

Against orders, I walked to the top of the hill on the Kingswear side and looked out to sea, which was crammed with the long low craft as far as one could see. It is as if someone had emptied many boxes of matches into a bowl of water. I went to the 10.15 Mass at the St John's Catholic Church in Dartmouth. The priest remarked, 'What an ominous silence there is over everything.' It hung heavily, and depressed everyone. I walked to the top of the hill: out to sea, on the horizon, the landing-craft still bobbed and jostled throughout the day, waiting zero hour. And during the afternoon the wind rose more and more and a gale warning came through. After all the fine weather we have had, it has to break on this the greatest day perhaps in history!

The Silent Day: 'Not a soldier was to be seen.'

Margaret L. Smith

SCHOOLGIRL

I was thirteen and a half years old at the time, living in a small village seventeen miles north of London, and had to walk three miles to school in Watford. A crowd of girls used to gather along the way, and I can remember the sky being full of aeroplanes pulling gliders; there were hundreds of them. The father of one of my friends, Kathleen, was in the army and she said, 'My dad is up there in one of those,' and we all started waving scarves, hats and hands and shouting 'Cheerio Dad' to all the planes as they flew very low over us. To most of us it didn't mean very much to see all the planes, but the next week Kathleen came to school and said her father had been killed that day. I remember feeling very sad. My own father was partially blind and unfit for the army, and for the first time ever, I thought I was glad he was blind because it kept him home with us.

Mrs Cecilia Hodgson

HOUSEWIFE

I was living in Gosport, Hampshire, on D-Day, in Ann's Hill Road, which leads to the harbour and Portsmouth. My husband had just been called up to serve in the Royal Pioneer Corps, and my brother was away at sea, in the Royal Naval Reserve, so there was just me and my little girl left.

We were in the kitchen at the time, and I think she had been having her nap, when all of a sudden we heard a terrible rumbling and clanging down the road. So I picked up my little girl in my arms and rushed to the front door to see what all the noise was about, and there they were, these great big tanks, rolling towards us. They were Canadian soldiers, all in their war gear, on their way to the harbour and the Channel, but of course we did not know their destination, though I guessed. And as they went by, my little one-year-old started waving and cried out ''Anks Mummie! 'Anks, look Mummie'; as she had only just started to talk, she could not say 'Tanks'. But the soldiers heard her and waved and grinned at us back. I'll always remember that afternoon and the way she called out.

Brian Selman

SCHOOLBOY

Then, one night back in Poole, our family was woken by a mighty roar. We looked out and saw the sky was filled with the lights of aircraft, each towing a glider. We knew the Day had come. All night long the roar of the aircraft went on and sleep was impossible. In the morning, formations of planes, newly painted with black and white stripes, flew out to sea, and singletons, some clearly damaged and some trailing smoke, came back. The battle was on.

Eileen Greedy

SCHOOLGIRL

One night my Mama awakened us all. 'It's okay, don't be frightened, you are quite safe, but I want you to see this.' Hearing the heavy drone of heavily laden bombers, I expected to hear the firecrackers of the fighter planes, but no. 'Look out of the window,' my Mama insisted. Looking out of the small pane of glass in the bedroom window at the dark sky, there were no lights, not a star to be seen. Then I saw them coming from the north, wave after wave. The unnerving drone of the bombers went relentlessly on and on. Mama, looking at our staring solemn faces, said, 'You are watching history at this moment. I don't know how or where they are going, but these are our planes. They will be turning this war around tonight. Say a prayer for all the men in those planes and remember them.' The next day the world exploded. It was D-Day. When I now see big, bright, twinkling stars hanging low in a dark velvet sky, I remember! And I say 'Thank you' to those who put the stars back in the skies!

Peter Carragher

SCHOOLBOY

I remember seeing the hundreds of aircraft and gliders flying over our school playground. All us boys, I was eleven, were very excited and wanted to stay outside and watch this great modern armada. History in the making we told our teachers, but they told us, school work had to go on.

Richard MacDonnell

SCHOOLBOY

And this is the bit which will stay in my mind for as long as I have a mind for things to stay in. Fifty yards up the road from our house, the Tavistock to Plymouth road had overnight been transformed into an enormous, endless convoy of American Army lorries. Dartmoor was being emptied into the waiting transports in the Sound. On and on and on they went: one after another after another after another. And there was only me and my brother to watch them, as we stood beside the road. Our mother called us in to lunch and when we went back; they were still rolling on and on and on. Then teatime and then bedtime, even though our mother called us, we stood quite still and watched and watched as that huge convoy just kept going.

The American soldiers, sitting in rows in their open-topped transports, must have been told to be friendly to the 'natives', which, on that section of the road, meant just two little boys, because they kept on throwing sweets at us. Or we thought they were sweets, until we tasted them. They were terrible-tasting Horlicks tablets. They were revolting. Let-downs don't come bigger than that to small boys. And we had thought rationing had come to an end just specially for us two, right beside the Tavistock to Plymouth road, courtesy of the American Army.

Doreen Pyne

WAR EFFORT WORKER

After a great few days and evenings we were woken in the early hours of Friday morning, it was still dark and the ground beneath us was shaking. We could hear heavy vehicles on the move and orders being shouted. My goodness, we thought that we'd left this all behind in London, but we stayed abed as we didn't want to trip over the ropes in the blackout darkness. Off to work for our last day, looking forward to our farewell dance that night.

What a shock; we were stopped at the gate and met by a few older men on security watch. Everyone else and the equipment had vanished; the lively camp was empty and lifeless. The soldiers were off to their embarkation ports. We were sad for them, as we had been seeing our troops go by at home. Now they were all going into danger.

We don't know how many came back, but like to think that we had been fun to be with in return for a lovely slant on life that they gave us. Not to mention that wonderful food. I can still see and taste it all these years on.

Kate White

CIVILIAN

Dad was a great rose grower; we had over a hundred in the garden. Bushes, standard roses and a couple of climbers, just coming out, some in bud, some in full bloom, so Dad stripped the garden and as the tanks and lorries went by he handed them to the soldiers, who put them on their tanks and in their hats. I remember later that day it was mentioned on the news and in the newspapers: the red rose of England was going to France.

Parked US armoured vehicles waiting for the order to move, a common sight in English towns during the lead-up to D-Day.

The Americans were kindness in themselves, so good with children; they had time for them. They were miles from home and friends and they were only too grateful to the British people. Our front door and back door was open all the time; they were just in and out. The lady of the house, they sat with her, they talked with her.

Harold Jackson-Seed

CIVILIAN

During the early hours of the morning there was a dickens of a row in our road but when I looked out later all the tanks had gone, everything had gone.

I looked in our front garden and there was a jerry can at the back of the garden wall; it was petrol. They'd left it as a present for me, but my near neighbour was a police sergeant; he said, 'That's very dangerous having that old boy, I'd better take it.' So I said, 'What are you going to do with it?' 'Well, I can't get enough petrol to keep the lawns mown up at the police hostel.' So I lost my five gallons.

Natasha Drewry

CIVILIAN

My great, great aunt, Julia Bell, was about ten years old in 1944 and was walking along Southsea Beach, Portsmouth, on the morning of the preparations for D-Day.

Her father was a bank manager and he had given her a little suede bag of shiny new pennies. This was a real treat as they were very hard to come by. Soldiers were in the process of boarding the boats and one saw her playing with these pennies. He asked her if he could have one for good luck. She happily gave him one. Being a very warm-hearted little girl, she ended up giving all her pennies away to soldiers in the hope that it would bring all of them good luck. She always hoped they did come back safely and would have loved to have known for sure.

Yvonne Oliver

CIVILIAN

Some of the troops that were to take part were camped in and around our part of Essex and gradually they moved in waves to get down to Tilbury Docks. I say exciting, but it wasn't really. It was very sad. But at least we began to feel that we were helping the war effort. Occasionally when a convoy was held up in our road, the soldiers came in and had a cup of tea and read the paper until their NCO called them out again. He used to blow on a bugle! One morning when we got up, there was a box of lard and two legs of lamb under the hedge in the front garden! The invasion had actually been announced on the radio after I'd left home to get the train to the City. My friends on the train were anxious to know how I had been able to tell them the date a week or two beforehand. I remember hearing the phrase, 'Always attack on a waning moon', and 6 June was the first time we'd had a waning moon. So I was not surprised. But everyone thought it was marvellous that I had been able to tell them. I remember going through my diary and saying, 'Can't happen till June the 6th.'

Harry Patch

WWI VETERAN AND MAINTENANCE WORKER

In the weeks before D-Day I knew the time and date of all movements in and out of every camp in my area, except for one, and that was the 6 June, which was kept secret by everyone. I went away on the evening of the 5th; everything was normal, camps full of Americans, everything as it should be. I came back in the morning and not a soldier was to be seen, they were all gone. It was quite eerie. Fires in the camp's ranges were still burning. There were urns of cocoa, coffee, tea, all hot. Cheese, butter, bacon, it was all there in the dining room, half-consumed meals on the table.

Anon

SCHOOLBOY

Boys are always interested in guns and we were no exception. One soldier unloaded his pistol and demonstrated how to take it apart. A request for some bullets as a souvenir was greeted with a knowing smile but firmly rejected. We stayed with those young men most of the day, but when we returned a week later hoping for a repeat performance, the Green was empty with only a few empty ration packs blowing about in the wind.

David Maker

PAPERBOY

Apart from the night-time puffing and clanking sound of an ammunition train busily shunting its load between Priddys Hard, Gosport and Bedenham, a strange sort of silence, full of anxious anticipation, fell over the area. The contractors and their machines had departed and it was as though a newly built gallows awaited the condemned. It was a moment during this time of tense expectation and suspense that I was sitting on our low brick front garden wall with my pal, 'Boy' Hodgson. Together we chatted and idly stretched our legs over the roadside pavement. The road was unusually quiet. No vehicles. No military. No residents. I looked down Priory Road and noticed three chaps wandering along the middle of it towards us. We followed their progress and when almost abreast of us I noticed them glance our way without interrupting the flow of their conversation. Their slow pace had not hesitated, and it was amusing to Boy and me that all three of them walked with hands clasped behind their backs. 'Did you see who that was?' I said to Boy. 'No,' he replied. 'Well,' I said, 'the one nearest to us was the King, the one in the middle was Mr Churchill and him on the far side was Monty.' 'Coo,' said Boy, quite unimpressed, 'don't they walk funny,' and then, with a bit more spirit he stood up and said, 'Let's walk behind them.' The suggestion seemed a bit forward to me but Boy was already up and on the trail. I quickly chased after him to take up a position some five yards behind the trio. Boy and I walked along with our hands behind us, nodding silently and seriously to each other in mock conference as smoke from Churchill's cigar wafted by us. We slipped out of the routine as the men, on whom our very lives depended, moved on still deep in conversation.

Alan C. Atkins

SCHOOLBOY

After my father had gone back to work, in the afternoon, we set off. It was quite a long walk, and every step was strange. There were no uniforms. Nobody left. The parks we walked through were empty of soldiers, not one around. The barracks in the cricket park was empty, nobody to be seen: just one door banging in the wind. A strange silence had settled over the whole town. No sound of trucks or Jeeps. No shouting out. No laughter. Really, one doesn't appreciate just how noisy armies are – until they're gone.

Peter Stockton

PAPERBOY

I carried on my paper deliveries and social calls to the barracks during spring 1944. Troops sometimes went away for a few days and would return very tired and dirty but would still pay me for the papers. One morning, sometime in late April, I called at the barracks as usual but no one was there except two or three sentries on the gate. The place was empty and they wouldn't let me into the barracks. When I asked where the troops had gone they just said 'Away'.

Very upset and with tears in my eyes I turned back from the gates and cycled down the road to continue on my round. Then I saw dozens of army trucks in a nearby field. Going into the field I searched for my special friends and found them sitting in the rear of one of the trucks, fully kitted out complete with rifles. They lifted me into the truck and I spent about ten minutes asking them where they were going and when would they be back. They couldn't tell me where they were heading for. They all shook my hand, hugged me and then lowered me back to the ground. As I stood there watching, orders went out and the vehicles fired up, and away they went down the road, out of my life forever.

Sometime later the news broke on the wireless that D-Day had started and British and American troops had landed on French soil. As we sat listening my dad said to me, 'That's where those Yanks of yours will be.' I followed the news about the fighting every day hoping that they were safe.

Trevor Butler

SCHOOLBOY

I don't know how long they were there, my sister thinks about two weeks, but our days were filled with wonderful excitement. But on leaving one morning I noticed the vehicles were no longer outside our house and when I walked into the road I could see that they were all gone, hundreds of different types of army vehicles just disappeared. 'Where had they gone?' I asked everybody.

Edward Bram

WAITER

For some months I was serving as a waiter in the officer's mess of No. 2 War Office signals at Purbrook Heath House. Two weeks before D-Day a tented camp sprang up overnight and was occupied; we were not allowed to mix with the men – security reasons I suppose.

On the night of 5 June I walked back to where I was staying as usual and turned in. Our beds were in the hay-loft of a stable and we slept with all the doors and windows open. On the way back there was hardly a noise apart from my own footsteps. The next morning I awoke to hear the radio announcement saying how the invasion forces had landed in Normandy. It appeared that during the night, dozens of tanks and support vehicles had been parked in neighbouring fields, but no one in our billet had heard any noise. When we had some spare time we wandered around the tented camp. What a shambles! There were odd items of clothing, part-written letters, screwed-up books, magazines and ammunition, mainly 300 and 9mm.

John Hobbs

CIVILIAN

Up at the end of Aldermoor Road they covered the grass each side with brick rubble and ashes and things to make a standing ground for the tanks. This was all the way round the Rownhams area, north-west of Southampton. These convoys of tanks and things with tracks, they camouflage them, and then they'd move off and go on manoeuvres in the area and they'd come round again. Then one morning they were gone. I'd slept through the night; I didn't hear the planes going over, I didn't hear anything.

Joan Dale

WREN

Suddenly everything disappeared. We woke up and troops, tanks, guns had gone. They were all now crammed into those little ships and nothing of war was visible on the streets any more. I thought of the men packed into those tiny craft, waiting, wafting and still no order, no movement.

All mail from the port was censored, and this resulted in long delays, so not a card, present or letter on my twenty-first birthday! But the coxswain made up for it. He gave me a tot of his rum, and I rode up Southampton High Street between the tram lines on my bicycle in an ecstatic state.

Still no news of an invasion, but Kathy and I went to bed on the night of the 5th, confident that it would be tomorrow as the coxswain had said. And so it proved. When we went down to the Hard in the morning there was not a craft to be seen. The sea was empty. We went back to the Wrens' quarters, for there was nothing for us to do in the office. There, crowded round the wireless, the quarters' staff, cooks and stewards were gathered to hear the news, some of them weeping as they knew their boyfriends had gone to France. Because of the careful secrecy, and in spite of the evidence of their eyes, they had not guessed that the night before, while they slept, D-Day was about to begin.

On the morning of 6th June 1944, a force of 380 US planes flew over the Allied invasion fleet gathered off the Normandy coast and bombarded villages with access roads to the beachheads.

Lawrence Cooper

SCHOOLBOY

Late one night we were woken by our parents and brought down stairs in a very serious moment. Colonel Story and a colleague had specially come to say goodbye, as they were embarking that night – the significance and importance of that probably not understood at the time, but I have never forgotten the incident. The next morning we climbed the stairs to the top window again, and sure enough, the fleet had gone.

Mary Strong

FACTORY WORKER

My younger sister and I, both naval wives, lived together during the war, sharing each other's joys and sorrows. There came a quieter time when we were both confident that our men were in home waters and my sister's husband managed to get word to her that he would meet her under the clock in Glasgow Central Station. Lying awake in the early hours of the following morning I heard footsteps at the door, and running downstairs met Phyllis coming in. She burst into tears as she had waited all day in Glasgow station and her husband hadn't turned up, so she made the journey home again as she knew no one in Glasgow.

I worked in a radio factory's office and one of my perks was a radio on my desk so that I could listen to the news bulletins. A few days later on 6 June I switched on as I started my day's work. Over the air came General Eisenhower's voice, telling the French people that the Allied armies had landed in the early hours. I reached for the phone and called my sister. I said 'here is the answer to where our men are' and held the phone to the radio.

Anon

SCHOOLGIRL

Our house was about a quarter of a mile from the main London to Portsmouth rail line, and just outside of Woking on the Guildford side was an extremely large rail freight shunting yard, which was always a hive of activity. This yard could be seen from a path which ran between two roads and was a frequently used access to all the allotments that people cultivated on the adjacent land.

Early in 1944, the freight yard was emptied and filled with passenger carriages – mainly Third Class – to be filled with soldiers who used them to live in. Of course we were told not to talk to or visit these troops – but being children we did and found that they were all Canadians. This was quite a coincidence as our mother had relatives in Canada. We got to know them quite well and used to take them food, particularly homemade Apple pies, as their food rations were a bit limited. In return, they gave us chewing gum which was almost unobtainable. One soldier in particular I got to know was named Howard. He was a dispatch rider and had the nickname of, 'Crash Right through Howard'.

We had got used to visiting these troops almost every day, as it was on the way to school, until that day at the beginning of June when on going to see our troops, we found that the whole yard was empty. There was not a carriage to be seen. They must have all gone away overnight. We were very disappointed as no one had said goodbye and went home to tell our Mother what we had found. She made no comment but when she told our Father on his return home in the evening, he looked as though he knew what the reason was.

Mary Brice

CIVILIAN

My mother, sister and myself were living in a gamekeeper's cottage in Hooksway, a hamlet in Sussex, nine miles from Chichester, several miles from any other towns or villages.

We had come from Portsmouth where my father was a pawn-broker. He became a policeman in the dockyard after our shop had been bombed and destroyed. My mother, sister and I had left Portsmouth at the start of the bombing and were living in this small flint cottage in a fairly deserted countryside.

Before D-Day hundreds of Canadian soldiers had suddenly appeared in the woods around us, camping out in tents with lorries and motorcycles and camouflage netting to cover them up. Every wood and hedge end had camps and tents for miles around. We had been told by my mother not to go anywhere near them and not to talk to them. Well, you know what children are like; when we walked to and from school two miles away, with several other children, we were given sweets and chocolate and our first chewing gum! In the time they were there we got quite friendly with them and they with us. They made gardens around their camps, and put up flagpoles and planted flowers. They built rustic fencing and had fires to cook on. I once saw a deer being roasted and they shot rabbits and made delicious smelling stews. I'm not sure how long they stayed but one night they just all vanished as if by magic. We were very upset when we woke up next morning and found them gone and were told they had gone for good and wouldn't be back. No more sweets, gum or anything; just the fences and flagpoles.

Mary Halpin

CIVILIAN

I used to walk along the Portsmouth front to go to the town to shop. And this particular day I'm walking along the front and I'm thinking, 'What is wrong? What's the difference?' I couldn't think what it was. The water was empty. There was absolutely nothing there and little if any sound. That was D-Day.

D-Day, 6 June 1944: 'I never loved England so truly as at that moment.'

Derek Hogg

ROYAL NAVY CADET

In the morning of 6 June, while we were in the dining mess hall having breakfast, an announcement came over the Tannoy telling us that the invasion had begun, and that the troops had landed on the beaches, that paratroops and glider troops had landed a few miles inland.

There were cheers from everyone in the mess. All day long, aircraft were landing, refuelling and taking off again, but in the meantime telling us what they could see of the landing and what progress was being made. It was all very exciting and a memory that stays clearly in my mind. I did go flying again later in the week, and troop movement on the roads was still very apparent, but now we know what it was all about.

John Bowles

CIVILIAN

Just before dawn we were awakened by the loud droning of aircraft engines and it went on for what seemed hours. No one knew what it meant, but one of the grown-ups said it was probably a thousand bomber raid on Germany. Later that day, I was on a train with Aunt Cissy going from Sturminster Newton to Blandford to buy some curtain material. Suddenly, there was the screeching of brakes, the carriage shuddered and the train slowed down to a complete stop. We were in a cutting and unable to see anything to the left or right. After about ten minutes, the train started to slowly move out of the cutting. To our left was a small copse and among the trees we saw a mass of bright splintered wood and olive-green fabric flapping in the morning breeze. Pointing straight up into the blue sky was a wing with a shining white star, brilliant in the Dorset morning sun. Everyone got off the train. Beside the tangle of wreckage lay some soldiers in the uniforms that we had come to know so well. They seemed to be sleeping, their faces covered with pieces of fabric. They did not move.

Another American soldier sat near the wreckage smoking a cigarette, staring straight ahead. Several soldiers stood nearby, silent, and two or three used their rifles as crutches for support. Some women passengers, including Auntie Cissy, started to cry and then the full impact of what had happened struck me, too, and I began to cry. I understood why those American soldiers in their snazzy uniforms were lying on the ground and not moving. I heard the train guard say to one of the women, 'It was one of them invasion force gliders, Missus, and they was supposed to land in France, but the poor blighters didn't get very far, I'm afraid.'

It was D-Day, 6 June 1944.

W.R. Nicholas

BRITISH ARMED FORCES

In the middle of the night we marched out of our camp, along the road through Southampton. It was rather eerie, everything dark – no street lights – you could feel the people were watching you out of their bedrooms. At the quay, we got onto the ship and sailed soon after. We anchored in the Solent, which was absolutely full of ships! It must have been a marvellous target for the enemy if they had been able to get there.

We were all rather excited inside. I do remember the chaplain having a Communion service and I thought 'I'd better go to this but I don't suppose many other people will.' The place was crammed! It was down in the hold and the chaps were sitting, standing, on coils of rope and that sort of thing – it was quite amazing! Then, of course, we turned round and came back – and we thought of just another exercise. And then the same thing was repeated the next day. That morning after we had anchored we had a marvellous breakfast of bacon, eggs and a lot of rum. Then the scrambling nets were put down the side of the ship and they lowered the LCAs and we scrambled down into them and off we went. It was quite extraordinary; it was rather like the front row of the dress circle – you could see these ships coming into view.

Soldiers of No 4 Commando, 1st Special Service Brigade, under the command of Lord Lovat, who under fire, instructed his personal piper to play the commandos ashore. They are seen here marching to Southampton.

Flight Lieutenant Alec Blythe

RAF

I had met the Royal Engineers, whom I was to drop on D-Day, and they seemed jolly nice chaps. However, when they came up to the Dakota on the night of the operation with blackened faces they looked a fearsome lot. One pulled out his dagger and said that it was going to find a German that night. I was rather glad they were on our side.

Ron Plater

RAF SPECIAL BEACH UNIT

We were responsible for all RAF stores, petrol, oil and ammunition, for getting them off the landing-craft, and then from the beachhead to forward dumps and thence to the first available landing strip. This allowed aircraft to land, refuel and rearm so that they could give troops immediate air cover without returning to England.

This was the third invasion we had taken part in, the others being Sicily and Salerno in Italy, so we knew a little bit about it all and I think it's safe to say the novelty had definitely worn off!

Rosemary Davis

FIRST AID NURSING YEOMANRY

I was part of the First Aid Nursing Yeomanry – FANYs. The Americans had a great laugh about that because that meant something quite different to them! I was posted to Baker Street. On D-Day there was a tremendous atmosphere. I remember so vividly we were receiving messages from these groups who'd been dropped behind the lines in France. I remember on D-Day this message came over: 'Thank you very much for information you've passed to us.' That was a group that had been taken over by the Germans.

Captain A.D.C. Smith

NO. 4 COMMANDO

We embarked in a grotesque gala atmosphere more like a regatta than a page of history, with gay music from the ship's loud hailers and a more-than-usual quota of jocular farewells bandied between friends. It was a perfect summer evening; the Isle of Wight lay green and friendly, and tantalisingly peaceful, behind the tapestry of war ships. At 21.00 we set out to war with Lord Lovat's piper playing in the bows. It was exhilarating, glorious and heart breaking when the crew and troops began to cheer and the cheers came faintly across the water, gradually taken up by ship after ship. I never loved England so truly as at that moment.

Ralph Rayner

ROYAL ENGINEER

As the formation moved closer to the coast, the heavy warships, including HMS *Warspite*, suddenly opened fire as one on a given signal: this bombardment of the French coast continued until just before touchdown when the barrage crept forward to the area beyond the beaches. Combined with the explosion of incoming German artillery shells the noise was deafening and a number of our own craft were hit, causing many casualties. On this occasion I was operating an armoured bulldozer and my job on reaching dry land was to immediately join up with a team of sappers and a unit of Royal Navy Commando divers; our task was to clear all the beach obstacles, most of which contained explosives and were under water at high tide. As my bulldozer crept out of the water two Royal Engineer tanks immediately in front of me were both hit by German shell fire, each simultaneously catching fire; I saw only one survivor jump clear before each tank exploded.

Rifleman Robert J.G. Comber

QUEEN'S OWN RIFLES OF CANADA

My closest pal, William Cuthbertson Calbert, Bill to us, had not seen his new English wife, Alice, for a long time, so he decided he would steal away home for a few hours. This was a breach of regulations that called for severe punishment. Nevertheless he went to see his wife. While he was gone I kept a watch on both our carriers. All the while he was gone I complained about him leaving me to this task. It was not long after that though I was glad that I had let him go. That was the last time he was to see his wife.

As Bill and his crew left the barge in their carrier on heading for the beach at Bény-sur-Mer they fouled a sea mine and became a blinding ball of flames and twisted steel sizzling in the sea. It was a hard thing for me to watch. Only then did I realise what was taking place around me. The wreckage was vast and startling, the terrible waste and destruction of war, and loss of human life. Anything and everything became expendable.

Catherine Green

NURSE

We all met at Goodwood House and waited with hundreds of troops around Portsmouth. Eventually we were put on an LST and tied up in the Solent for three days waiting for the Mulberry to be taken over and for troops to take over the beaches. Finally we went to the Mulberry and one of the trucks with all our kit and belongings went over the side into the sea!

At last we landed and were sniped at by Germans. One of our doctors was killed and an orderly was shot and we had to amputate his leg at the side of the road.

Allied ambulances driving along a 'Mulberry Pier', part of a portable, temporary harbour designed to facilitate the rapid disembarkation of men and cargo onto the French beaches.

Captain Mike Crooks

CHAPLAIN

There were exciting days and infernally noisy nights, with vehicles, tanks and armoured cars pouring ashore past our high-and-dry landing-craft in a constant stream, everybody blazing away with their guns at the sound of aircraft passing over. It is impossible to describe the volume of noise, and flak going up like a firework display to end all — and of course our own shrapnel coming down like rain. We were all in danger of being killed by our own gunfire.

William Thomas Baxter

SCHOOLBOY

My father carried this poem on a rough piece of paper, written in pencil, inside his wallet from his time serving in the Second World War.

He died a number of years ago and Mum and I have often wondered who wrote this poem.

INVASION

No sound was heard on that cold grey morn
When the life of France was once more born
No bugler played his victory note
Just a lap of a wave against the boat
Swiftly silently on we spun
At last the great day had begun
We peered and watched with bated breath
Watched what we all knew might mean death
Our hearts stood still, the air grew tense
Who could endure this cold suspense?
Then with France within our reach
We softly slid upon the beach
I grasped my rifle in my hand
And softly crawled along the sand
I prayed to God then felt secure
With his strength I could endure
With the coming of the dawn
We all assembled and marched on
Victims of this circumstance
Yet liberators of mighty France
With one mad charge we cleared the hun
Watched him, scorned him, saw him run
And then upon that scene so gory
The sun shone with all its glory

Shone upon the place we stood
Shone on rivers red with blood
Our hearts were lifted high with pride
We knew that God was on our side
Now we'll fight with never a care
Fight in the fields, fight in the air
Fight in the mountains and on the sea
Fight for God and for victory.

6 June 1944: US and Canadian Perspectives: 'I knew that it was going to be the war of the war.'

Leo Garrieppe

CANADIAN SOLDIER LANDING AT JUNO BEACH

I was frightened when I left Canada in 1940. I didn't stop being frightened until I got back home in 1945!

Anyway, on 5 June at seven o'clock, we got the signal to go ahead, so we were preceded by two minesweepers – two lonely little minesweepers. There is nothing more harmless-looking than the minesweeper. But behind that were some 4,300 ships of different shapes and forms.

We crossed the Channel – well, we ventured into the Channel – and about twelve o'clock at night the weather condition changed very, very suddenly – so the weatherman wasn't at all wrong. It was a very, very cloudy night, but we knew what was waiting for us in the morning, and not too many of us were sleeping. As a matter of fact, the majority of people we were with were all seasick like dogs all through the night. We could hear the bombers, we heard paratroops flying, although we couldn't see them because of the clouds – but you train an ear in warfare that tells you the sound of the motor which belongs to you and the one that belongs to the enemy – so we knew they were ours. It gave us a little bit of a morale builder.

Edward C. Boccafogli

B COMPANY, 3RD PLATOON, 508TH PARACHUTE INFANTRY

On the night of 4 June we loaded into C47 aeroplanes at Falkingham aerodrome. Everyone was very nervous, very tense. We took off, being as we were in the first lead group. We flew around for about an hour, and then word came that the invasion was called off for twenty-four hours due to the bad weather. They said that there was one of the worst storms in many years in the Channel.

When we landed back at the airfield it was really a let-down. It just seemed to take everything right out of your stomach. That night there were very heavy rains and a couple of tents collapsed: one was hit by lightning. Next morning, the fellows were trapped underneath the canvas because of the weight of the water.

One thing I remember very well was one young kid, I don't think he was more than seventeen years old; his name was Johnny Daum, a blond, tow-headed kid. In the morning he was standing there, staring into space. I went over to him and said, 'What's the matter, Johnny?' I get emotional just thinking about it. He said, 'I don't think I'll make it.' I said, 'Nah, you'll be all right.' I sort of shook him, because he was like in a daze. As it turned out, he was one of the first men killed in Normandy.

Leo Garrieppe

CANADIAN SOLDIER LANDING AT JUNO BEACH

There was quite a controversy going on in High Command concerning the weather. The DD tanks had been conceived for a sea force 4 – and on D-Day it was 7 – sea force 7. Therefore, the ship's officer told us we would be dry-beached – to which we refused absolutely to be dry-beached; because of the construction of DD tanks, we were absolutely powerless to fire from the LCT. We absolutely had to get off the LCT; in water, we couldn't fire. We had to be on dry land to fire. In other words, in our minds, they had sacrificed us totally – and we refused. We almost came to a point of, I would say, mutiny. So they decided to come closer to about 1,000 yards because we insisted on it. We had voluntarily offered our life to do what we had to do, but we figured we had the right to choose the way we were going to die. We didn't want to be impaled on the beach – we knew exactly what was waiting for us on the beach. So we finally were launched – however, we were told that losses would be approximately 80 per cent, but we figured that at least 20 per cent of us would make it.

Frank Lawson

CANADIAN FIELD REGIMENT ARTILLERY

As we sailed down the Solent, we passed some Royal Navy destroyers and the men ran to the saluting stations to honour those who would make tomorrow history. Our regimental padre conducted a short service and led the singing of 'Abide with Me', which quite upset me, as I was leaving behind my wife, who was expecting our first baby any day.

The weather had improved slightly but it was still very rough, and everyone was seasick, with the vomit and the waves splashing over the side onto the steel floor, which made it a job to stand up. We had been told that we were landing on Juno Beach, on an uncleared minefield, and that 50 per cent casualties were expected. I am sure no one got any sleep.

Samuel Schmidt

AMERICAN ARMED FORCES

The only time I really had action with the British was when we left England to go to Normandy. We went aboard a little British boat and, although I hate to say it, I found that the British were a very dirty and sloppy organization. The boat was so unclean and seemed to be badly operated; there was junk lying all over the place. Naval men are supposed to be dressed in a certain manner: you wear your uniform with pride, but these guys, they were dressed like stevedores. One afternoon, as we were crossing the Channel, we could hear on the loudspeaker system, 'Attention, Flotilla, rum ration.' So we figured, 'What the heck? We'll get in line, too', but we were stopped. We were told it was only for the British seamen. That sort of cemented our relationship.

Stuart Brandow

AMERICAN ARMED FORCES
I was fine until the guy next to me, he upchucked, and you want to know what dying is, that's when you want to die. Boy, there's nothing like seasickness.

Dr Harold L. Baier

AMERICAN ARMED FORCES
The two Merchant Navy ships that were sunk were torpedoed but we kept steaming ahead. At five-and-a-half knots, you steam ahead. We were in the last column, the outside column. The ship that was sunk was right astern of us and the other one was twelve miles across the convoy. There were twelve columns of five ships in the convoy. One of the escort ships, they stayed back, I suppose to look for survivors.

Clifford Kingston

AMERICAN ARMED FORCES
All during the night, the British Spitfires, and all the US planes that we had, bombers and towing gliders full of paratroopers, were flying over the Channel. The ships had barrage balloons on them to prevent strafing by the German planes. I don't know if they were effective, because the ships didn't move very fast. They were going eight or ten knots. These things were on a winch back on the stern, so, they could run them up, or run them down, because if a plane tried to come through to strafe, and their

wings hit the cable between the barrage balloon and the ship, they would crash.

Clarence Riker

AMERICAN ARMED FORCES

We were on an LCVP. It's a landing-craft, personnel and vehicle. The English Channel was very rough. It was terrible. This little, tiny boat held about thirty, forty men, bobbed up and down like a cork. That was only one of, I don't know, hundreds. Some had tanks in them, artillery; all had men in them. So they all circled around and, when the order was given, all of them, everything at once, took away for the beach.

Assault troops massing behind the protective front section of their landing craft as it approaches Omaha Beach early on D-Day morning.

Lee Eli Barr

EIGHTH AIR FORCE, 306TH BOMB GROUP

Oh, yes. D-Day – I felt it was something extremely important; that it was going to be the war of the war. D-Day – I knew right away that it was going be a hell and that there would be thousands of casualties: we lost 2,500 killed on D-Day alone, with so many more to come.

Captain Cyril Haworth

ROYAL ARTILLERY

I can still remember the overwhelming feeling of apprehension as we crossed the sea towards Normandy. One of the men on board was a vicar, who gave a short service, and as we approached we all sang together, 'Onward, Christian soldiers'. Ironically, I later found out the same song was also being sung by the Germans who were waiting for us on the beach. We were captured by the Germans. Unfortunately our driver was shot and killed but the rest of us were taken captive. My wife was sent a telegram informing her I was missing and presumed dead, but in fact I had escaped after eighteen hours. Luckily a news reporter was travelling with the first group of Allied troops we came across. He took down our story and had it printed in the British newspaper, the *Daily Dispatch*, which thankfully my family and wife had read before they received the dreaded telegram. You never forget some of the more horrible memories.

Raymond Bodnar

AMERICAN HIGH SCHOOL STUDENT

I came home from high school and we knew that my brother was in France. As a matter of fact, 6 June is my birthday and when my mother woke me, she said, 'The Allies have invaded France.' Well, we knew that Steve was still in the United States at that time, or maybe on orders to go overseas, and so I went to school and everything was abuzz. We heard from him, that he was in England and in the 95th Division, and then, when I came home for Thanksgiving break, and we lived in this duplex house, my mother opens the door, and she's crying, and I said, 'Mom, what's happened to Steve?' She's walking through the hall and I'm saying, 'Mom, what's happened? What's happened?' She goes into the kitchen, she's still not talking, and I knew that something had happened. The worst we could hear is that he was killed. So, she showed me this telegram. Well, before she received the telegram, she had a letter. The mail used to be delivered, like, at two o'clock in the afternoon, and here she was, all alone, and my brother wrote to her, and I'll never forget that letter; he said, 'Dear Mom and Dad, you'll have heard by now that I lost my leg.' Well, like about an hour later, the telegram comes, delivered from the War Department. So, then, she showed me the letter and I said, 'Oh.' I remember, I was crying with her. I said, 'Look, Mom, he's okay,' and then, she was worried about how she's going to tell my father when he came home. So, she finally calmed down, and, when my father came home, we waited for him in the kitchen, because, normally, she'd be there cooking supper.

He was pretty strong. He felt that, 'Oh, well, what can you do?' but it set in later.

Clarence Riker

AMERICAN ARMED FORCES

Yes, it was all very noisy and guns going off every place was terrible. It was terrible. I never went back, because I had such memories of that, all the people getting killed and everything right on the beach, but we went into the beach.

Sergeant Frank Murray

HQ COMPANY, 18TH INFANTRY

That night, I was lying on my bunk next to my best buddy. We had received a mail from home prior to leaving. Before we embarked he had taken a furlough to Scotland and met a girl who he fell in love with. When he returned to Weymouth, his girlfriend followed him and got a room nearby in Dorchester and they managed to see each other. He had written to his former girlfriend in the United States and her reply was the letter he read to me that night. She had written that 'Instead of being a war bride, I hope your girlfriend's a war widow.'

She got her wish; he was killed in Normandy.

Peter Daly Campbell

US NAVY

The news of D-Day hit me in Belfast. I was on one of those long, dark piers, and I saw these thousands and thousands of soldiers and everybody knew what it was all about. I'm very happy that I wasn't part of it, because those guys really had it tough.

George Aiello

AMERICAN ARMED FORCES

We get on this ship and the commodore of this transport gets on the Tannoy and says, 'Now, hear this. It is such an honor to have you people on my ship. This ship is your ship. My men have to wait on you hand and foot. You remember, they're your guests, you take care of them. Whatever you want you got.' He was so proud to be part of the invasion and to hear him talk over the thing was like, 'Oh, boy.' He said, 'If any of our men do anything to aggravate you, you let me know.' Wasn't that nice? I'll never forget that. That was amazing.

Richard G. Wagner

AMERICAN ARMED FORCES

There wasn't one experience I had that was unhappy. No assignment that I had was the wrong one. I mean D-Day and Normandy, they were harrowing experiences, but I knew why I was there. I had opted for it, didn't have anybody else to complain about, lucky as all hell, I was.

At six o'clock on D-Day morning, it was a clear day. I saw the battleships, the cruisers, the planes overhead. I mean, it was like the 4th of July times 500,000.

You knew it was a big operation.

Louis Russomano

AMERICAN ARMED FORCES

They sent us in as decoys to draw the fire. The invasion started at six o'clock and twenty minutes later we were in the water. We got hit right in the forward engine room, which split it in half. The ship went up in the air and then went down and hit bottom. When we came up, my turtleneck sweater had sand all around my neck from hitting the bottom.

We then found ourselves hanging on to a life raft waiting to get picked up. That's when the son of bitches started to shell us. You had no time to react. It was bad. I knew all the guys down in the engine room had been killed, about six or eight of them. The rest of them were shot in the water.

After about three hours another destroyer picked us up. They gave us blankets and stuff, and we had to stay there another four hours yet, then we headed back to England. We were heading back with a cruiser, and I remember they were racing across the channel; that cruiser beat our ass boy, for a big ship it was fast.

Edward Bautz

AMERICAN ARMED FORCES

The convoy started out and that first night was real nice as it assembled. The weather was good and everything, but, the next morning, it started to get rough and I realized that there weren't too many ships around as there were in the beginning. All of a sudden we were by ourselves, and the skipper, who happened to be British, asked me to come up to the bridge. He said, 'We've lost both engines, but we're working on it. My orders are to take you to Omaha Beach.' I said, 'Well, my orders are to go to Utah Beach. He got the engines working again but it was a rough voyage. As we approached the beach, the skipper, using flags, asked, 'What beach is this?' and the beach master said, 'Well, you're on Omaha Beach,' and the skipper said, 'Well, I'm supposed to go to Utah Beach,' and then the beach master said, 'You better land while you can,' but the skipper said, 'No, I'm going over to Utah.' So he backed up, found Utah, and we pulled in; he dropped the ramp and said, 'Okay off you go.' I said, 'Just a minute.' Again, being at the Assault-Training Centre was good training. I said, 'Let's check the depth of the water,' and so we got a bamboo pole, and sure enough it just kept going down. So we backed off and he tried again. This time we were able to debark. As I jumped down I told him that he ought to stay and get some repairs. He said, 'No, I've got a date with a Wren.' Those are the British ladies in the navy. 'I've got to get back to that.' He took off.

Private First Class Robert Koch

C COMPANY, 116TH REGIMENT

In my particular ship, a sergeant raised himself up to see how far we had to go to reach land – and was struck right in the forehead by a bullet, and fell back dead. He was the first man I had ever in my life seen dead in combat. This also made me pray more and think of home, but I never sat down and wrote a letter home or made any farewell speeches or anything, because I still had confidence in, I would say, the Lord and myself, that He was going to watch out for me.

Robert Slaughter

CANADIAN ARMED FORCES

We had trouble going in. We were taking a little bit of water and we were bailing out. We also had to stop a couple of times to pick up some people – boats had capsized and we picked up some survivors. We were pretty well loaded down, and that delayed us a little bit, and we finally got in close with the shells and the machine-guns. We could hear and they were hitting the water; the 88s were hitting, and there must have been a few mines exploding. We naturally kept our heads down. They were telling us to stay down. They took us all the way, maybe twenty-five yards off the beach, and dropped the ramp. We were in the surf and it was real rough – and the front of the boat was going up and down and the enemy were shooting at us. I know some got shot as they were going off it. By the boat being so rough and up and down, I think it probably saved some of us.

Canadian troops hold their weapons aloft while wading to shore during the Normandy landings, the largest single-day amphibious action in history.

Some of them went over the side. One man went off the ramp and got hit by the ramp – it was way up in the air and it came right down and hit him in the head and killed him – but I jumped off the side and was bobbing around in the water. I think we were about twenty-five yards out – the water was still way over my head.

Colonel Edward Wozenski

E COMPANY, 2ND BATTALION, 16TH INFANTRY

We were horribly overloaded and, incidentally, just before the landing, all our web gear – standard web gear, issue gear, fine, battle-proven gear – was taken away from us because some theorists figured that it would be far easier to carry a hunting-type jacket. So at the last minute, we were issued these canvas jackets with these fantastic pockets all over the place, and we transferred all of our gear into these pockets. So the picture – you hit the beach, and you're up and down – you're in the water, and then you're ducking the small fire all around – so you duck down. You're terrified, as anyone would be – and every time I got up, I thought that it was just pure terror that was making my knees buckle – until I finally hit the shingle and I realized that I had about a hundred pounds of sand in those pockets that had accumulated, on top of maybe the fifty- or sixty-pound load that we were all carrying in. So it wasn't just pure terror that was making our knees buckle. Our pockets were full of sand.

Private First Class Robert Koch

C COMPANY, 116TH REGIMENT

We were about 300 feet off the beach when our LST got hit, so we had to swim in, and the water was, oh, I would say twelve feet in depth – so therefore, when you went off, you were over your head. When I arrived on the beach, believe it or not, the only thing I had was myself. My rifle I had dropped in the water, and I had hit the beach and laid there and thought to myself, 'What am I going to do here? Am I going to wrestle or fist-fight – or what?'

My buddies had been shot and were lying near me. Of course I took their rifles and their belts and moved along.

Lieutenant Rany Nance

LANDED OMAHA BEACH

I do remember my radio operator calling out from my left, saying that he'd been hit. And he called to me for help, but I couldn't give him any help – that's the pity of the whole thing – because we all had a mission, and that came first.

Leo Garrieppe

CANADIAN SOLDIER LANDING AT JUNO BEACH

We took them totally by surprise. When we came to shallow water, our DD tanks started to touch sand and naturally we rose out of the deep – and when we came to hold our position, we deflated our screen – and at that particular point, an incident which will always be vivid in my memory is the fact that machine-gunners scattered in the sand dunes were standing up in their machine-gun-nest, looking at the tanks coming out of the water – so we just mowed them down like corn. They were just standing there and couldn't believe their eyes to see tanks coming out of the water. I think it was then they realized the mistake of not firing at us.

Robert Slaughter

CANADIAN SOLDIER

I really didn't think I would make it. I didn't think there was any way that you could get across that beach and survive. I mean, I really thought it was my last day, but I had a job to do, and you know you're scared to death, but your friends – you don't want your friends to know you're afraid. You bluff, you act big and tough, but really you're scared to death.

Private First Class Robert Koch

C COMPANY, 116TH REGIMENT

Now, we had brought flame-throwers and machine-guns with us on this LST, which were vital to us in making our attack – but we had to let go because the weight of them would have taken us under and we couldn't possibly have gotten in. Then, in coming in, there were mines around – small mines that were scattered in the water, and were blowing some of the men up. Then, when we made our run for cover on the beach, we were being machine-gunned – and this is a miraculous thing about life in such a situation: when men on the right of you would drop, and the men on the left would drop – but you seemed to keep coming – you weren't getting hit at all.

Patrick Donnell

BRITISH ARMED FORCES

The unit by then had managed to rearm itself from weapons taken from our casualties on the beach, and, indeed, from the Germans. I think my German rifle stayed with me for the rest of the campaign, and it was a very good rifle. On the way towards La Rosière, sitting in a hedge, there was my commanding officer and a naval officer, who was our naval support fire-controller. They had achieved getting through the little village of Le Hameau near Arromanches, by riding on an ammunition sledge behind a tank, but obviously one tank wasn't able to take a unit of some 400 men through.

I have always said that British troops are very inventive. We kept saying to ourselves, 'Well, we've got to get on with the job.' The beach was a shambles and vehicles were lying all over the place – and the original beach which we should have landed on would have been impossible. One couldn't have got in there. On the other hand, one had a terrific sense that we'd get there. That we'd do it. And those tanks up on the skyline were, you know, a great boost to our morale. All we had to do was pull ourselves together and get on with the job.

Private Joe Minogue

7TH ARMOURED DIVISION

When we reached the first corner there was a dead German there – he was just like something from a film. His helmet had fallen off, and he was very, very blond. You know, this seemed so stupid in its way, that there should be a blond dead German on the very first corner that you saw.

Robert Slaughter

CANADIAN SOLDIER

The first thing I can remember was the odour of the gunpowder: the artillery fire. It's a distinct odour you don't forget – and it was the first time I'd smelled anything exactly like that. Then you're aware of the crack, crack, crack of our machine-gun. Then you heard a German machine-gun, with its burp, burp, burp – just a steady drone. There were traces of cross-fire across the beaches – you could see the tracers just hip-high. Then, from the cliffs, the snipers and the 88s were shooting down.

Colonel James D. Sink

AMERICAN ARMED FORCES

There were just so many people on the beach that you could literally walk on the bodies from one end to the other. Either they're dead, or they're wounded. The Germans really hit us hard, and my regiment lost around a thousand men that day.

You saw bits of people lying around – a leg or an arm – but the water itself wasn't bloody because most of the wounded men were up out of the water. I saw that those who were still able-bodied tried to pull the wounded out of the water. In fact they even pulled the bodies out of the water – the ones that were dead.

Some of the first American casualties awaiting evacuation.

Colonel Edward Wozenski

AMERICAN ARMED FORCES

I ran into this sergeant who had sent up the smoke flare. He was one of my platoon sergeants, and he was the first one off the beach and it was the path that he took that I picked up. The rest of our battalion followed; I think almost a whole corps went up that path. As I'm climbing the bluff, I see this sergeant coming down, because he's happy to see me – and he's got a grin on his face. As he steps down, he puts his foot on a Teller mine, right in front of my nose. I say, 'How stupid can you be?' He says, 'Oh, don't let it worry you, sir – it didn't go off when I stepped on it going up.'

We got up to the top of the cliff and I had a head-count. I landed with 180 men and eight officers and now all I could count was thirteen men and one other officer and myself. And one weapon – one M1 rifle that would fire. So we put a man on guard with it and the rest of us sat down right at the top of the bluff.

Lieutenant Rany Nance

LANDED OMAHA BEACH

There was no cause for elation. I think it was saddening. It was the most heart-rending experience that I ever had. I hope I never have one like it – to see the remains – to look back and see the remains of crack battalions, strewn over the beach – equipment and men floating in the water, face up.

6 June 1944: D-Day is Announced to the Civilian Population: 'A very small sense of hope.'

Mrs Mattie Minords

CIVILIAN

I was sitting facing the window; suddenly there was this slow kind of engine noise, and then high in the sky there appeared hundreds and hundreds of planes, each with a glider attached. They reminded me of large flocks of geese high in the sky, but with a much more purposeful mission. It reminded me of different kinds of planes over Aston, Birmingham, where I was in 1941, where they night after night devastated our city.

Barry Smith

EVACUEE

I was an evacuee on a farm in Montgomeryshire to get away from the heavy bombing of Birmingham. I remember clearly 6 June. When the farmer's eldest son John visited and excitedly asked, 'Have you heard the news?' 'No! The accumulator is not charged.' Radios in those days had to have a battery (accumulator) charged up regularly or they wouldn't work. John connected a bicycle-lamp battery to the radio and we heard the one o'clock news. That the allies had landed in Normandy.

Mollie Reed

CIVILIAN

On D-Day itself, I was listening to the radio and heard that the invasion had taken place. I remember saying to my daughters, 'I expect Daddy is there.'

Morely Wolfe

SCHOOLBOY AND ROYAL CANADIAN AIR CADET SQUADRON

For me on 6 June 1944, my war was over. No need for preparation or concern as to military service, only follow events to final victory.

Joan Short

CIVILIAN

I was on the east coast at Clacton-on-Sea; the weather had been lovely, and we had heard that something was in the wind, but of course had no idea what. In those days we were not able to get many cakes, and our local baker baked beautiful doughnuts just once a week. To get to the baker I had to run through the church-yard and on to the road as the shop was only about thirty yards away. A policeman stopped me and said, 'Can I see your identity card?' I knew it was silly of me, but I had not thought of bringing it just to get some cakes. The outcome was that I had to appear before the court on 6 June. I was a war widow – my husband had been killed in '42 – had a very young baby and was all on my own. The night of the 5th the troop planes were going over head all night, I could actually see them passing over; I knew this was to be a terrible battle. I was sick with fear not only for this awful fight that was going on, but for all the wonderful men like mine who would lose their life and the nagging fear in my stomach concerning the case in the court next morning. None of us had slept a wink; we knew that the war had taken a big step. I was sick on the way to court. I came before a lady magistrate who told me not to go anywhere on the King's Highway without my identity card, and fined me five shillings and asked if I wanted time to pay. Now it seems like such a small thing, but then I was alone and very frightened, it seemed terrible. So I shall not forget 6 June and every time I see a doughnut my mind flies back!

This is a small thought about those terrible days, and this only one of my awful nightmares. I was bombed out of two homes and lost my husband, but for those wonderful men on 6 June who helped to bring all that horror to an end, and are still with us, I say thank you.

Mrs Barrett

CIVILIAN

I cannot forget that day the friend living downstairs called out, 'Mrs Barrett, the Second Front has started.' I said, 'God help those men.' Then I kneeled to pray for them. How I wish I had the faith that I had then.

From the Diary of Gertrude White

CIVILIAN

6 June 1944 – D-Day – made tea, took my shutters down. Quiet day. Cold. Very little sunshine.

Molly Lawson

CIVILIAN

I can remember D-Day as clearly as if it were yesterday. I hadn't heard anything from my husband since he returned from a twenty-four-hour leave ten days or so beforehand, and neither did I know that when he returned from leave, his entire regiment were put behind a barbed wire compound and cut off from any contact with the outside world. But I did know that when the invasion happened, he would be going in with the assault troops.

Our first baby was already two days overdue on 6 June and I hoped against hope that his daddy would be able to see him when he was born, but it was not to be. I got up that morning to hear that landings had been made on the beaches of Normandy and the bottom dropped out of my world. Our son wasn't born until the 18 June, and at that time I hadn't heard if my husband was still alive, but he was one of the lucky ones.

Our son John was seven months old before he saw him for one precious week's leave, and fifteen months old before he came home to us permanently.

Simon Agmann

PARISIAN REFUGEE

We were refugees from Paris, hiding in the village of Lignières to escape from the Gestapo. I was only twelve years old but was carrying messages between different factions of the Resistance. I clearly remember two dates. The first is Pearl Harbor. When we heard about it, we didn't consider it a disaster: our first reaction was one of immense hope: THE AMERICANS ARE COMING! The second date, of course, is 6 June. Our feelings were so intense, it was like our hearts were burning, screaming: hold on, now they are really coming.

Kathleen Cooper

CIVILIAN

June 6th – I was then living near Watford and was woken in the early hours by an unusual continuous roaring sound of aircraft. I dashed to the window to see the amazing sight of a sky full of aircraft-towing gliders, so I grabbed my two-and-a-half-year-old daughter Jill out of her bed to see a sight that would be one of the turning points of the war.

A short while later the first invasion communiqué from General

Eisenhower's HQ was given out over the radio, and I realised that, after many anxious years, there was the possibility that my husband would soon be released from a PoW camp in Germany and see his daughter for the first time. We had another year to wait for the reunion, but on that day there was hope.

Angela Austin

CIVILIAN

I woke up on a grey, drizzly morning and was just getting out of bed when my father, who had already gone downstairs to make early morning tea, called upstairs 'The invasion's started!!!'

That excitement! What relief that at last invasion day had come! All our thoughts were of joy and certainty that we would win. I regret to say we thought little of the dangers that our men would face.

George Ince

CIVILIAN

I came home from work on the two-forty bus in the morning; changed at the bank and got the ninety-eight to Romford Road. Then I got the three-twenty-one. So the conductor's looking round for the others. He said to these printers, 'Where's all the others?' 'They won't be here this morning. It's the off.' That's all they told us. It's the off. So I went home, went to bed.

My mum woke me up about half past nine and said, 'They invaded France.' I said, 'Mum, I knew that at twenty past three this morning!'

John Hammond

SCHOOLBOY

Although I was only eleven years of age in 1944, I can still recall the day vividly.

I was a pupil at South County Junior School, West Bridgford, Nottingham. On the 6 June the headmaster, Mr Angrave – normally an extremely strict disciplinarian – assembled a group of us together in the hall and gave us a talk on the significance of D-Day. History, he said, was not just about kings and queens and battles long ago. History was being made here and now. He advised us to save that day's newspaper as it might be rare one day. I wished I had taken his advice! He drew a map of Normandy on the blackboard and explained the significance of the landings. He left us in no doubt of the importance of the day and said it would live long in our memories.

That talk, by a usually forbidding headmaster, has remained in my mind all my life. He was the first teacher I ever knew who really made history come alive.

English newspapers adopted a pacey, upbeat tone to announce the invasion of Western Europe on the morning of D-Day.

Frank Dickinson

CIVILIAN

At about 6am on the morning of the 6 June I was travelling upstairs on a Bradford Corporation bus while on my way home following a night-shift stint as Fire-Watcher-cum-ARP Messenger.

As the bus trundled past Undercliffe Cemetery in Otley Road, Bradford, I looked out of the window and saw to my amazement hundreds of aeroplanes – some towing gliders – flying across the valley towards Shipley. Someone said, 'It's the invasion.' The bus stopped and we all got out to watch this air armada flying, as it seemed very low in the sky. We watched until they were all out of sight, leaving the skies above Undercliffe's 'Swamp' empty.

Later, at home, while the kettle was boiling, I turned the wireless set on and heard the announcer say, 'We are receiving unconfirmed reports that the Allies are attempting a landing on the north-west coast of France.' Later of course, this news was confirmed. D-Day had arrived! I was fifteen years old.

Alan C. Atkins

SCHOOLBOY

When my father came home for his dinner, he was very excited. 'It's on Rose,' he kept saying, 'we're going for sure. Take a walk up London Road this afternoon. Take the nipper. This is history in the making.' Even my mother was smiling. 'It will soon be over,' she kept saying.

After my father had ridden his bicycle back to work and my mother had washed the dishes, she helped me put on my shoes and socks. We didn't need coats, as it was quite warm, in spite of it being cloudy. We walked together up the road. All the women seemed to be outside their houses, talking to each other. They were passing lumps of chalk to each other, making a 'V' mark alongside their front doors. I asked my mother why they were doing it; she told me it stood for 'Victory'. I asked her what 'victory' was; she said it was to help us beat Mr Hitler. 'I shall put one on our door-post when we get back, if someone will lend me some chalk.'

By the time we got to the top of our road we could hear a continuous roaring sound. There were lots of people going the same way as us and some were carrying little flags on sticks. Everybody was talking, even to people they didn't know. Some even spoke to my mother. 'Good news, missus. We're going.' 'Yes', my mother would reply, 'it would seem so. I hope it is not just an exercise though.' 'Not this time, missus,' another man replied. 'I heard that the docks are full of boats: full of them, three and four deep at each berth. It's on for sure.'

What's on? Nobody would tell me. Something big and beautiful was happening it seemed. Everyone walking around had big smiles on their faces, but nobody would tell me why. 'What's on, mother?' I asked. 'The invasion. Our soldiers are going to invade France and drive the Germans back to their own country. It will be peace soon. No more war.' 'No more war? Why ever not? War is normal. What are we going to do if there is no more war? All of the soldiers will be unemployed. They'll have nothing to do.'

We walked from Bedford Place to London Road and what a sight met our eyes. The roaring had been getting louder and louder – then we saw what was causing it: two continuous lines of trucks, roaring down the road towards the town and the docks. Some trucks had tarpaulins covering huge piles of boxes and crates, but most had soldiers, standing up smiling and waving at us.

No other traffic except that of the army is being allowed onto London Road. At every junction there are men in uniform with armbands and white helmets; they stop every car and make it turn around and go back, unless they are army. A lot of Jeeps, full of officers, join the trucks from the side streets. The officers are smiling and waving as well, a bit undignified really.

We stand there for over an hour; the trucks and Jeeps still keep coming. Some of the trucks have a large gun towed from their rear. 'This is no bloody exercise,' says a man, 'this is the real bloody thing.' Then he puts his hands to his mouth and shouts at a passing truck of soldiers, 'Give them bloody hell, mates.' The soldiers are pleased and stick their thumbs up at him.

'Come on,' says my mother, 'we've seen enough. Let's go home and have a nice cup of tea.' I can't believe my ears. Here we are watching history and my mother wants a 'nice cup of tea'. What a way to win a war.

Henry N. Giguere

GERMAN REFUGEE

On 6 June 1944, I was a nine-year-old child of a family that had fled the Holocaust, and understood that war was ugly and frightening. Listening to the war news on the radio was a daily ritual for us, as it was for many Americans. I remember so very clearly that on that historic day we listened to General Eisenhower speak to the nation about the 'Allied troops' having landed in France. There was no joy in my house that day. But there seemed to be a very small sense of hope that the war would end. But, more indelibly, I recall going to school the next morning and hearing my fourth-grade teacher talk about D-Day. She asked the class what we thought the 'D' stood for, and I will never forget the first two answers offered by my classmates. One said 'Death Day' and the other offered 'Dooms Day'. Mrs Perkins then explained that the 'D' was simply a code letter for the army, and not a symbol for any word. Still, even as children, we understood that so many young men had died to liberate Europe. And so they did.

M.J. Cope

SCHOOLGIRL

My memories of D-Day are still very vivid although I was only a twelve-year-old schoolgirl at the time. The school was fortunate in having a radio, which in those days was quite unusual, and I remember the whole school filing into the assembly hall, each carrying a chair, and sitting in complete silence while listening to the reports. We later had a chart up in the school hall and plotted the progress of the Allied Armies.

J.S. Godsell

POST OFFICE WORKER

I was sixteen at the time, a girl probationer in the General Post Office, and on 6 June I was sitting the Civil Service Exam. We had a break for lunch and took a walk outside, and there for everyone to see on the placards was 'Allied forces land in France' – the big breakthrough at last. We returned to the building, congregating ready to return to the exam; great excitement abounded as we talked of the landing and I said, 'It's smashing; now the war will soon be over.' One of the girls who was unknown to me said, 'It is all right for you. My brother has gone over in that lot.' I felt dreadful.

Anon

CIVILIAN IN A LETTER TO A FRIEND

Dear Anne,

Well this is it! The invasion I mean, and it leaves us with mixed feelings, and mostly with the sick feeling at the pit of our stomachs.

We have looked forward to it for so long. People cried in the street, and everybody wanted to be at home – partly because they wanted to be near the radio, and partly because so many of them had sons and husbands who would, at that moment, be risking their lives on the beaches of France.

A friend of ours bought a newspaper in the street, which came out as soon as the official announcement came through on the BBC and she was immediately surrounded. Where and when and in what part of France had the invasion begun? She seemed to be very pleased. She was rather bucked at being able to tell them something so much to their liking. But reading a bit further on, a woman cleaner at the cinema burst into tears and was immediately joined by other women also crying. There was nothing for it; we had to join them. Nan and I had a good weep. Later we were eating our tea – listening to the six o'clock news – when without any ado we both started to weep again. Though exactly why, we didn't know. I don't think we felt much like weeping when we were in the midst of air raid – but now we felt bitterly sorry for mothers and wives who were worrying so much about their lads.

But we are proud of the people here – who are taking all the worry so bravely. There is no complaint about the uselessness of all this slaughter – but a quiet 'waiting' for news, good or bad. The news keeps on coming through – the radio talks of the preparations made, and the men.

These poor, poor lads – it's tragic to think of them and we pray the war won't last long; we can't afford to lose all the best of this generation.

Then, this morning, we hear the official announcement that Jerry had sent over a number of his pilotless planes, and damage and casualties had occurred. So now we are faced with this horror, but we hope that, as in the case of the magnetic mine, and those tanks in Italy which were piloted by radio, we shall find a remedy. If we can't, it opens up a tremendous danger – not only to civilians, but to the second front, and to the fighting forces in general. We don't know enough about it at the moment; we only know that we are told to get into a shelter when the sirens sound, and that after the light appears in the plane, or whatever the revolting thing is, there are only fifteen seconds before it explodes, and blast is the thing which causes the damage. I suppose I ought to get up now when the sirens sound – usually I wait until the guns open up. Blow Hitler – he can't do me out of my sleep!

From the Diary of May Hill

CIVILIAN

Tuesday 6 June, D-Day 9.30pm

An Ordinary Day

So, at last the long-talked-of Second Front has begun. I have not even given it a new page and that seems a fitting symbol of how it appears to me. What excitement there may be in towns or elsewhere, in the country it does not seem to have touched us here in Chapel St Leonards. It is just an ordinary day; after nearly five years of war it takes a lot to make us demonstrative. I went on with my ordinary work and made my first toy for sale, a white duck with green wings and yellow beak and feet. It is for Mrs Russell to give to a baby friend. I must make the rabbit for Emmie next and try to send an extra one too. Ciss cleaned her pantry and Rene washed. Jean went to school; indeed she had gone before the announcement.

Listening to the Radio

Four thousand ships and a great many smaller craft crossed the Channel. Great airliners took airborne troops behind the German lines. Montgomery is speaking now, a message to the troops of which he is the head. The Archbishop of Canterbury has spoken and now they are singing 'Oh God, our help in ages past.' At nine o'clock the King broadcast a call to prayer, not for just one day, but all the days of crisis.

In the news afterwards we heard that all was still going well in France. I fear the 'little people' like us would not just go on with this ordinary work. However pleased they may be at the thought of deliverance, at present it means danger and hardship and war. Many will have to leave their homes and many I fear will lose their lives. The service is over, a beautiful service, ending with the hymn, 'Soldiers of Christ arise.'

At the End of the Day

We are in bed. A motor cycle has just gone by and a swiftly moving plane. Percy was with the Home Guards last night. I am pleased he is at home next door tonight. God be with us all, those sons or husbands or other dear ones who have already fallen in this new front. Be with the wounded and comfort the dying and those who are afraid. We had twelve letters from Ron today – a record. I had six, the others three each. In the most recent one, only a week since he wrote it, an air mail letter, he says his hopes of return are practically nil. I am almost pleased, much as I long to see him, but somehow he seems safer there at present. I must try to sleep now. The longed-for D-Day has arrived. Deliverance Day, Jean says it means.

Troops Continue to Leave, 6 June: 'Even as children we knew this was something special.'

Brian Selman

SCHOOLBOY

A few days later, back in Southampton, the relentless loading of the American army continued, but now, every few hours, a white-painted hospital ship docked. Down Hill Lane, a continuous stream of ambulances slowly moved to the docks while a similar but faster-moving column flowed up The Avenue on their way to the hospitals. Going in the other direction past these ambulances marched battalions of apprehensive American troops on their way to the battlefront. To us it seemed as if a great gloom had lifted: victory would clearly be ours sometime in the future.

Everywhere one was surrounded by organisation on a stupendous scale: floating harbours; petrol pipes across the Channel; thousands of ships, planes and tanks all flowing in ordered formations; ammunition; food; and the evacuation of the wounded to the waiting hospitals. I learned then that if a nation devoted everything to a single objective, almost anything was possible. This was a lesson I was never to forget.

Later, when the American soldiers abandoned the camp on the common and set fire to it as they left, we found the ground white with condoms and the accompanying packets of tubes of cream. Thus the Americans advanced our education.

Nellie Nowlan

WAR EFFORT WORKER

I remember D-Day very well. I was eighteen and working in Plessey's Underground Tunnel at Redbridge, Wanstead, making Spitfire vacuum pumps. I was walking to the top of the road towards East Ham High Street to get my 101 bus from Woolwich when I heard such a noise and thundering. I reached the High Street and thousands of lorries and tanks loaded with soldiers all waving their hands were making their way to Woolwich. Mrs Larkins from her sweetshop was throwing them packets of cigarettes and chocolate and peanuts. They were catching them and saying 'Thank you, darling.' The older people were standing by the kerb crying and saying, 'Good luck boys, God bless you.' I walked across the road to get my bus. They all gave me the wolf whistle. I smiled and waved my hand. Needless to say, I was crying too.

Len Bellows

CIVILIAN

I worked with another chap on the sewage wagon in Southampton and Bournemouth. There's an American camp at St Leonards which was a hospital and, of course, we serviced that as well. But doing the job we were doing, we were allowed into areas where other people weren't allowed to go. There weren't a lot of other fourteen-year-olds doing the same job. But it was quite an experience. You could say that, on D-Day, we were knee-deep in sewage! That's it, really.

John Keegan

SCHOOLBOY

The sky over our house began to fill with the sound of aircraft, which swelled until it overflowed the darkness from edge to edge.

Its first tremors had taken my parents into the garden, and as the roar grew I followed and stood between them to gaze awestruck at the constellation of red, green and yellow lights, which rode across the heavens and streamed southwards towards the sea. It seemed as if every aircraft in the world was in flight, as wave followed wave without intermission, dimly discernible as darker corpuscles on the black plasma of the clouds, which the moon had not yet risen to illuminate. The element of noise in which they swam became solid, blocking our ears, entering our lungs and beating the ground beneath our feet with the relentless surge of an ocean swell. Long after the last had passed from view and the thunder of their passage had died into the silence of the night, restoring to our consciousness the familiar and timeless elements of our surroundings – elms, hedges, rooftops, clouds and stars – we remained transfixed and wordless on the spot where we stood, gripped by a wild surmise of what the power, majesty and menace of the great migratory flight could portend.

Vera Lawrence

LAND ARMY GIRL

D-Day saw me working as a Land Girl doing field work and feeding the animals on a farm. Overhead the bombers were roaring in a never-ending stream. My land army girlfriend, Jo, and I leaned on our hoes and waved up at them, saying a silent prayer for their safety. I thought sadly of my lovely brother-in-law recently killed at Anzio, and yet in the next field were Italian prisoners of war also working the land. I also thought of my other brother-in-law, a Canadian tank sergeant. We subsequently learned that his was one of the first tanks to land at Normandy; he was later wounded at Caen.

Betty Boorah

CIVILIAN

We knew it wasn't far off as the cages for prisoners had been built on Southsea Common and there was the ceaseless roar from boats along the sea front. The morning of 5 June, I emerged from the shelter at 6am and started down the hill. There was a constant stream of army vehicles, tanks and lorries carrying sections of Bailey Bridges.

The troops were waving and calling out; as a lorry drew abreast of me, one of the soldiers threw a football to my eldest son. He was only small and couldn't catch it properly, and another boy picked it up. On it was written a lot of names and a message: 'We have no further use for this and hope it will give you a lot of pleasure.' I tried to buy the ball off the boy, but he wouldn't part with it. I would have treasured it always.

Stanley Jones

SCHOOLBOY

Suddenly they had gone – the streets and lanes were strangely empty – and then we knew that D-Day had dawned; now the activity was in the air. Keevil Airfield had always been so important during the war – Spitfires made in the Trowbridge area were assembled and tested there, but now lines of aeroplanes towing gliders were taking off all day. My most vivid memory is of listening to the six o'clock evening news. I listened to the voice of the newsreader coming through the open window into the back yard where I watched in the clear blue sky, the lines of gliders going over.

Hilda Scarth, née Brock

SCHOOLGIRL

At home, we watched late into the evening of 6 June. Because of Double Summer Time and being near mid-summer it didn't get dark until well after 10.00pm. We didn't go to bed; it was much too exciting to miss. This was the beginning of 'The Second Front' about which we had been hearing for so long, and we could see it actually happening. Even as children we knew this was something special, and I am glad I was old enough to be able to realise the importance of what was going on.

David

SCHOOLBOY

D-Day stood vividly in my tender eight-year-old mind. Around the area where we lived in Liss, Hampshire, there were many military camps and so, on D-Day, thousands of men were passing down the roads in the area in all types of vehicles. It all seemed very exciting to my young mind to see so many soldiers going off to war. Thoughts of thankfulness were also in my head as I was told they were going to defeat the enemy in Europe.

I, with my family, was standing outside our house when one particular noise caught our attention: the sound of aircraft engines. Within minutes the sky was full of aeroplanes. The roar was deafening, but also reassuring. Wave after wave of aircraft came into view and then disappeared over the skyline. Suddenly one plane began to veer to the left and lose height. It was obviously in trouble. We saw two very small figures shoot from the plane and two white parachutes open, and my mother said, 'Well, at least they are safe.' Hardly had the words reached our ears when the plane blew itself to pieces. The parachutes seemed to take ages to very slowly drift to the ground. Later we learned the two airmen had been blown off their parachutes when the plane exploded.

At an early age I experienced how tragic war is when lives are lost even before they reach the enemy.

The Silence: 'We would never see those men again.'

Bernard Knowles

AUTHOR

Day after day, truck-load after truck-load, column after column, of white and coloured troops surged through the town and, entering dockland, were lost to sight. It was a poignant scene. Inexpressively inspiring, it was as inexpressively sad. Neither among the townspeople nor among the troops themselves was there any appearance of levity. There were no flags, no drums, no music and no huzzahing. Every citizen without exception seemed to be awed into silence by the gravity and immensity of the occasion.

Mrs Peggy Jessey

CIVILIAN

I remember being in Fareham one day and seeing columns of men marching down the High Street on the way to embarkation. Everyone was waving them off, but there was no cheering and no sounds, just a total pervading silence as people watched the men away.

Shirley Jeanne Bridger, née Glanville

CIVILIAN

From where we lived to the middle and north of Hampshire, as far as Haslemere, was full of Canadian soldier camps, in fields, in woods, in fact anywhere they could find space for them! Early on 6 June, I remember hearing a loud drone, which was all their tanks and armoured vehicles moving all the soldiers and equipment for the evacuation to the continent for the invasion. By the end of that day they had all gone. I very often wonder how many of these young men came back from the war. We never heard anything from any of them again.

Winifred Joan Pine

WREN

Then suddenly one day all ships disappeared from the river and there was silence. No more Glenn Miller music that woke us up in the morning, and when after a few days they didn't return we realised that this time they had gone for good. Going on duty on 6 June we heard that the invasion had started. What happened to the Dartmouth contingents we were never to know.

John Bowles

SCHOOLBOY

As the weeks went by, we became better acquainted with the Yanks, who would put on little parties for us and give a film show (they called them movies) of Laurel and Hardy and The Three Stooges. There were always plenty of good things to eat and every child left with a couple of chocolate bars. We got to know many of the men well. There was Lonnie, from New Jersey; he was a terrific artist and used to draw pictures of Spitfires and P-47 Thunderbolts. He would also draw pictures of American soldiers attacking German machine-gun emplacements. We thought it was terrific and wished and wished we were grown up and could put on those snazzy uniforms and shoot down German bombers and attack their machine-gun nests. Oh my, how we envied them. Then there was Tex; he was big and tall. He would tell us about his spread in Montana and how he wished he were back there with his horses and his kids. He showed us photographs of his two daughters, who were very pretty and older than we were. We asked the soldiers when they would be going back to America and they said, when the war was won.

There came a day when all the soldiers went to some movies that only soldiers could see. They told us they were propaganda movies and we wondered what that meant. They took over the Scout Hall and no civilians were allowed. We asked what the movies were about and were told 'tactics'. We didn't know what that meant either. A few days later, the artist Lonnie said, 'Well, kiddo, we leave tomorrow. The show is on the road,' and he gave me a big hug. I did not want to say goodbye to my American friend and his buddies and I wept hot tears. We had all grown attached to these kind men from that far-off country. But leave they did the next day, in long columns of lorries and tanks. It took several hours before they were all gone and we stood at the side of the road waving and waving and missing them so much. We would never see those men again.

Francis Reginald Lovell

CIVILIAN

I was quite moved the next morning when I arrived at work at 7.15 going down to the beach looking out across the Solent and noted just one landing-craft, which had obviously broken down, being attended to by a Tid Tug. We then heard later that morning on the radio that the invasion had begun.

Anon

SCHOOLBOY

We were all assembled for Morning Prayers, at the Devonshire Road Junior School, which was an everyday occurrence. On this occasion we sensed that this was to be a different assembly to the usual one. The headmaster, Mr Powell, told us that we were living through an event which we would remember for the rest of our lives. He proceeded to advise us of the landing of the Allied Armies on the beaches of Normandy. We were then asked to sing our National Anthem, which we all did with great enthusiasm, with everyone standing rigidly to attention.

Mrs Sylvia Kay, née Needs

SWITCHBOARD OPERATOR

On D-Day itself, we were on duty, the board was very quiet, hardly any lights showing at all, then suddenly it was bedlam – we were receiving the very first Allied calls from Cherbourg! 'Operation Overlord' completed! It was nice being in on a piece of history!

Margaret Hartrey

CIVILIAN

On that fateful day, I was walking to work – a 'normal' day in all respects, except for the fact that the sky was full. There were so many planes and gliders you couldn't see a patch of sky between them! Day turned to night, so to speak. I went on to work, waiting for the news. A few of the friends I had made in our forces died that day. My boyfriend was killed later in the fighting.

Patricia Roach

SCHOOLGIRL

I went to school as usual and at 9.30 that morning we heard the voice of John Snagge on the wireless telling us that troops had either landed by glider, been dropped by parachute, or gone across the channel by boat, and were now on the beaches in Normandy. One thought, at last, the end of the war might now be in sight. There was a feeling of expectancy, of hope, tinged, of course, with a feeling of anxiety, wondering what was happening to our lads 'over there'. We were sent home from school early that day and the wireless was never turned off just in case there would be more news. My brother, Michael Long, was in the Glider Pilot Regiment, and at the time we had had no word from him. Around 8.oopm that evening, we heard the sound of aircraft approaching so we all made our way onto our balcony overlooking the sea.

Within minutes, the sky was filled with gliders and the tugs (aircraft that towed the gliders). I think 'armada' is the only word that can describe this scene. It was an amazing experience and one I shall never forget. We put up the Union Jack (always kept at hand!) and waved our hankies madly. The aircraft were flying fairly low so they could easily see us.

There was a strange silence after they disappeared over the horizon. We were still anxious for my brother, as the phone had remained silent.

I remember we had a marvellous sunset at about 9.30 to 9.45pm. I went up on the balcony by myself and listened to the lapping of the waves. Suddenly the drone of aircraft could be heard – the tugs were on their way home. It was a very poignant moment. There were tears pouring down my face as I thought of all those young men who were now in France, wondering what was happening to them. Was my brother among them? It was a very sad moment and one I will never forget.

Around 10.oopm, the phone rang. It was my brother, Michael, telling us he was still in England. We were very relieved. He went to Arnhem three months later, was shot through the leg and taken prisoner.

6 June 1944: Casualties Begin to Arrive: 'I will never forget the suffering, pain and fear.'

Thomas R. Hiett

TELEGRAM BOY

On 6 June the town was deserted and I was on a district round. The distant rumble of guns could be heard in Southampton. At 11am I had the first 'death' telegram. The lady came to the door. She was horrified. I muttered, 'No answer' and fled. I could hear the crying all down the road. Good God, I thought, how many more?

Mary Verrier

BRITISH RED CROSS

For two days before D-Day, and even before that, wards had been cleared, as well as possible; people had been shoved somewhere, I don't know where they went. The chapel, the big dining room, church hall, schools, were all cleared out. Schools were allocated for walking wounded, or shell shocked, or people like that. So, about a week prior to that, we knew something was on the move. Laundry was everywhere, loads of sterile equipment for theatre, loads of equipment ready and handy. All leave was stopped for forty-eight hours, so you were incommunicado. Matron spoke to us all, in the big hall; she said, 'In the near future, we are going to be tried to our capacity. Just remember what you have been trained to do. Do it well, and do it with courage; like all things, it will last for a certain period of time, and, in that time, you must not be found wanting. But should any of you feel that you are unable to cope, you must report immediately how you feel and it will be understandable.' But nobody did.

We were getting all the blood and serum banked up and checked and rechecked and rechecked. Our big blood packs, which we started to work with that day when the boys came back, were supposed to last for twenty-four hours, they didn't last an hour! But then you didn't have to worry about that, because you would just put up your right hand, and someone would come and put down another pack. But you stayed at your post.

We were off. But there was a gentle air of quiet determination, and at last we're going to hit them back. But at what cost, we were going to learn that during that day. We had twenty-six nurses at South Parade Pier. We had our big mobile hospital unit there. In the harbour all the ships were there, all the barrage balloons were up there, planes were going, troops were going; the movement was colossal. I can remember the silence when they'd all gone. I remember Sister Mitchelmore said, 'We will now kneel and pray.'

A lot of them went from the pier, where we were, down the wooden gangways and got into small boats. It was fast, quiet, but efficient movement. The beach masters, of course, were responsible for everything, and they would tell sister if somebody was hurt. It was very, very moving. There were no silly heroics from the men. You had the one or two wags who'd crack a saucy joke, but that would be frowned upon by those in command. They all went knowing that we were going to be there when they came back. And I think that was one reason why the presence of the nurses was important; not so much for the minor injuries and odds and ends, more to let the boys know that we were there and we would be waiting when they returned. Psychologically, I think it was a very clever move.

When they had gone we moved to the Queen Alexandra Hospital to await the return of the wounded, and that day they came. Of course the fellas had terrible, terrible injuries, gunshot and blast wounds, and they were covered in dirt and sand.

Wounded soldiers arriving back in England immediately after D-Day.

Deafness was very prevalent from the shelling going on. Men don't speak much of events like that, they very seldom will say anything, but they would say, 'Hell does not describe it nurse.' And I don't think it did really. Some of the time all we could do was give them tender loving care and a kiss and a hug. That's all we were able to do for them. But it was pretty awful. That took a bit of sticking.

You'd have the mishmash of all the men on the stretchers, all bad, really, really bad injuries. But if there was a German, say, next to a couple of English Tommies, then the Tommy who had a cigarette would share it with the German, or one of them would go over and pat the poor old German soldier's arm. Of course they were separated; they had to go to special wards which had armed soldiers at the doors.

We had the new 'Wonder Drug', penicillin. I'm sure we quite often gave too much in a dose, as their hair would fall out for a while. We were told it was the miracle drug; it was going to kill all the known bugs. We had to give it where you had deep injuries, and after surgery, where the need for sterility is at the highest. The priority was for the most seriously ill and the burns.

Margaret Phillips

TRAINEE NURSE

I was a young nurse in a large teaching hospital and was looking forward to being able to go home to see my family for the weekend. Work was hard but extremely rewarding, and spare time was a luxury, and a leave weekend a great event. A few hours before I was to leave my shift, the ward sister informed us that our ward was to be cleared and that all the beds had to be cleaned and remade. Any patient who was able to be discharged was, and without any reason being given, my weekend leave was cancelled. We instinctively knew that something big was about to happen, but we had no idea what. There was a deep sense of anxiety and I am still aware of how silent and still the ward was. That in itself was unusual, as the ward was never that still. It sounds clichéd to say it, but it really was the calm before the storm. Then it happened: the allies stormed the beaches, and later the next day the first casualties arrived, in huge numbers. We worked solidly for three days, snatching sleep and food when we could. And I will never forget the suffering, pain and fear of some of the young men I was fortunate to be able to help. We must never allow the world, or future generations, to forget the sacrifice of so many people for the good of the world.

Anon

BRITISH RED CROSS NURSE

Prior to the day there was a funny quiet and a funny calm before the storm. We could see there were a lot of people; we were preparing a lot of packs of dressings, and stocking them away with the dates on: we were being trained so that we could do it blindfolded. The staff nurses training had put us in good stead when D-Day arrived. I remember we had coaches, converted into stretcher carriers all down to South Parade Pier. I went down and was waiting beside my allotted coach with all my little drums stacked beside me, and chaps in a very grim state were being loaded on. Dr Roberts, the medical officer, came along, stopped and looked at me and said, 'Are you going with this charabanc?' and I said, 'Yes, Dr Roberts,' and he said, 'Are you?' I said, 'I am here and more than capable of doing this job and I should go with these boys.' I was barely nineteen, and he looked at me aghast and well he might. I stepped on that vehicle a bright-eyed bushy tailed young girl, and stepped off it a woman.

Jean Rouse

VOLUNTEER

D-Day itself was full of excitement and apprehension. I recall that in the afternoon when the first hospital ships arrived bringing in American wounded and they transferred to waiting trains at Southampton they were greeted by a US Army band playing the Stars and Stripes. This went on night and day for nearly a week and drove the occupants of the South Western Hotel nearly mad.

In the evenings I did a bit of canteen work on the station, handing out cups of tea and cigarettes to the wounded. Quite an eye-opener and made one think how futile war could be.

June Martin

VOLUNTEER

I remember going with a group of girls to St Mary's Hospital in Portsmouth to visit wounded – and they were tank fellas that were terribly badly burnt and they were covered in a kind of plastic; they must have been in agony. What could we say to them, these poor men lying with the skin burnt off them in these sorts of plastic things? God knows whether they ever survived. That was horrendous. I shall never forget them.

Naina Cox

TRAINEE NURSE

I attended Red Cross classes in the local Baptist church hall. This was the Hants 28th British Red Cross Detachment and our Commandant was Miss Hobbs, who had been a VAD in India during the First World War. She did everything possible to make our attendance interesting. This included asking any army or navy doctor with half an hour to spare to come and talk to us – and help us through our First Aid and Home Nursing exams. I am glad to report that I took and passed every exam going. This was a small thing in the eyes of the world, but a big thing to me.

About 2pm on D-Day Miss Hobbs came into the office where I was working and said that I was needed up at Queen Alexandra's Hospital, because there were so many wounded coming back from the beaches that they desperately needed help. I ran home to tell my mother, got my uniform and then rushed up the hill to the hospital.

Another girl who I saw once a week at lectures checked in shortly after I did and we reported to Matron together. She told us to go to a particular ward. It took us some time to get there because all the corridors were laid end to end with stretchers. Lorries were coming up from the dockyard so quickly that there wasn't room for all the wounded. The army stretcher-bearers knew who was badly wounded and those who were less seriously wounded were put on the floor.

When we got to the ward we were told to start cleaning people up, giving them drinks and things. Many of them were filthy –

well, they were quite young and when you're frightened you know what happens, you're all messy and dirty – so the main thing was to clean them and bed-bath them. We didn't have to treat their wounds but if you took somebody's filthy battledress off and found a bad wound, then you would call a sister.

Mostly they were conscious, but not talking much; they were really, really tired and later on in the day we were told that they were the first exhaustion cases. A lot of them were so completely exhausted they didn't care one jot what happened to them. Some of them could speak, but when you are too tired to care about anything, you just want to be cleaned up and have something to drink. They weren't hungry.

As I worked with these poor exhausted soldiers, I was thinking, 'How long will it go on? If I come tomorrow and the next day, will I still be doing this?'

Cyril Walter Crain

BRITISH ARMED FORCES

MY BUDDY

In memory of a man from '43
He came from a land across the sea
'Hi there, Limey!' he yelled with a grin
'Hallo!' I replied, 'how've you bin'
'Go inside and stow your gear,
Bring your pals, we'll go for a beer'.
From this moment a friendship grew.
We ate, we trained, and socialised too.
Then one day the orders came
Realising now this wasn't a game.
We boarded ship, then on our way
And during the night we gathered to pray.
Landing-craft lowered seven miles from land.

We scrambled down nets, hand over hand
Into the boats, a fearsome task.
Look after us Lord, that's all I ask
The sea was stormy, we had a rough ride.
I looked at my buddy who sat by my side,
'Take care Limey, you'll do fine,
Good luck Canuck, old friend of mine.'
The ramp went down, we plunged into the swell,
The beach before us a living hell.
Our feet on the ground, we dashed to the wall
From the corner of my eye I saw him fall.
Again and again I still ask why!
My friend from Toronto, why did he die?

This poem is dedicated to Freddy Harris, a sergeant in the Queen's Own Rifles of Canada – killed in action on D-Day 1944 – 'My Buddy'.

Casualties after D-Day: 'We had not been taught how to cope with dying young men.'

Francis Reginald Lovell

CIVILIAN

It was sad to see several days afterwards the wounded being disembarked from landing-craft into ambulances which were parked the full length of Broad Street, Old Portsmouth.

Mary Ritson

CIVILIAN

My parents received two telegrams almost at the same time. I was married by then and living at Scilly Banks and I had my eldest three daughters to look after. So I don't know what it was like when my Mam got the telegrams. I went to see her as soon as I knew, but Mam and Dad didn't want a lot of talk about Robert and Joseph being killed. It was really bad. Everyone was upset. My other brothers came back, but we've always remembered Robert and Joseph. Even now I still remember them. And Mam, even years later, would get really upset.

Stoker Terence Mullee

HMS *FORT YORK* MINESWEEPER

I was sent to Aberdeen to join HMS *Fort York*, which was being turned into a minesweeper. I met my wife-to-be there. When I saw her walking up the street I asked her for a light and she told me to 'Go fly your kite!' But we fell in love and a week later we were married!

On 6 June we set sail for the D-Day landings. The captain told us we would be minesweeping from dusk until the following dawn. All night we could hear the noise of hundreds of bombers – it must have scared the life out of those ashore. We were near Gold Beach. As dawn came and we pulled out, we had a grandstand view of the soldiers landing and the big Royal Navy ship shelling the Germans.

It wasn't long before shoals of dead soldiers were floating by and out to sea. They were British and Canadian boys. It was just heart breaking.

Ralph Rayner

ROYAL ENGINEER

On the second day we had the unenviable task of recovering many bodies that were floating in with the tide; most had drowned, unable to keep afloat due to the heavy equipment they were carrying.

Peter Carragher

CIVILIAN

My next powerful memory was the next day seeing the Red Cross ambulance trains slowly pulling up the line from Southampton and into Andover Junction for onward transportation to many hospitals in the south. There were hundreds of wounded soldiers on those trains and in my mind's eye I can see them to this day. The junction staff wouldn't let us boys onto the platforms, but we managed to by various means. My mother was allowed on and she helped dish out cups of tea and sandwiches to the injured troops. I shall never forget those sad days.

Rosemary Davis

FIRST AID NURSING YEOMANRY

Well, I had a boyfriend; I met him in Dunbar. He was a lieutenant. I don't even know what he was in. But he was a Brighton boy who did art, and was very clever. So we had a lot in common. We had one leave and he said, 'Rosie, show me the places in London.' I always regret that we went to a rather dreary little pub, which was one of those pubs where the people in it just felt they owned it. Even though he was an officer, what the hell were we doing in it? Anyway, Jack went back to his regiment and I never saw him again, as he was killed on the D-Day landings.

Rozelle Raynes

WREN

The following day more ships came alongside the pier to unload their cargoes of wounded British soldiers, and the only thing which relieved the horror of that day was an inspection of our quarters by Superintendent Curtis. No doubt all the preparation involved for this event was specially designed to keep our minds and eyes off the unhappy scenes around us.

Gunner Percy

6TH/7TH BATTERY OF THE 20TH ANTI-TANK REGIMENT, ROYAL ARTILLERY

In 1944 I was aged twenty-four and was one of the crew of four self-propelled anti-tank guns mounted on a Sherman tank. The guns were three-inch American naval guns. For approximately three weeks prior to embarkation we were camping in tents at Waterlooville, just north of Portsmouth. We had little to do and so took to a form of gambling which consisted of attempting to toss half-crowns or whatever into a mug, and whoever succeeded scooped the pool of coins which had missed.

The luckiest gambler was 'Crash' Heelbeck, so nicknamed because he was so modest and retiring. We all liked him and pulled him into all our goings-on. Unfortunately Crash's luck did not last; shortly after D-Day the M10 tank, in which he was a gunner, received a direct hit. While the surviving crew members recovered, all that remained of Crash was something resembling the burnt stump of a tree. If you ever visit Douvres-la-Délivrande cemetery, inside the wall safe, where records of everyone buried in the cemetery are kept, you will find the information of all the servicemen interred in this cemetery – all except Crash! I think there was nothing of him to bury. His name and rank are on a headstone, but, unlike all the others, there are no nice comforting words at the bottom of the stone. In the register there is no mention of his father or mother or where he came from, so I came to the conclusion that poor Crash must have been an orphan. How little we knew of each other after all those years training together.

American walking wounded disembarking from a US LCT at Southampton docks.

Mrs Ramsey

ROYAL NAVY NURSE

Then the casualties came. It took about three or four days after the invasion before we started receiving casualties. I was an operating room supervisor. We had two operating room theatres, one upstairs and one downstairs. At first, we started out with one and then we required two because we just couldn't handle all the casualties in one theatre. When I say theatre, I mean several rooms, each room with its own surgeon and nurse, and corpsman, enlisted navy medical personnel. I was in charge of the one downstairs. I remember how busy we were and how they kept coming and coming and we had no place to put them. We put them out in the halls and everywhere. We were only there as a receiving hospital. We received the casualties, removed the bullets and shrapnel, did the debridement, cleaned them up, poured penicillin and sulphur into the wounds, wrapped them up, and sent them to the army or to British hospitals inland, or by air to the United States, especially if they were bad-burn patients. So we didn't keep them very long. The operating room nurses would pitch in and help the doctors do debridements and remove bullets.

Captain Mike Crooks

CHAPLAIN

And then the journey home on the third night, all bunks filled with wounded. We did our best for them, but there was always a feeling of inadequacy – we wanted to do more.

At theological college we had not been taught how to cope with dying young men, whose bodies were beyond recall. But in those college days wise men were there who were able to detonate the latent ideas in our minds, of how to come to grips with the purpose of existence. My own concept of God had a long way to go in order to comprehend the mystery of our Christian religion. In that process the Hand of God was with us.

The Crucified One was strangely with us – and was still there on D-Day when the support of His strength, His suffering and His Holy Spirit were desperately needed. He was with us. Looking back upon the momentous events of that time, unequalled in history, I maintain that the troops were marvellous. Remember, those soldiers, sailors and airmen were businessmen, teachers, bus drivers, lawyers, factory workers, writers, road sweepers – you name it. They didn't want war. They didn't want to be there. Their place was at home. But we were all called upon to fulfil a function, a necessary task, no matter how awful. The chaplain's role was one of rare privilege, carrying out duties of compassion, healing, evangelism, moral support.

These are the words of a BBC announcement broadcast about a week after D-Day: 'Many thousands of men went forth for righteousness' sake and no other reason. The chaplains were asked, and strongly asked, to make our men as Christian as we could.' Today, I have a golden opportunity to turn that the other way round and declare – as I remember the fortitude of those young men, their devotion to duty, comradeship, laughter and winning sense of humour – they were the ones who made me a better Christian than I ever was before.

And now, my final words to you for the present and the future. What better than the quiet Celtic benediction of that splendidly chosen anthem: Deep peace of the running wave to you; Deep peace of the flowing air to you; Deep peace of the quiet earth to you; Deep peace of the shining stars to you; Deep peace of the gentle night to you; Moon and stars pour their healing light on you; Deep peace of Christ, the light of the world, to you; Deep peace of Christ to you. Amen.

Elsie Batho

SEAMSTRESS
Geoffrey was the love of my life. I was only seventeen but we

were madly in love. He got his orders to go out to D-Day and asked me to marry him.

I desperately wanted to be his wife so I said to my father, 'Pa, I'm going to get married.' But he soon told me I wasn't to.

My father was a veteran of the First World War and knew what happened to boys who went to fight. He'd been injured in the leg and lost his brother Arthur in the North Sea. Pa was terrified of war. He didn't say as much, but I knew.

He told me to wait until the boys came home. 'Then I'll give you the biggest white wedding ever,' he told me.

Pa didn't want me to become a widow at seventeen so he said I should wait till the war was over before I married Geoffrey. Geoffrey and Percy were in A Squadron 24th Lancers, and were in the same tank landing at Normandy. Their tank was attacked and Percy and Geoffrey died. We knew nothing for a long time. First of all the letters stopped. Then Doris got a telegram saying the boys were missing. We were devastated.

I never did get my white wedding, to Geoffrey or anyone else. He was my first love and I just never got over him. Every anniversary it all comes flooding back. I will never forget him.

The Return

John Goldsmith

ROYAL NAVY

Homeward bound, there was now time to tune in the radio to the BBC, to see if we were famous. After hearing the first sober and restrained account, I went excitedly to the skipper. 'Sir, it's all on the radio, about D-Day.' Amiably, the skipper asked, 'And did they say that 442 and its crew pushed on?' Recalling the craft that rammed us, I replied, 'No, sir. They said we was bloody pushed on.' He seemed to enjoy that, and shared our combined glow of achievement, as our craft limped back into harbour, the blackened hole in its side clearly advertising to the spectators lining the wharf where we had been and why.

While LCT 442 was docked for necessary repairs, the crew were given leave to return home to families anxiously awaiting news of their sons. And if our high-flying seagull had followed this crew member to a Surrey council house, where the key, in those trusting days, was still in the front door, the gull could have observed me turn the key and quietly enter, to see my father, a small but indomitable veteran of the war to end all wars, with ghosts of Flanders in his memory, seated in his chair by the window, peering through spectacles at newspaper stories and photos of the battle across the Channel, unaware that the one face he wanted to see was standing a few yards away.

'Dad,' I said quietly.

'BLOODY GAWD ALMIGHTY!' My father started up from his chair to greet his first-born son, home safe and unharmed from Normandy.

Prisoners of War: 'Some of them were only kids.'

Rozelle Raynes

WREN

Three days later we were jerked out of our selfish brooding by a scene which I shall never forget. An armed merchant ship came alongside the Royal Pier and several hundred German prisoners disembarked from her under the supervision of a strong military escort. We stood outside the band-room watching them as they shambled down the gangway and lined up along the whole length of the pier. I am not sure what I had expected to see, but in that precise moment I suddenly became aware of the indescribable tragedy and horror of war. These were no proud and noble specimens of the Aryan race, but a pathetic collection of under-fed, tired and ill-looking youths wearing the ragged remains of their uniforms, with a forlorn and hopeless look in their eyes which made it impossible to view them objectively as the dreaded Huns, the greatest enemies of the human race.

Last of all a mangy black mongrel came down the gangway, one more bit of flotsam and jetsam in the tide of war; he trotted up to one of the prisoners and fixed him with a look of such single-minded devotion that I almost burst into tears when the wretched beast was hustled into a police van and the black doors shut irrevocably behind him.

An order was given at the far end of the pier and the hordes began to move. Many of them were wounded and the stretcher-cases were carried by those prisoners who were strongest among

254

them. A great silence seemed to fall on the dock area in Southampton, broken only by the shuffling footsteps of hundreds of miserable Huns.

A glum group of German prisoners of war arriving in England and starting the long march to a prison camp.

From the Southampton Echo

10 JUNE 1944

A trainload of German prisoners passing from the coast north today, stopped for a few moments at a South of England town. One onlooker from the platform addressed a German looking out of one of the carriage windows.

'Well Jerry, what do you think of England?' he asked.

Another German quickly thrust his head out of the window and answered in broken English. 'Three years ago,' he said, 'Herr Hitler promised we come to England.' He shrugged and placed both his fists together as if they were handcuffed. 'Vell,' he added, grimly, 'V haf come.'

This lot looked exceptionally young, average age about twenty, and all were wearing soft-peak service caps.

There wasn't a steel helmet among them. Their clothes looked exceptionally clean and tidy, and they did not give the impression of men fresh from the battlefield. It was rather as if they had just come off ceremonial parade.

Later, another trainload, which appeared to be loaded with officers only, passed through the town, and they were waving cheerfully and appeared to be very happy.

Michael L. Ryder

CIVILIAN

At the time of D-Day in June 1944, I was not far off my seventeenth birthday and nearing the end of a 'gap year' working in a medical laboratory before going to university. This was in my native city of Leeds, where we knew virtually nothing of what was going on in the south until sometime after D-Day. The blood transfusion service was in the same building in which I was working and there was soon much activity taking van-loads of glass bottles of blood to the local aerodrome to be flown direct to France. The planes must have brought back wounded soldiers, including German prisoners, because I occasionally had to go on the wards of the adjacent hospital to collect specimens or deliver reports, and one day I was amazed to see a young German prisoner in a bed being guarded by a rather scruffy British soldier sitting on a chair with his rifle between his knees. Until then the war had been a long way from the north of England and here was a German in our midst!

Albert Carter

CIVILIAN

The SAU only stayed a year before the British reassumed possession of the barracks.

In wartime some farmers had Italian PoWs placed with them and there was one who would appear in the field adjacent to the box who would shout up to my father for a newspaper. This fellow remained for years afterwards.

There was a German PoW camp at Watchfield three miles away. We used to see the prisoners wandering about in clothes with big patches on them to denote their status. The Germans would make things like ships in bottles, which my father obtained for two shillings and sixpence each. My brother still has one of these at his home.

Naina Cox

TRAINEE NURSE

While I was washing and cleaning up filthy and dreadful and horrible messes and giving out water and cold milk to people who were allowed such things, two sisters came round and asked if I would be willing to work in the German prisoners' ward. They needed the same kind of help, but some nurses refused to go into their ward.

I had to go and see Matron first. I went with my friend, Win. Matron said, 'You know we have a lot of German prisoners – they were picked up very early from the beaches.' I said I didn't know but had just been told. She said, 'Well, a lot of people won't work with them; they are either walking out or refusing to work with them. Will you do what you're doing, for them?'

Well, I was a bit meek and mild and I didn't say anything and Win looked at me and Matron said, 'Hurry up and make up your minds, because if you are not going to do it, I'll try somebody else.' Win looked at me and said, 'Oh, come on, Naina. My

Eddie is out there and if somebody said they wouldn't clean him up, Mum would feel terrible.' So, with that, I felt that if Win was going to do it, I'll do it. We would do it together and protect each other! I also couldn't bear the thought of my commandant saying, 'One of my girls wouldn't even give a prisoner a cup of water.'

Once we got to the Nissen hut where the Germans were being kept, we found there were four armed guards, two on the outer doors who had rifles and two on the inner doors with pistols. The guards checked who we were, checked the papers Matron had given us, then the sister checked us and said, 'You know what you are here for, don't you? Get on with it.'

These people were just lying on top of their beds in an assortment of dirty clothes. None of them was particularly badly wounded, but they were filthy dirty, absolutely stinking dirty, very white, unhealthy, unwholesome-looking people. They had the dirty pallor of tramps, a horrible yellowy-grey unhealthy look. And nobody said anything. None spoke English to my knowledge; they just pointed.

I sat somebody up – in those days you had feeding cups – and the smell was awful, but by then it was too late to say you didn't like it. The main thing I remember was them staring, a sort of a glazed staring. They hardly talked to each other at all – I hardly heard a word, just the odd grunt or the odd word; nobody had any brightness or any life. Everybody was lying down; nobody sat up unless we propped them up. It was very silent. I remember Win saying how strange and how quiet it was.

I don't really think I felt sorry for them and I didn't hate them or anything like that. I know that when I gave them a drink or a wash or cleaned them up a little bit, there was a feeling of humiliation. Some of them were only kids; they weren't really much older than me. One of the rules of the Red Cross is that you are there to help everybody. I'm glad I didn't refuse to help those men.

My small contribution to D-Day gave me a wealth of inspiration for the future.

Kay Childs

WREN

My husband went down with his ship and I just felt that it was the end of the world. For example, when it was a question of going into the air raid shelters, I did my damnedest not to, because I just, well, I don't want to sound melodramatic, but I just wanted to die myself, but I was only twenty-three and life had to go on. So I began driving an ambulance in Portsmouth. When the wounded were put in you'd go and talk to them and usually offer them a cigarette or something like that. But one day I offered a cigarette to one of them who looked at me very blankly and obviously didn't know what I was talking about. I then realised that he was German, which slightly knocked on the head all the vows I'd made of what I would do if I ever met a filthy German. But of course when it comes to the point, you don't, do you.

The War Continues: British Perspective: 'This wonderful feeling of belonging to a cause worth fighting for.'

Rozelle Raynes

WREN

Once the first thrilling news of the invasion had been received and absorbed by all of us in Southampton, a period of waiting ensued which was enshrouded in a grey blanket of depression. Up and down Southampton Water the mooring-buoys bowed and curtsied to the flood and ebb, the only physical objects in sight on that long monotonous stretch of water. All the ships that used to swing to those buoys – all our favourite ships and the ones we did not care for so well, and our tea, chocolate and rum ships – had gone, and no one knew if or when they would ever return.

We scrubbed and polished our boat until it shone like an oriental sunrise; I drained the oil out of the sump and filled it with fresh oil, cleaned the plugs and carburettor and did a few other maintenance jobs on the engine. We returned to Bridell Lodge in Shirley next afternoon and immersed ourselves in vast piles of dhobying; but to do any of these things required an enormous effort of will-power, as a lethargy born of too little sleep and a sense of unutterable anti-climax had gripped us in its powerful embrace.

Terence C. Cartwright

SCHOOLBOY

We had decided to take a 'bike-ride'. So, with tyres resembling python snakes that had swallowed a colony of rabbits, we set off along 'Cut-throat Lane' (Coleman Road) towards Evington Village. We rattled and clanked our way past 'Blacky Fields', scene of many 'raids', onto farmers' potato clamps to supply requirements for our campfire feasts, and then eventually Shady Lane PoW camp. On to Stoughton Airfield, scene of many a fascinating hour, watching the Dakotas and gliders taking off and landing in almost round-the-clock training for D-Day. With the absence of traffic and petrol fumes we were able, above the rattle of our bikes, to take in the fleeting sounds of *Family Favourites* on the radio, hand-pushed mowers, cows mooing and lambs bleating. Which mingled and blended with the tantalising smell of roasting beef, evidence that the locals and farmers were not restricted to the meat ration. Newly cut grass, blossoms and farmyard manure all produced a cocktail of sensations, which could only portray a typical peaceful English summer Sunday. The war was coming to an end, rations were easing and it felt good to be alive.

We arrived at the junction of Station Road and Uppingham Road. Our bicycle inner tubes were porous, as well as being the wrong size, so we decided that we needed to stop for a rest. Looking over the countryside towards Scraptoft, there was a simmering haze covering the rolling green fields and in the distance we heard, then saw, a Lancaster bomber with an accompanying Spitfire tagging behind, droning majestically towards us. We had seen many bombers over the years, but, as always, the sight never failed to arouse our interest. We turned our attention back to our bikes.

A minute or so later the drone of the engines changed abruptly to a high-pitched scream. We looked up in alarm and to our horror we saw the Lancaster in a vertical dive, descending at terrifying speed towards the ground, only a few yards from where we stood. We tried to run, but our legs could not move. We were rooted to the spot. Just when we thought that our end had come, a miracle happened; with engines howling, the plane suddenly began to pull out of its dive, as if trapped inside a giant invisible U-bend of a waste-pipe. The wings bent to breaking point as it swooped over Station Road at tree-top height and began a vertical climb over Coles Nurseries. Our fear changed to relief and then to anger and indignation where we found ourselves shouting abuse at the pilot for 'acting the fool'.

Our anger, however, was short lived, and quickly turned to horror when we witnessed the plane, high over Thurnby Railway Station, turn on its back and plunge earthwards once more in another vertical dive. We saw its black silhouette disappear below the horizon of the railway embankment and a split second later a tremendous orange/red/black mushroom of fire clawed its way into the blue sky, followed by a delayed, hollow, booming thud. Our legs came back to life, and with childish visions of heroic rescue of airmen from burning wreckage we sped down Station Road, over the embankment, and ran along the back of gardens where people were standing like statues. I passed a woman with a baby in her arms. Tears were falling from her cheeks.

The site of the crash was covered in a layer of smoke, but as we got nearer we were confronted with an incredible sight. There, in the meadow, stamped as if by a giant's hand, was a scarred outline of the Lancaster. A large crater was created by the fuselage, with four others made by the engines. Unbelievably, the leading edge of the wings, tip to tip, could be clearly seen, marked purely by scorched but otherwise undamaged grass. The field was strewn with small pieces of debris no larger than the page of a newspaper.

Our hopes of rescue vanished as we jumped over the small brook and ran to the edge of the main smoking crater. As we looked into this pit, ammunition was exploding, sending puffs of ash into the air like a volcano ready to erupt. We were not sure if any bombs were in there, so we retired to a safer distance. It was then that I saw that the local 'Bobby' had arrived. He was looking at what I thought was a meaty bone a dog had brought into the field. He had a strange shocked look in his eyes and when he said, 'Don't touch it' the tone of his voice prompted me to look again . . . With a numbing sense of shock I realised I was looking at what appeared to be a human shoulder blade! I then saw a sock . . . inside was half a foot . . . Up to this point it had been as if it was all a dream, but now reality and shock began to filter through my brain and I felt sickened, sad and helpless.

The accompanying Spitfire returned to check the scene . . . I could clearly see the pilot as he banked his plane to view the smoking craters below. The sound of bells announced the arrival of the fire engine and at this point the 'Bobby' asked us to leave.

The day had changed . . . Sounds of music, animals and mowers were abruptly replaced by the thud and crackle of exploding ammunition, fire bells and tears. The smells of the countryside had dissolved into an unforgettable stench of burnt fuel and flesh . . . The summer haze was now acrid smoke . . . We made our way slowly to Station Road. The woman with the baby was still rooted in the same spot . . . I found myself thinking of the unfortunate families of the airmen, who were soon to receive those awful, heartless, Buff Telegrams . . . . . . We regret to inform you . . . I don't remember the journey home.

Marion Ainsworth

SCHOOLGIRL

The weeks wore on; still the tanks continued to throw down their 'E' rations, their cigarettes and their money. Because of the continual build-up of traffic, for reasons best known to the powers that were, every few hours the dock gates would have to be closed. As the docks were overflowing with the military, convoys of troops and equipment had to wait in the street for hours, sometimes all day.

All the kids used to climb over the Jeeps and lorries. All the ammunition was there; it was all covered in canvas then but we used to lift it up and have a look – kids would get everywhere.

Many times, a GI leaning over the side of his lorry would ask me if I could fetch him something to drink. Once I answered that I had nothing to carry the drink in. Stretching down, the soldier handed me his helmet. Dashing into the nearest pub's snug bar I managed to get the helmet filled with beer. As I reached up on tiptoe an officer marched up to me and, after calmly taking the container away from me, poured the liquid down the drain.

I used to get fish and chips for them. Often, when I brought it back, the convoy had moved on so I sold it to another convoy. I'd already been paid for it, paid about three times over. I was quite rich from the bombed buildings as I used to collect all the planks of wood there. We used to chop them up and go round people's doors and sell them a small tin bath full of wood for threepence.

Brian Bailey

SCHOOLBOY

For the last six months of the war I found myself in relatively normal circumstances. There were four other evacuee boys already living with Miss Howlett when I arrived. I was the youngest and we all got on well together. I was almost seven and school was a big problem because I don't think I had ever seen the inside of one before. So the problems started. I couldn't read or write. It was considered that I was just lazy. After a tussle with a new schoolbook which tore the cover right off, my fate was sealed. I was beaten in front of the whole school during assembly with my trousers down and on a podium. So my loss of interest in school was complete and understandable. It was because teacher's pet did not want me to have a new book.

Jimmy Mead

CIVILIAN

The Yanks arrived in big numbers and I well remember two incidents in the docks. Directly behind where we were working we saw an American soldier called Paul Shimer, who was standing on a box with a placard placed around his neck, 'The Millionth Yank', being congratulated by all sorts of top brass. Later on it was the 'Two Millionth Yank'. This was to mark the number of Americans who passed through on their way to France! Shimer was killed three weeks before the cessation of hostilities.

'The Millionth Yank', Paul Shimer, enjoys his fifteen minutes of fame with Southampton's mayor, Rex Stranger.

R.J. Stranger

AT THE TIME MAYOR OF SOUTHAMPTON

I was down at the docks at Southampton one morning to watch the ships, the ships that took the Americans and the British into the fighting across the Channel. I always tried to be around to wish the men good luck, but this particular morning I was waiting for the man who would be the one millionth Yank to leave

Southampton for the Battle of Europe. The olive drab line marched past me up the gangplank, and then one man, a sergeant, was called out. He was the millionth Yank. We had our picture taken together. It all happened so quickly that we didn't have much time to talk. I didn't even get his name, but I do remember he said he had a wife and a three-year-old girl at home. I told him to come back when the war was over and visit my wife and me and I would help to start his daughter in life. He said he would, and then he was gone. I never saw that man again. United States Army Headquarters told me that he was Sergeant Paul Ed Shimer of Chambersburg, Pennsylvania, who lost his life on 14 April 1945, just twenty-four days from cessation of hostilities. He was killed by the blast of a shell as he led his men against a fortified German hill. He had served in the US Army for just fifty-one weeks. By a cruel twist of fate, Marian Shimer received the telegram informing her of her husband's death about one hour after reading an article in the Chambersburg local newspaper, *Public Opinion*, that her husband had been the 'Millionth Yank' to embark from Southampton, the British censor having only just passed the information to the USA.

Connie Hayball

CIVILIAN
My husband landed on D-Day. We were all frightened for our men, frightened. We were worried. But I can remember we used to go down New Street in Birmingham where there was a big stationer's shop and they used to have a map outside. The staff would put flags in to where the Allies had advanced or not. I thought that if we don't win and Hitler comes here, I'll have to join the Resistance.

Sylvia Wilde

SHORTHAND TYPIST AT THE ARMY GENERAL HEADQUARTERS IN LONDON, AND A VOLUNTEER
And once the invasion began on 6 June 1944, I decided I could

contribute far more if I volunteered to follow the forces to Normandy rather than kicking my heels back home in London. So it was six weeks after the first troops landed on the French beaches that I found myself on board a ship with 6,000 Canadian soldiers heading out of Southampton and bound for Normandy. I was part of the very first group of servicewomen sent to France as secretaries, cooks and hairdressers. And at the age of twenty I was the youngest of them all.

We knew there had already been a great number of casualties from the initial D-Day assault and we knew the fighting was still going on, but I can honestly say I was never frightened. There was this wonderful feeling of fellowship and of belonging to a cause worth fighting for. People talk of the 'all for one and one for all' wartime spirit that typified the time – and it's absolutely true. It really did exist.

Everywhere you went in Normandy there were thousands of little white crosses in fields and along the sides of the roads where the dead had been hurriedly buried. When two of our officers had to spend a day further along the coast I went with them. We were almost alongside a German unit firing V-2 rockets across the Channel. It was an awful thought to know my own family might be at the receiving end.

Mrs Ramsey

QUEEN ALEXANDRA'S ROYAL NAVAL NURSING SERVICE
After D-Day, the Germans began shooting V-1 rockets at England. The V-1 was a relatively slow-moving rocket-propelled flying bomb with stubby wings that made a loud buzzing sound while in flight. We knew them as 'buzz-bombs'. Although we had air raid shelters I don't think we ever used them. At the foot of every bed hung a gas mask and helmet, and if we were bombed we would push the little lad under the bed, putting his helmet on first. We would hear the buzz-bomb whizzing and suddenly the sound would cease as its engine stopped and the

rocket fell. There would be a breathless pause as we waited until the explosion was heard. Although parts of Southampton were destroyed, thank goodness the hospital was spared. Then, after the buzz-bomb attacks were over, came the V-2s guided missiles carrying a one-ton explosive warhead that flew high and fast and were impossible to shoot down. I am told that more than 1,350 fell on London. One of the things that struck me so emphatically was the British people. They would be bombed out of their homes and they'd salvage what they could and get on with life. I was so impressed with that. They had been very nice to us and we had made friends. They were able to share with us what they had and I just admired their spirit so much.

Rescue workers pulling a victim from the ruins of a bombed out building in London, July 1944. It had been hit by a V2 rocket.

Daphne Meryon

WREN

We had had air raids for over three and a half years, but in the summer of 1944 the infamous V-1 pilotless planes started to come over the coast and make for London. One recognised the unmistakable noise of their engines and, if they got too near, scrambled down onto the floor or, preferably, under a desk. One selfishly hoped that the engine wouldn't cut out until it was past, because, if it did, it meant it was about to descend in the near vicinity.

I had an elder brother in the navy, as well as a fiancé – both involved in the D-Day landings – so I remember great anxiety about what was happening to all our forces in general, but about them in particular. But then there had been anxiety for friends and family for so many years that it had become an accepted state of mind. It became a ritual, if possible, to listen every evening to the nine o'clock news, preceded always by the chimes of Big Ben and all nine strikes.

On 24 June my fiancé's frigate, HMS *Nith*, was hit and badly damaged, with the loss of nine lives, by what was subsequently identified as a German unmanned bomber, released over the target by a piloted fighter aircraft and known as Mistel. The ship came back for repairs at Samuel White's shipyard at Cowes. On 28 June I had a telegram from Peter saying 'fix our wedding for July 8th' – not much notice but, with much family help, we managed it, with a week or so in hand, before he had to return to the ship, which then went back to Normandy.

Jeanne Law

QUEEN ALEXANDRA'S ROYAL ARMY NURSING CORPS
I had only been working at the Queen Alexandra Hospital for a few weeks when I was told there was going to be a dance up in the officers' quarters, which was right on the top of Norfolk

House, Portsmouth. I had been late on duty, I was terribly tired, but I was told I had to appear. The only thing I could do to make myself at all respectable was to put on a different tie. So sometime after nine I went up the stairs and at the top of the stairs there was a very decorated elderly officer, Rear Admiral Creasy, standing there talking to a whole lot of people, and he saw me coming up the stairs and came towards me and he said, 'Hello, my dear, have you come to dance?' and I said, 'Oh Lord, no, I am absolutely rattling, I haven't had anything to eat all day.' So he said, 'Well, that won't do. I must try and get you something to eat.' I said, 'That is very kind,' and I followed him and I was rather put off by the looks on the faces of the people he had been talking to. So I followed this gentleman into the bar, where he asked me what I wanted to drink and I hadn't the faintest idea, so he got me something and a ham sandwich. And he said, 'Well there, my dear, I shall have to leave you; I'm so sorry, I hope you understand,' and I said I did.

A rather battle-axe of a Wren officer, when I nervously reappeared on the dance floor, asked me what the devil did I think I was doing going up to the Chief of Staff and telling him that I was rattling! I took this lesson to heart, but a day or so later I was in the lift and the lift man held the door open longer to let an officer in. Older than Creasey, and I thought, 'Oh my God, I'd better make myself scarce.' So I pressed myself to the back of the lift and stood to attention. And when the lift man said 'third floor' I didn't move, and he repeated it, 'third floor', and the man in the lift didn't move either. So I just stood there. And then this man turned to me and said, 'After you, my dear,' and he took me by the arm and we sailed out together, and there waiting to get into the lift was the battle-axe, who nearly died. I think she thought there was no hope for me! That gentleman was Admiral Sir Bertram Ramsay, who was in charge of the Allied Naval Expeditionary Force!

Ralph Rayner

ROYAL ENGINEER

During the next months my unit was attached to the Canadians, who had the task of clearing the Channel ports; then in November I survived another sea-borne landing on Walcheren Island in Holland. In January 1945 I was fortunate to be among the first troops to return to the UK on seven days' leave. I was naturally both anxious and apprehensive about meeting Georgina again after having had only one previous date and a year in between, although we had kept in touch by writing to each other as often as possible. In that seven days we were happily able to confirm our love for each other and we eventually married on the 27 April 1946. My happiest memory of the war years was of that seven days' leave in January 1945.

Rita Weiss

CIVILIAN

My husband Manny – well, he'd gone over on D-Day +3 and I was still in London. Lily used to bake her own bread and cakes and we used to send them over to wherever he was in France, Belgium and later in Germany. But he was very lucky in a sense. He'd learned German while he was in the Forces; I used to have to send him books. He could speak German fluently. They put him in charge, because he was mine-lifting with German PoWs. He always said that they treated the older ones differently to the younger ones because the younger ones went in on their own accord, but the older ones had to go in. He didn't treat them ill; all he did was swear at them.

Our nearly-three-year-old daughter, Tamara, used to collect the letters as the postman came down from the village. And she always used to know they were Daddy's letters because they had no stamps on. One day she came running in. 'Daddy's home! Daddy's home!' I said, 'Daddy can't be home.' 'Yes, he is! Look!

There's a stamp!' Now, she couldn't read or write, as far as I know, but she knew it was Daddy's letter.

Elsie Horton

WREN

In our free time, walking around Fareham could be quite interesting. There was a constant stream of lorries, full of young soldiers on their way to embarkation points, and of course they all had a wave. After a while we learned to be careful, after we found we'd waved to a lorry load of German prisoners who had the nerve to wave back! Another common sight, both before and after D-Day, were Queen Marys, very long, low articulated vehicles, which were used to transport crashed RAF aircraft.

It was amazing that in only a few weeks, life settled down into routine. Convoys continued to come from both east and west, made up of both naval and merchant ships, Mulberry harbour parts, landing-craft, and heavy battleships and cruisers on their way to bombard the French coast. Aircraft continued to cross the skies, and we saw our first Flying Fortress.

Dorothy Brown

CIVILIAN

My family moved in August 1944 down to Bournemouth and I went with them and I remember seeing where we lived near King's Park. It still had all the vehicles and things that were going over the Channel and they were all stacked in rows as reinforcements.

Southampton Forces Newsletter

The WVS, Women's Voluntary Service, supplied personnel to do domestic work in emergency medical services hospitals. One of these workers was eighty-two years old and she worked from midnight to 3am twice a week.

The War Continues: The US and Allies Perspective: 'The war is not over.'

Terence Nickolette

CHILD

I was not yet born but my father, an American GI, landed with the 467th Combat Engineers on D-Day +20. He was first stationed in Belfast, Northern Ireland, and had married an Irish girl from Belfast. I was born later in Belfast during the Battle of the Bulge. My mother travelled with him to England when his company was transferred to a base in England. She actually stayed in a cottage in the Cotswolds near his base. His job was to waterproof all the vehicles that would land with the troops. She told me he arrived on D-Day and kissed her goodbye. It had started. She said the streets of all the villages were filled will all manner of war vehicles heading to the sea. She didn't know if she would ever see him again. She travelled back to Belfast through towns bombed by Nazi buzz-bombs, windows broken, curtains blowing out. My dad told me about riding in the LST towards the beach and how some guys threw up all the way in, and seeing the dead in the water and on the beach. Sleeping in a foxhole, and hearing bombs exploding. Once, while he was eating a meal, he wandered off, and looked in a big pit that was being dug. It was filled with amputated limbs of GIs.

Barbara Gwynne

COMMANDING OFFICER WAC DETACHMENT AT STARK
GENERAL HOSPITAL IN CHARLESTON, SOUTH CAROLINA

I was made commanding officer of the WAC detachment at Stark

General Hospital in Charleston, South Carolina. It was a receiving and evaluation hospital for our wounded coming in from Europe. The wounded soldiers would come in on hospital ships. We had wonderful doctors there who would size up and reassess each patient and figure out all the problems with each patient. In about three or four days they would be shipped out by plane and train to the nearest hospital to their home that was equipped to take care of their particular problem. We were there during the Battle of the Bulge. We could sometimes get a thousand amputation cases off one ship. Most of the kids were eighteen, nineteen, twenty years old. There were bad amputations, minor amputations. As one can imagine, it's not easy to see all those thousands of kids so injured. Then we might get a whole ship-load of neuro-psychiatric cases.

Stark General Hospital was really big, about 2,400 beds. I had about 250 girls working throughout the hospital. They did all kinds of jobs, from secretarial to ward work to anything one can think of that anybody would do in a hospital. I saw to it that they were all housed properly, clothed, and were fed. I was completely in charge. I really liked this job a lot.

During my whole career in the army, I was paid twenty-one dollars a week. The army provided just about everything else. First of all, they gave us our uniforms. We were very conscious of the fact that we always had to be in correct uniform, and that we were representing our government.

During the war, I got to know some people pretty well. A great number of WACs had brothers in the service, or even a husband in the service. Since we were at war, many of their friends, relatives or husbands were killed. When something happened to one of the girls or her family, the whole platoon would rally around and try to help her. War is no joke. When we went to the officers' club, we'd get to know these boys in all these different squadrons. Then there would be somebody who would go down in the sea and that was it. He'd never be seen again, and it was very hard for the rest of the squadron to see this happening all the time.

John Pino

AMERICAN ARMED FORCES

At our base, where we were located, we knew that things were going bad. We were near an airfield and there were a lot of hospital aeroplanes coming in with hundreds of wounded, and that was about the time of the Battle of Bastogne.

We knew this was the big invasion and, of course, we were all hoping that this signalled the beginning of the end, and everybody was kind of looking for Christmas to be kind of an end of the war. It didn't happen that way.

Edward Barry Jr

AMERICAN ARMED FORCES

When D-Day was on, we were busy digging out a thousand-kilogram bomb (that's 2,200 pounds), that had fallen in a US Army Replacement Depot in England and failed to explode. It had fallen in chalk soil, which, naturally, is white and wet. The bomb had gone down quite a ways: we had to dig down twenty-five feet for that bomb, which meant we had to use planking. We had a regular set of timbers with us to sink a shaft and shore up the walls. But the men had to shovel dirt from one level to the next, and when they came out of that hole they looked like wet goblins! We had spars coming out to a pulley and the winch cable went down the hole. It was beautiful for pulling up the bomb, after which we loaded it onto a truck. We got a big round of applause for doing that!

Later, when I was in France, I came across something very interesting. I saw a GI come out of a house; it had a big red light on it, and in the window was a girl with her bra showing, and this poor soldier comes out of this house and he had no shoes on, no stockings, no pants, no jacket and no shirt. He was carrying everything in his hands. He walks up to an MP and says, 'That is no American Red Cross.'

William Biehler

AMERICAN ARMED FORCES

Well, we had a very experienced platoon sergeant at that time, a tech sergeant who was the platoon sergeant, and, at the end of that battle, he just says, 'I've got to go,' and walked back to the first aid outfit and we didn't see him again. He came back about two months later and lasted about another couple of weeks, and then he was gone again. He never was shot, never wounded, but he just couldn't take it mentally. Nobody ever told us what happened to these people. We don't know whether they returned to duty. I really don't know what happened to them, but they were no good in the infantry, that's for sure.

So here I am, with blood dripping off my arm. So I told the rest of the guys, 'I've got to go back,' and another fellow was wounded, too. The rest of the platoon went on and got into the building, but that's all I know. I went back and the company first aid man guy took care of me and the other fellow. We all had these first aid packets. You know about them, with the morphine, yes, and a big bandage, and it had the sulfadiazine powder. We sprinkled that on it. The Germans didn't have any of that. As a matter of fact, they used to gather those from the dead American bodies, because their medics wanted that medicine so much. The sulfadiazine was something they didn't have, and then they took us by Jeep to the battalion surgical department, where I knew a couple of the doctors. He says, the captain there said, 'Okay, I think you're going to be okay, that you're not going to lose the arm. I'm pretty sure they can save it, but you're going to have a nice rest and sleep in some sheets for a while.' That's the first time it hit me: I wasn't going to be in a foxhole for a while. So I went to an evacuation hospital in – can't remember the name of the town, but further back towards Paris – and they operated that night and they gave me pentothal, sodium pentothal, and the anaesthetist said, 'Count to ten.' I think I got up to three; that's all I remember, was three. So I woke up about twenty-four hours later and saw an American nurse walking by and I said, 'This is pretty good.' So she said, 'Oh, you're finally awake.' My arm was all bandaged up, I couldn't see anything, but it was painful, but they gave me morphine and they had put a penicillin pack in. They cleaned it all out and packed it with penicillin crystals. I'd never heard of that before, and they were giving me penicillin shots every two hours, night and day, but you got good, warm food there and I was just there two days. They gave us the Purple Heart the next morning, all three of us – the other two guys, I never saw them again. They took me and a couple of other fellows to a hospital in Paris and did another operation there and they took us by troop train to Le Havre and across, via hospital ship, to England, and I was in a hospital in Kidderminster, England. That was a real big one, huge hospital, a lot of guys from the 90th Division there, and they did a third operation there. By then, I could see how big it was, but I was considered 'walking wounded' by that time. I could go to the

Home at last: RMS Queen Mary arriving in New York harbour, bringing thousands of exhausted American troops. June, 1945.

mess hall and everything. The food was wonderful and I regained the use of my arm. They gave us exercises and everything, did fine then, and, right away, I was able to see the fingers still worked, everything still worked. So, I was very, very fortunate.

Lee Eli Barr

EIGHTH AIR FORCE, 306TH BOMB GROUP

They did, finally, tell me that I had flown thirty missions and was going to be separated from the Eighth Air Force and that I would be awarded a Distinguished Flying Cross. They told me to go to the orderly room and that was it. Nobody pinned the medal on me, shook my hand or kissed me – nothing. A few days later I was put on the *Queen Mary* and eventually arrived back in America.

Flying Officer Johnny Smythe

RAF

I was fêted by the Russians because I was black. They took me to a town near the camp and I watched as they looted. A pretty German woman was crying because they had taken all her valuables. I wanted to help her but the Russians wouldn't listen. I had hated the Germans and wanted to kill them all, but something changed inside me when I saw her tears and the hopelessness on her face.

Frederick A. Almerino

AMERICAN ARMED FORCES

There were light moments just after D-Day. We had built a latrine, a slit trench in a field, but it wasn't encased. You sat on this and we didn't have any screening around it and we're there one Sunday with two other guys and we're sitting there, doing our duty or whatever, when out of the blue come these two girls, across the fields walking towards us. One of the guys says, 'What should we do?' I said, 'What the hell are you going to do? Sit here, what else? Where else am I going to go?' They came up to us, the two girls, shook our hand and said, 'Ça va? Ça va?' 'How are you?' and then they walked on. They were going to church.

Melvin Silverman

AMERICAN ARMED FORCES

The reason that D-Day succeeded was that the GIs decided that the guy next to him was important, and they just kept going. The reason we were thrown out of Vietnam was the same reason: that our opponents had a psychological bond with the guy next to him and just kept going. That's what we did; we just kept going, knowing that we would die for our buddy and that he would die for us.

Lieutenant Murray Rosenthal

ROYAL ARMY MEDICAL CORPS

At Wolverley, near Kidderminster I had fifteen technicians working in the laboratory in bacteriology, biochemistry and serology. We did all the blood transfusions work. In fact, I was responsible for getting blood from whatever source I could as we needed vast amounts of blood, especially after D-Day. I had a list of about three hundred-odd enlisted men and they were allowed to give every thirty days and we made sure that they did donate. There were four blood types. It was necessary, especially with the ones that were the most rare, that we had somebody on hand that could give that type of blood. I donated because I had a rare blood type, A2 positive. I think the most vivid memory I have of D-Day was our complete change of lifestyle. Up till then we were doing our job and working hard doing it. But after D-Day we realised what our guys were going through on the continent and we got into that long working day. I felt that if I had to, I'd give them twenty-four hours, if it were necessary. Everyone felt the same.

David Sive

AMERICAN ARMED FORCES

I was evacuated to southern England, where there was a hospital in a very beautiful area, as is so much of rural England, about ten miles from the town of Torquay. It is a port on the southern coast, and the hospital is in a rural, pastoral area, very beautiful. It was like the classical country which you read of in novels and travel books, and which I was familiar with from reading. It took about forty or fifty days for them to surgically remove the shrapnel, which was very easy and simple, and then for me to convalesce.

Near the end of my stay I noticed some men in the hospital also recovering from wounds, feigning injury to delay return to the front. I wrote a lot of letters home and did a lot of thinking about English literature and the poetry of Wordsworth and the other Lake Poets, which I always had a passion for, along with Percy Bysshe Shelley and John Keats.

At the end, they gave every person a three-day pass before going back to the front. Instead of going into a town and looking for women, which most men did, I rented a bicycle and cycled for a couple days across the area known as Dartmoor, one part of which is the location of *The Hound of the Baskervilles*, the Sherlock Holmes story. It was very romantic and interesting and scenic.

Edward C. Piech

AMERICAN ARMED FORCES

After D-Day you were, I suppose, respected quite a bit. You were appreciated for doing what you had done and been through. Now looking back, I guess we did a pretty good job. But for that time, it was your job.

At D-Day I saw so many people killed. You just kept going. You're trained, you know, to do that. There isn't anything else you can do. Well, yes, but you got your honor, for one thing. I suppose maybe that's the difference. That's a powerful force. You have your integrity and you have your honor. You have to face people back home, you know. You wouldn't want to fail them.

Lois Manning

AMERICAN NURSE

The fact that I had my health and my freedom and made my choice to do what I did without consulting my family. I had a very strong feeling of being an American. The fact that we were in this fight and, if I could help in any way, I was more than pleased to be able to do so, and I wasn't scared. Many folks say, 'Weren't you scared?' Well, you're young and you just don't have those thoughts. I mean, I didn't know that much about what could happen, and naturally, being the only one in the family that could serve meant a lot to me, too.

Richard E. McKeeby

AMERICAN CIVILIAN

My three brothers all enlisted and served on active duty in the Second World War. My oldest brother, Benjamin, was killed on D-Day in 1944 in St Lô, France. He was a paratrooper in the 82nd Airborne Division and had been a prisoner of war. He was being moved in German supply trucks, which were not marked for prisoners, and he was strafed and killed by American planes. He had enlisted in 1939, and had fought in the battles of Sicily, Salerno, Holland, Africa and Normandy. I remember the first telegram that came to our home when he was missing in action. All the hopes and fears of my parents and the rest of the family and friends came to the surface while we waited for further news. Then we got the second telegram, which said he had been killed. My mother became very depressed, cried a lot, stayed in bed, and lost her interest in the world around her. She underwent treatment at Greystone Psychiatric Hospital in New Jersey for several years. That day I lost a brother and a mother. A memorial service for my brother Ben was held in Newton Presbyterian Church and a stained glass window was dedicated to him and also to a neighbour of ours, William Sanford, who was also killed. My brother is now buried in Beverly National Cemetery in New Jersey. His body was brought back in 1948.

My oldest brother, Benjamin, who was killed, had been shot in the head with a .22 rifle while he was woodchuck hunting and he was not supposed to live. In fact, when he went in the service, the bullet slug was still in his skull and he was denied enlistment in the navy, and in the marines. My mother and father had to sign special papers for him and I think that was on their conscience all their life after he had been killed.

He wanted to go in the service. He was fresh out of high school and Hitler was on the rise and some of his friends had joined and, I guess, my brother just wanted to join up too because, as a young guy, it probably sounded exciting to him to go in service.

His death was a big shock. I can remember exactly each time. We had been out on Bertram's Island and we came home from there and the telegram was stuck in our door. Then, of course, that was the big terrible thing but then my family had hope because the telegram said he was missing. Everyone was hoping, 'Why, he's okay. He's really okay. He's just missing,' but then, I guess, it was a while later, almost a year, before we knew for sure that he had been killed in the Normandy invasion. I came home from school, and got off the school bus, and my mother said, 'Benny is dead.' I thought she said 'Betty', which was my oldest sister's name, and I didn't understand what she was talking about, but she was saying 'Ben' or 'Benjamin', and then she said, 'Look on the table,' and I saw the telegram.

That was another thing: I always hoped that my brothers would come home, and I always hoped that mother would be better, but she never really was. She, of course, received cheques, money, after my brother was killed, and she always referred to it as blood money, and she would hardly ever spend it on anything. So, those were tough times.

Now the War is Over: 'The feeling of deep sadness is almost overwhelming.'

Jane Pook

SCHOOLGIRL

My father told me that, throughout the war, his mother refused to lock the back door. Her children tried to persuade her that she should, but she refused, saying, 'I'll never lock that door in case one of my boys comes home.' For seven years it remained open. Her boys did come home but Dad's brother, James, never did come home.

I was surprised at the bravery of the people affected, and their tremendous spirit and ability to keep smiling.

Dad never spoke much about the actual landing. Maybe his happy nature suppressed any desire to dwell on the cold, hard images of that day.

Lawrence Cooper

SCHOOLBOY

Sometime later we heard that Colonel Storey had survived the landings, but tragically the colleague he had brought to our house did not. After the war the colonel returned safely to his family and job in the States, and they kept in touch with us for many years afterwards.

Brian Bailey

SCHOOLBOY

Fifty years later I found out through Barnardo's after-care the name of the village and revisited. My first school is now converted and is the home of a businessman who has the old punishment book. My name wasn't in it. Later, I realised that Miss Howlett (my foster parent) had given me her name. I had become Barney Howlett. Her plans to adopt me failed. I found her 300-year-old house and was invited in by the new owner. After a look around and a chat, I visited the village pub and spoke to an old gentleman who was sitting near the fireplace nursing his pint. After I'd introduced myself and told him that my wife and I were visiting from Holland, he was only too willing to help. So my first question was: fifty years ago and six years old I was walking down the road a few yards from where we were sitting. The whole sky was full of aircraft. What was I looking at? Without hesitation he said, 'Our boys on their way to Arnhem.' I have lived at Eindhoven for forty years, which is about one hour's drive from Arnhem. I had spoken to some of the vets from Arnhem and was pleased to hear that I had seen them flying over to free the country that has become my home. Another small piece of the puzzle slots into place. The old gent knew Miss Howlett and that she had fostered many Barnardo boys during and after the war. She was a nice caring person. We tried to find her grave, but without success. She came to London to try and adopt me. That was the last I saw of her.

It must have been a terrible time for many hundreds of thousands of families. The feeling of deep sadness is almost overwhelming when I think of the scale of it all. God must have shed a tear or two when he saw what was going on. All I can say is we were given a free will to make our own choices. That is what it was all about: the right to be free. Our freedom was worth the sacrifice that we all made. Many of us carry a heart full of tears. Sometimes they overflow and bring relief in various ways. Not just to ourselves but to others too. We gain a certain sensitivity that is not easy to describe, and use it to put a smile on the others' face. Happy people don't make war.

The great thing about being a kid is the feeling of adventure. There is so much to be discovered. The greater problems of the world are for grown-ups. Our world was just starting to get bigger. The postman in his horse and buggy takes me to the station and I am going to a place called London. Miss Howlett reminds me to tell my mother that she had used some coupons to buy me some clothes. This is all new to me. Coupons? My mother? What's a mother? 'You will soon find out. Go with the lady.' The excitement of travelling in a train soon changes, as I look out at the miles of devastation as the train moves slowly towards wherever we are going. 'What's this place called?' I asked the lady. 'This is London,' she answered. I was wondering what to say next. If this is London, why doesn't the train stop?

But it did many times with a lot of shuddering, shunting, and many other strange and fearful noises. I don't like it here, I thought, as the train finally came to a halt. All I could see were legs of people rushing around in a sort of panic. The shouting, the pushing, the noise and the half-broken everything. Then that terrible wailing that made everyone do everything faster, some people falling over in the rush to go through a little door. We ran down a white tunnel, probably to the Underground. Then a long ride in a big red bus with eyes on the front. I was handed over to another lady at a huge building where I was taken to a roomful of tables and left alone. Suddenly a cupboard door banged open and a voice shouted, 'Are you hungry, my darling?' I saw the friendly round face of a woman peering out of the cupboard. Before anything could register, the door slammed shut. The couple of sandwiches on a plate were quickly eaten.

It seemed like hours before that dirty green door opened and two ladies came in. 'So you're Brian?' 'No, my name is Barney Howlett.' 'That's not your name. Your real name is Brian Bailey.' That name did sound familiar. 'Who are you?' I asked. 'I am the auntie who will take you to your mother.' All strange women were called auntie in those days. But I still didn't know what a mother was. I was curious to find out so I went with the auntie on another red bus which also had eyes on the front. Later I was taken into a room where a woman was lying in bed. 'Give your mother a kiss,' I was told. Puzzled, I answered, 'I haven't got one.' I was seven years old and just stood there wondering what a kiss was.

Mary Brice

CIVILIAN

Years later I still remember where they camped; odd rustic poles rotted away in quiet green corners of fields in Sussex and you could pick up old shell cases and rusting Gerry cans.

Norma Pepper

SCHOOLGIRL

My father was a soldier during the war and used to write letters to my brother and me whenever he could, from Italy and North Africa. He was a gunner in the Royal Artillery. When the war ended in 1945, I was ten and looking forward to him coming back home to hear of his exploits. Sadly, right at the very end of the war we got a telegram to say he wouldn't be coming home. He went away when I was seven and I never saw him again. The telegram came at breakfast time and we still had to go to school that day as usual. No counselling for children then. We just had to 'get on with it'.

Angela Bridget Christian, Civilian, on her Father, Private Gilbert M. Bush

175TH INFANTRY CO. M, 313TH INFANTRY CO. H AND
313TH ANTI-TANK

My dad spent almost eighteen months taking part in vigorous training in England and at some time met my mother in the

London area. Sadly, Mum didn't tell me much about him other than his love of music, dancing, gambling, being incredibly romantic and having an eye for the ladies. He was just your typical GI Joe full of charm and brimming with confidence. There are still many gaps to fill in concerning the short life of my father, but I know that he lived life to the full and literally swept my mum off her feet with his boyish good looks and charm. He was awarded his Combat Infantryman's Badge on 9 December 1944 while assigned to 313th Infantry. At this time he was fighting in France and sustained injuries which warranted being shipped back to England for treatment. He was eventually sent back as a replacement and joined the Anti-Tank section. On 8 May 1945 (VE Day) while on security duty in the Dortmund area of Germany he was invited to join the Russian soldiers for a celebratory drink to toast the end of hostilities; this toast to victory and freedom tragically ended the life of my father, some of his buddies and a number of the Russians. I think the drink had been poisoned. How would my life have differed had this tragedy not occurred? Thinking back to my childhood in bombed-out London, being shunted from one homeless centre to another. Mum not knowing where the next meal was coming from, no family to turn to for help and eventually marrying someone who was not a bad man, but who was unable to show me any sort of affection whatsoever. We were eventually given a council flat in South London. I remember sharing a bedroom with my half-brother, and my step-father would creep in after finishing work and take my brother out of the bedroom to play with whatever new toy he had bought for him. I would just lie there thinking, 'Why does he never buy anything for me?' Not knowing then that he wasn't my dad. Then one particular night he said, 'Angela, are you awake, I've got something for you.' I was just so excited when he handed me a little man made of beads with bendy arms and legs. The excitement was so much that as I was bending the arms and legs in all directions, the whole thing just fell to bits. I was devastated and I heard him saying to mum, 'See, that's why I never give her anything.' I eventually started to think that maybe I was bad and undeserving and then as I got a bit older this changed to a complete dislike of my step-father, so when Mum eventually told me at the age of twelve that he wasn't my real dad, I was overjoyed! This euphoria was short lived; I became a victim of sorrow. Why did I not have a real dad to love me, to kiss me goodnight, to give me encouragement and tell me how precious I was; how I yearned for all those things – the hurt was indescribable.

'Sorry Jean, had to go. Johnny'. A poignant farewell scrawled on a tent by a US soldier as he left for D-Day. Many Anglo-American romances ended on the morning of June 6th, without even the chance of a proper farewell because of the secrecy surrounding the preparations.

Clifford Kingston

AMERICAN ARMED FORCES

So, anyway, we spent about two weeks there on the beaches on exercise and then we went back to Plymouth and met the girlfriends that we had said goodbye to. They all knew where we were going, and then we sailed to America. We broke a lot of hearts. I left one there, too!

She finally wrote to me, and she said, 'Don't send me any more mail; my husband's come back.'

Thomas R. Daggett

AMERICAN ARMED FORCES

Going home was quite a trip. We were shipped to Southampton. From there we were to be shipped home. And we were put on board the original aircraft carrier *Enterprise*. I remember this very well, too, because I thought, 'Oh man, this is going to be a nice smooth trip.' Well, it turned out it was anything but. We turned back to England two or three times because of the weather. And they literally – and I mean this – they literally welded twelve-inch I-beams on the forward end of the flight deck to break the waves as they came in the flight deck. And the water just bent those things over like they were hardly there. So that was quite a trip.

Reflections and Remembrance: 'I don't stand up for the Queen, I stand up for all my old mates that died.'

Carol Schultz Vento

CIVILIAN

They didn't talk about it. Talk about what we call post-traumatic stress as we call it today. There wasn't any good treatment. When I got my dad's VA files, I saw how long he had been trying to get help and they pretty much dismissed him for a long, long time. He finally got 100 per cent disability rating when he was eighty years old. He had been trying since 1946. They really did not acknowledge it, so we, the children, didn't even know. When the veterans were going for help back then, they should not have been dismissed. They were dismissed constantly and it caused more and more problems. I know in my own situation, my mother's family basically thought that my father was a failure and a bum. There was no support or understanding. The children were sort of caught in the middle. I just wish there had been a lot more support, understanding and discussion about it.

I think it was because they saw combat. They didn't get any more help after the war than anybody else did and they didn't get any more understanding. It just happens to be documented. What sort of struck me with that is, that they had lots of parades and welcome homes and honours, but that hid the problems.

Howard Lee Ball Jr

AMERICAN ARMED FORCES

Yes, it was a considerable number, and it kills me and it brings tears to my eyes to think that, on D-Day, thousands of them died. I have to convince myself that it was worth it, and it was, it was, but it's difficult. When you look at what's happening now, with the wars in Iraq and Afghanistan, and the people's attitude towards it, they have no idea what's going on and they shoot off their mouth and they don't know what's going on, but some of these old guys that were there, do know.

Clarence Riker

AMERICAN ARMED FORCES

Just the remembrance of what happened on D-Day. That was bad. That was bad, guys lying all around, screaming. It was just, you know, a terrible thing. That's the only remembrance. That's the only thing. I didn't want to go back there, try to bring that up any more, but I guess I should, you know, just to show respect to all the guys that died.

Nancy Potter

AMERICAN HIGH SCHOOL STUDENT

I think for girls and women, and perhaps boys and men, of my generation, the war forced them to grow up prematurely. It made them far more serious about the bare realities of life: life, death, values. It robbed them, in a sense, of some child-hood. Perhaps it was a good thing. But it made us more critical of later generations, who seemed to have a somewhat easier time.

Barbara Gwynne

COMMANDING OFFICER WAC DETACHMENT AT STARK
GENERAL HOSPITAL IN CHARLESTON, SOUTH CAROLINA

Now that the war was over, my plans for the future were just to survive. I got married, and my husband and I had a baby. We just did what was in front of us. I can tell you, though, women had become much more independent because we had the experience of standing on our own two feet while husbands or fathers were overseas. We had to do it, and so obviously we were used to making decisions for ourselves and were more independent. I suppose that it was a surprise for some of the men. Yet my husband took care of me. He took such good care of me and spoiled me that it was hard for me at first to get accustomed to being spoiled like that, I must say. It's something one can thoroughly enjoy, once used to it, though.

War is terrible, and I hope that I never have to get any closer than I was when I was at that hospital, because you could see the results of war. You know, old men make the war, and then the young men have to fight it.

Commander Charity Adams Earley

CENTRAL POSTAL DIRECTORY BATTALION

The future of women in the military seems assured. What may be lost in time is the story of how it happened. The barriers of sex and race were, and sometimes still are, very difficult to overcome, the second even more than the first. During the Second World War women in the service were often subject to ridicule and disrespect even as they performed satisfactorily. Each year the number of people who shared the stress of these accomplishments lessens. In another generation young black women who join the military will have scant record of their predecessors who fought on the two fronts of discrimination: segregation and reluctant acceptance by males.

Brigadier General Hazel W. Johnson-Brown

USA NURSING CORPS

In the past, women, particularly minority women, have always responded when there was a crisis or need. We acknowledge all minority women in uniform. You are the strength of our success. You represent the patchwork quilt of diversity which is America – race, creed, color and ethnicity.

Lilian M. Bader

RAF AIRCRAFTWOMAN

My father was in the First World War, his only three children in the Second World War. And then I married a coloured man who was in the Second World War as was his brother who was even decorated for bravery in Burma and their father had been in the First World War. And our son was a helicopter pilot, he served in Northern Ireland. So all in all I think we've given back more to this country than we've received.

Anon

CIVILIAN

We have known terror and heartbreak, frustration, strain, the unbearable joy which unexpected happiness amid war can mean; in all, a worldwide testing of limb and spirit which was never imposed on earlier generations. We matured more rapidly and emotionally than any previous generation.

Jane Pook

SCHOOLGIRL

When I complained as a teenager about being overweight, Dad would tell me I should try rationing – there was no obesity during the war.

My father was fifty-three when I was born. Not many of my peers had an old soldier as a father. As a child in the 1970s, I would join my mother in the kitchen and she would say, 'What's up? Nothing on telly?' I'd reply, 'Dad's on about the war again.' We would exchange knowing glances and change the subject. My father liked to relay his old stories, but was never one to dwell on sadness; I found out after he died that when they all lived at home with their mother, his brothers and sisters had relied on him to smile through bad times and bring them cheer. He was one of those people. I think that's why it took me a while to realise the enormity and importance of what he was saying. As I grew, I became more aware of the enormous impact that war has on lives. I became more interested in what my father had to say in his own muted way about the poverty, fear and desperate uncertainty that war brings to a family. Years later, at the British Legion after a few pints, a tear would strike the corner of his eye as the National Anthem played. I once asked him why he didn't sing the words. He said, 'I don't stand up for the Queen. I stand up for my old mates that died.' He never forgot. I think he just realised that if he let it affect him, he'd crumble.

A popular tale was 'The Day He Shot the German'. At Dad's funeral, as we waited for the hearse, someone mentioned this. It was one of his proudest moments. It was in France. The British Propaganda machine had done its best on a simple, country lad who never had it in him to hurt a soul. It stirred enough hatred in him to make him actively want to kill a man. The German had shot at Dad but the bullet ricocheted off a wall and a piece of it hit him in the thigh. He saw the man at a window and took a snipe. The German fell out of the window to the ground, struck in the chest by my father's shot. Dad lay there hoping that his wound would get him a ticket to Blighty; the MO pulled the small bit of brick out with tweezers and told him to 'Get on with it'.

Trevor Butler

SCHOOLBOY

It was only in later years that I learned where the American troops went and what they did. Those wonderful men who shared their food with us, many of them not making it back to their families. I and many like me owe them a great debt of gratitude, and I, who met them, will not forget them.

Mr Davies

CIVILIAN

As a child of the 50s, I found that memories of war were still fresh in the minds of many people, including my parents, who both served during this conflict. During my childhood, my twin brother and I were familiar with the odd remnants of 'bomb shelters' in our locale near Bristol, and television was awash with many a film depicting the Second World War.

We knew that our father, Joe, had fought in Europe during the war in both the 'King's Regiment' and, at some point, the 'Dorsets' as a Bren gunner. I often remember asking Dad how many Germans did he kill, but I never got an answer. Once when I posed the question he got out an old army photograph of himself with many of his comrades taken on the successful completion of his basic training. He told me that from all those I could see in the photo, only twelve came home alive!

He would never talk about his experiences, but would only say that he hoped that my brother and I would never have to go through what he experienced during the war. The only time he told me what happened was regarding D-Day, after we watched an Audie Murphy war film on television.

He simply said that he went into D-Day after the initial landings of the first day, with a wave of reinforcements; he was twenty years old at the time. As they proceeded up the beach they came under German mortar fire, with a mortar round landing directly between him and his best friend.

His friend was killed instantly and my father received serious shrapnel wounds to both his head and body. He was evacuated back to Britain and I understand spent many months recovering. I only recently discovered that he never even told my mother or his family what happened that day; they said he simply refused to talk about it.

He never collected his medals.

American soldiers enjoying the ancient British tradition of dancing around the maypole, June, 1942. One of many memories that both the children, and the soldiers who survived, would cherish.

Anon

CIVILIAN

Over many years I have thought that some of those young men, our hosts for a day on that tranquil English village green, perished on Omaha beach.

Anon

CIVILIAN

We never found out what happened to our friend 'Crash Right through Howard'. We can only hope that he survived.

Ian Roy

SCHOOLBOY

I shall always remember those days as very exciting and memorable. Boys living in those days will never forget those momentous times.

Ron Plater

RAF SPECIAL BEACH UNIT

So let us not forget those times when our loved ones have been reported 'missing' or 'killed in action'. Those of us who have been fortunate enough to have survived sometimes perhaps say, 'Was it all worth it?' The answer is, of course, 'yes', although at times we question the moral standards of our lives these days. But then what would it have been like had the tyranny of the evil regime we fought against not been conquered?

Sharon Jensen

CIVILIAN

My daughter, aged thirty-three, watched the BBC coverage of the D-Day anniversary and was moved by the sight of the veterans to write this poem.

OMAHA

Seas of white crosses
Stretching for miles
Memories of heroes who lost their lives
On that fateful day
They had come so far,
Blood on the beach,
Slaughter at Omaha.
Many never reached the sands
Fear in their eyes
Guns in their hands.
Destined to a watery grave
Forever young, forever brave.
No one can thank them
For the sacrifice they made
For a better today, for the price they paid.
Many had never left home before
But would never again step back through their door.
Never forgotten as they lie side by side
June 6th 1944, together they died.
We'll always remember the sadness they saw
Slaughter at Omaha, the horror of war.
Today, a beach that stretches for miles
Calm and still, clear blue skies.
Nothing to hear but the ripple of the sea
A beautiful, peaceful place to be.

Anne Rosa Coward

SCHOOLGIRL

On 6 June 1944 my Uncle George jumped out of his boat and
landed on a beach in Normandy. He was one of the lucky ones
and survives to this day. His uniform was saturated with sea

water, and covered in sand and mud and then worn for several days before being rolled up and stuffed into his kitbag.

When he finally made it back to Lyndhurst Road in Portsmouth, my nan greeted him rapturously, and then exclaimed in horror at the state of his uniform as he pulled it out of his kitbag. She got it out, shook it, sponged it down and hung it on the line to dry. All to no avail as it remained stained and crumpled. So she took it to the dry-cleaners at the end of the road, and I went with her.

Inside the shop she took out the uniform and put it on the counter. 'I'd like to have this dry-cleaned, please,' she said. The dry-cleaning lady looked with distaste at the muddy bundle. 'I don't think we can do anything with that, Madam,' she said. 'Whatever happened to it?' 'It's my son's,' explained Nan; 'he was in the Normandy landings.' 'Oh,' said the lady, 'leave it here and we'll see what we can do.'

A week later my nan and I went back. And there on a hanger, where everyone could see it, was a newly cleaned, freshly pressed and totally immaculate uniform, buttons gleaming. 'Your son's uniform, Madam,' said the lady. 'That's amazing,' said my nan, getting out her purse. 'How much do I owe you?'

'There is no charge, Madam,' said the dry-cleaning lady.

Acknowledgements

I would like thank my editor, Rupert Lancaster, at Hodder & Stoughton, for his immense enthusiasm for The Silent Day, from its inception to final proofs. His assistant Maddy Price was also of enormous help with the various drafts of the book. The photographs were selected with an extraordinary empathy to match the personal accounts by Juliet Brightmore. I would also like to thank Ashleigh Crilly for her excellent research and for her particular skill in finding rare source material. Vera Meuret provided additional research and ideas. Sincere thanks are also due to my agent, Gordon Wise, of Curtis Brown.

I am most grateful to the following museums, libraries and archives for permission to use extracts from their collections:

The Sound Archive of the Imperial War Museum; Rutgers Oral History Archive; Eisenhower Center, New Orleans, D-Day Collection; BBC WW2 People's War Archive; East Midlands Oral History Archive; The D-Day and Normandy Fellowship; 'What did you do in the war, Grandma?' [www.library.brown. edu/cds]; The Wartimes Memory [www.wartimememories. co.uk]; American WWII Orphans Network; Women in Military Service for America Memorial Foundation; Memorial Gates Trust; The Second World War Online Learning Resource for Northern Ireland; The Warren Tute Collections of the Portsmouth History Centre; Bristol Central Library; The Linfield Oral History Society Interviews at the Surrey History Centre; London Metropolitan Museum; The Voices from the Home Front Oral History Project, at The New Forest History and Culture Archives.

I am also indebted to the following authors and publishers

for permission to use extracts from the following books and periodicals:

Southampton and D-Day, by Ingrid Peckham, Southampton City Council, 1994

Maid Matelot: Adventures of a Wren Stoker in World War Two, Featuring D-Day in Southampton by Rozelle Raynes, 1971, reissued Castweasel, 2004

D-Day as the Newspaper Boy Saw It, by David Maber, David Maber, 2001

D-Day, by Sir Martin Gilbert, Wiley, 2004

The War at Sea, a Naval History of World War II, by Nathan Miller, Oxford University Press, 1995

Reconstructing Women's Wartime Lives, by Penny Summerfield, Manchester University Press, 1998

To Serve My Country, To Serve My Race, by Brenda L Moore, New York University Press, 1996

West Indian Women at War, by Ben Bousquet and Colin Douglas, Lawrence and Wishart, 1990

Love, Sex and War, by John Costello, Pan, 1986

Navy nurses remember the Invasion, by JK Herman, Navy Medicine 85 no.3, May-June 1994

We Remember D-Day, edited by Ray Freeman, Dartmouth History Research Group Paper 11, 1994

Lastly, I would like to thank the following newspapers for their invaluable help:

Mirror Group Newspapers
The Huffington Post
Southampton Echo

As always my work was encouraged and enhanced by the steadfast love and support of my brother Adrian, Deborah Moggach, Susan Jeffries, Don and Liz McClen, Lucia Corti and my dear friend Ruth Cowen.

Picture Acknowledgements

Index